THE MINOR RAILWAYS OF EAST ANGLIA

Fig 1: Saxmundham Junction Signal Box. A DMU, from which this picture was taken on 26 June 1965, is taking the Aldeburgh Branch which curves away to the right and becomes single track. The double track main line is the East Suffolk line from Ipswich to Saxmundham, Halesworth and Lowestoft.

THE MINOR RAILWAYS OF EAST ANGLIA

DEVELOPMENT DEMISE AND DESTINY

ROB SHORLAND-BALL

First published in Great Britain in 2020 by
Pen and Sword Transport
An imprint of
Pen & Sword Books Ltd
Yorkshire - Philadelphia

Copyright © Rob Shorland-Ball, 2020

ISBN 978 1 52674 481 4

The right of Rob Shorland-Ball to be identified as Author of this work has been asserted by him in accordance with the Copyright, Designs and Patents Act 1988.

A CIP catalogue record for this book is available from the British Library.

All rights reserved. No part of this book may be reproduced or transmitted in any form or by any means, electronic or mechanical including photocopying, recording or by any information storage and retrieval system, without permission from the Publisher in writing.

Typeset in Palatino 10.5/13 by Aura Technology and Software Services, India.

Printed and bound in India by Replika Press Pvt. Ltd.

Illustrations are from the author's collection or, with their permission to him, from Dr Ian Allen, John Aves, Tim Edmonds, Anthony (Tony) Kirby, David Lee, John Mann, Blake Paterson, Online Transport Archive (Peter Waller), Ken Penrose, Prof. Peter Rowlinson and Commissioning Editor John Scott-Morgan. I am a long-time keen photographer, and have accumulated my collection from my time working on BR in the 1950s and 1960s; at the National Railway Museum (1987-94); and as an active member of the Railway Study Association since 1988. I always try to contact all possible copyright holders and check any unacknowledged illustrations with forensic image search engines. I can be contacted at robsb@wfmyork.demon.co.uk

Pen & Sword Books Ltd incorporates the Imprints of Pen & Sword Books Archaeology, Atlas, Aviation, Battleground, Discovery, Family History, History, Maritime, Military, Naval, Politics, Railways, Select, Transport, True Crime, Fiction, Frontline Books, Leo Cooper, Praetorian Press, Seaforth Publishing, Wharncliffe and White Owl.

For a complete list of Pen & Sword titles please contact

PEN & SWORD BOOKS LIMITED
47 Church Street, Barnsley, South Yorkshire, S70 2AS, England
E-mail: enquiries@pen-and-sword.co.uk
Website: www.pen-and-sword.co.uk

or

PEN AND SWORD BOOKS
1950 Lawrence Rd, Havertown, PA 19083, USA
E-mail: Uspen-and-sword@casematepublishers.com
Website: www.penandswordbooks.com

CONTENTS

	Acknowledgements	7
	Abbreviations and Acronyms	8

PART 1: DEFINITIONS

CHAPTER 1	Where is East Anglia?	12
CHAPTER 2	What are Minor Railways?	13
CHAPTER 3	Great Eastern Railway – an East Anglian monopoly?	17
CHAPTER 4	Independent Railways defy the GER monopoly	19

PART 2: DEVELOPMENT

Railways for maritime produce and perhaps for tourists — 22

CHAPTER 5	King's Lynn Harbour and Docks railways	23
CHAPTER 6	Gt. Yarmouth and Lowestoft Docks railways and Southwold Harbour	29
CHAPTER 7	Kelvedon, Tiptree and Tollesbury Light Railway	47

Railways for agricultural produce and passengers — 52

CHAPTER 8	Three Horseshoes to Benwick Branch	53
CHAPTER 9	St Ives loop and Long Stanton Station	55
CHAPTER 10	Elsenham to Thaxted Light Railway	66
CHAPTER 11	Denver, Stoke Ferry & the Wissington Railway	70

Railways for industry — 78

CHAPTER 12	Leiston Works railway	79
CHAPTER 13	Snape Maltings	81
CHAPTER 14	Barrington Cement Works Railway	83

Railway Companies in competition – two stations to serve one location — 86

CHAPTER 15	Ramsey	87
CHAPTER 16	Fakenham	90
CHAPTER 17	Cromer	92
CHAPTER 18	Haverhill	94

PART 3: DEMISE – AND POSSIBLE RECOVERY

No more a 'Common Carrier'? Economics? Social changes? A public service?   97

CHAPTER 19	First to go. Great Chesterford to Newmarket Railway	99
CHAPTER 20	Mildenhall Branch	103
CHAPTER 21	Aldeburgh Branch	107
CHAPTER 22	Mid-Suffolk Light Railway	111
CHAPTER 23	Halesworth to Southwold Railway	114

PART 4: DESTINY

Some 'minor' railways have found a new purpose   117

CHAPTER 24	Sizewell C Nuclear Power Station – Aldeburgh Branch	118
CHAPTER 25	Preserved heritage railways	120
CHAPTER 26	Cycleways, Footpaths, a Busway	123

PART 5: MEMORIES

More illustrations of 'minor' railways   131

    List of Illustrations   135

    Select Bibliography   143

    Index   144

ACKNOWLEDGEMENTS

When my Commissioning Editor, John Scott-Morgan, suggested that I should research and write a book about the minor railways of East Anglia I was very tempted. This book has been a good excuse for revisiting memories from the 1950s and 1960s and sharing those memories in a form which, I hope, will perpetuate them.

I grew up and was at school in Cambridge so took the opportunity of watching, photographing and travelling on many of the 'minor' railways to and from Cambridge or further afield in East Anglia. BR was beginning to introduce diesel railbuses and diesel multiple units (DMUs) providing a unique opportunity to sit at the front and share a driver's eye view of the journey. **Fig 2** (below) shows one of the diesel railbuses that I remember and the front view it offered which was impossible in steam days.

My grammar school in Cambridge was the Cambridge and County High School for Boys and the 'County' in the title reflected the journeys that many pupils made by train to school. I had friends from Swavesey, Bartlow and Whittlesford, for instance, and some of their memories have enhanced the stories I am telling.

I have acknowledged several of these friends, and other contacts below, because they have given me pictures for this book. I am adding here several people and sources who have also been very informative and helpful: Graham Burling, whom I first met as a clerk at Long Stanton Station where I was a summer-contract cut-flower clerk; Robert Humm, suggesting a definition for a 'minor' railway; Honorary Minor Canon Daniel Jones for suggestions on the contextual meaning of 'minor;' John Jones (Association for Industrial Archaeology), with information on: '. . . *Brick Kiln, built by Major General Sir Robert Harvey, 1847 in which year two Millions of Bricks were burnt for the Railway*'; Michael Perrins, railway archivist, librarian, much respected and valued critic/proofreader; Ralph Potter, a former BR signal engineer; Peter Wakefield, whose father was Station Master at Swavesey, then Oakington, then i/c St Ives; and Robin Whittaker, BR 1959-1995.

If I have accidentally omitted anyone my apologies; any mistakes are mine and – when I learn of them – much regretted.

Fig 2: Bartlow Junction: 4-wheel railbuses offered interested passengers a front seat beside the driver's enclosed cab.

ABBREVIATIONS AND ACRONYMS

Abbreviations & Acronyms	Full name	Notes
©	Copyright	
ABP	Associated British Ports	
BLS	Branch Line Society	
BR	British Railways	
BTC	British Transport Commission	
CV&HR	Colne Valley & Haverhill Railway	
D&SFR	Denver & Stoke Ferry Railway	
DMU	Diesel Multiple Unit	
ECR/EUR	Eastern Counties Railway/Eastern Union Railway	
FONCS	Friends of Norwich City Station	
GER	Great Eastern Railway	
GNR	Great Northern Railway	
GRADE II*	Statutory listing of an historic building	
HMSO	Her Majesty's Stationery Office	
HSNGRS	Halesworth to Southwold Narrow-Gauge Railway Society	
IRS	Industrial Railway Society	
KLD&R	King's Lynn Docks & Railway	
KT&TLR	Kelvedon, Tiptree & Tollesbury Light Railway	
LNER	London North Eastern Railway	
loose-coupled	loose-coupled	A basic three-link coupling between coupling hooks on adjoining vehicles
LR&HC	Lowestoft Railway & Harbour Company	
M&GNR	Midland & Great Northern Joint Railway	
mixed train	mixed train	A train conveying both passenger and freight vehicles
MP	Member of Parliament	
MR	Midland Railway	
MSC	Manchester Ship Canal	
MSLR	Mid-Suffolk Light Railway	
NESNC	North of Europe Steam Navigation Company	
NRM	National Railway Museum (York and Shildon)	
OS	Ordnance Survey	
pick-up	pick-up	Railway term for freight trains which stop to 'pick-up' additional wagons
RSPB	Royal Society for the Protection of Birds	

Abbreviations & Acronyms	Full name	Notes
SM	Station Master	
SR/SRT	Southwold Railway/Southwold Railway Trust	
SSBB	Stamford, Spalding & Boston Bank	
sugar beet Campaign	sugar beet Campaign	Sugar beet factories are most busy when the beet has ripened and is ready to process. A 'Campaign' is that busy period from September to February
the Grouping	the Grouping	The Railways Act 1921 'grouped' the majority of UK railways into four
Vanfit	Vanfit	Covered (roofed) railway wagon fitted with vacuum brakes for express trains

PART I

DEFINITIONS

Fig 8: Railways in East Anglia (page 17) illustrates the pattern of railways which had developed in East Anglia by the beginning of the twentieth century. Parliament had to approve an Act for a railway to be built but, as the nineteenth century advanced, there were few obstacles to schemes which had capital, ambition and support from major land-owners. The railways in East Anglia developed from a number of competing and sometimes conflicting interests, ultimately serving most towns of significance and a number of smaller towns and villages which were often served by branch lines. There was no coherent vision or strategy other than to enrich their promoters. East Anglia lacked the minerals, especially coal and iron ore, which fuelled industrial development in other parts of the UK.

Railways in East Anglia tended to develop from London northwards, or by linking a principal town like Norwich with a port – Great Yarmouth (see **Fig 3**).

The first railways in East Anglia were built by small companies which were leased and absorbed by the Eastern Counties Railway [ECR]. A unified whole was created by the Great Eastern Railway Act of 7 August 1862. By this Act the ECR changed its name to Great Eastern Railway (GER) and the East Anglian, Newmarket & Chesterford, Eastern Union and Norfolk railway companies were absorbed.

The GER Act was an expression of Parliamentary good sense in bringing together in one Company a diverse miscellany of Company management and operational practices. The principles were good but the practices were more varied; many 'minor railways' were part of the GER mix and some few remained independent. This book is an exploration of East Anglian railway variety, which I enjoyed in the 1950s and '60s!

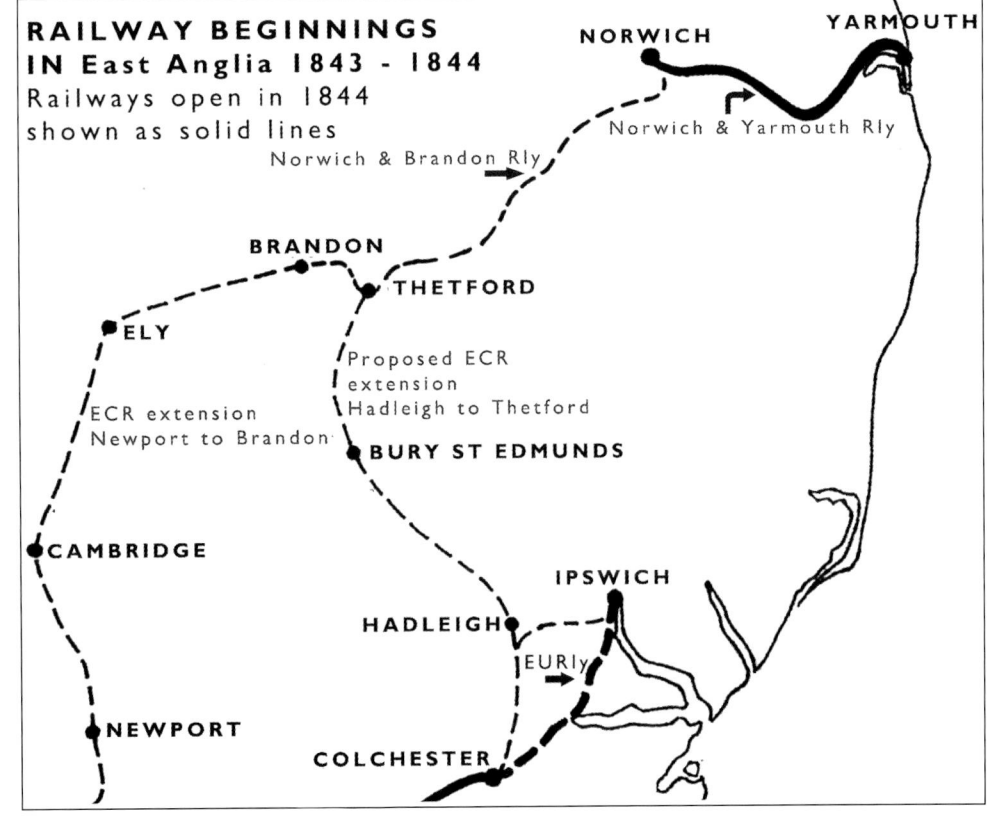

Fig 3: Railway beginnings in East Anglia in 1844. Edited, with thanks, from *East Anglia's First Railways*. Hugh Moffat. Terence Dalton. 1987.

CHAPTER 1

WHERE IS EAST ANGLIA?

I have previously explained that I grew up in Cambridge and considered myself to be living in East Anglia. I knew that the one-time Kingdom of East Anglia consisted principally of the lands of the North Folk and the South Folk – so modern Suffolk and Norfolk and little of what is now Cambridgeshire. Essex, the land of East Saxons was, in these early times, a separate Kingdom.

I was aware of the strong local loyalties in East Anglia and that Norfolk, Suffolk and Essex were considered to be very different, separate and independent areas by their inhabitants. When I worked in Suffolk I remember explaining that I came from Cambridge which, I believed, was 'the front door to East Anglia'. The elderly Suffolk man to whom I was speaking paused for a while and then said, with an unarguable finality, 'Here in Suffolk, if Cambridge exists at all, it is a back door and rarely used.'

A map outlining what I consider to be East Anglia is **Fig 4**.

To ensure that my definition of 'East Anglia' is not entirely arbitrary I have turned to *Civil Engineering Heritage – East Anglia*. Peter Cross-Rudkin. Phillimore. 2010 so, to quote Peter's Introduction, I can write – for the purpose of this book – East Anglia is taken to include the four post-1974 counties of Cambridgeshire, Essex, Norfolk and Suffolk with minor modifications to include the ancient county of Huntingdonshire and the Soke of Peterborough(neither shown on the **Fig 4** map) while excluding those parts of (southern) old Essex lost to Greater London.

Fig 4: Norfolk & Suffolk, which are the principal counties of East Anglia, the northern part of Essex and most of Cambridgeshire westwards.

CHAPTER 2

WHAT ARE MINOR RAILWAYS?

When John Scott-Morgan (my Commissioning Editor) suggested a draft title for this book about minor railways I welcomed the idea and thought that I knew what a minor railway was. I was sure it was like **Fig 5**.

Or, to come a little more up-to-date, like **Fig 6**.

Fig 5: Tollesbury Pier Station, Kelvedon & Tollesbury Light Railway c1930.

Fig 6: BR 4-wheel railbus leaving Wickham Bishops Station *en route* for Maldon East c1964.

But then my inborn pedantry began to influence my thinking. I was familiar with the terms 'Light Railway' and 'Branch Line' but where had I previously encountered the term 'minor railway'? Surely *The Re-shaping of British Railways* (the 'Beeching Report') HMSO 1963 must have used the term? But no; there are references to 'major amalgamations' of railway companies but no mention of any 'minor' railways which were not amalgamated. **Figs 5** and **6** which are visualisations of my concept of a 'minor' railway justify a second and perhaps more questioning look and more thoughtful analysis.

The Kelvedon & Tollesbury Railway (**Fig 5**) was opened as a 'Light Railway' on 1 October 1904. It was built to take advantage of the provisions for rural branch lines enacted by Parliament in the Light Railways Act of 1896. Passenger and goods traffic over the whole railway ceased in 1951 and freight services on the remaining Kelvedon to Tiptree section ceased in 1962.

The Witham to Maldon branch line (**Fig 6**) was opened for passengers and goods traffic on 2 October 1848. The passenger service was withdrawn in 1964; a residual goods service continued until 1980 when the line was closed.

Both these railways would seem to be minor railways but one was a Light Railway and the other was a branch line. I decided I must explore 'minor' as a technical term as used by railway men and turned, first, to Alan A. Jackson's *The Railway Dictionary With Index Of Themes* (3rd Edition. Sutton Publishing. 2000). No 'minor' railways there and the nearest was references to Miniature or Minimum Gauge railways.

Perhaps George Ottley's *A Bibliography of British Railway History* (2nd Edition. HMSO. 1983) could be more helpful? He was, but not entirely as I wished because he suggested alternatives in his very comprehensive index. See:

- Light & narrow-gauge railways
- Narrow-gauge railways
- Industrial railways

John Glover's *Modern Railways Dictionary of Railway Industry Terms* (Ian Allan Publishing. 2005) does not include 'minor railways' but does quote the Transport & Works Act 1992 s67(1) which is usefully pertinent for this book:

Railway
A system of transport employing parallel rails which:
(a) provide support and guidance for vehicles carried on flanged wheels and
(b) form a track which either is of a gauge of at least 350mm or crosses a carriageway (whether or not on the same level) but does not include a tramway.

The Dictionary also offers a definition of a Branch Line:

Branch Line
A secondary route from a terminus which acts as a feeder to the main trunk line. Terms based on the likening of railway infrastructure to that of a tree.

Next I turned to the several contacts who kindly responded to my request for help in defining a 'minor railway'.

Tony Jervis, my predecessor as Editor of the *R&CHS Bulletin*, is widely-read and a very good source of unusual railway information. He responded thus in August 2018:

'Rob, regarding your agonising over what could constitute a 'minor' railway, I thought the late Edwin Course might have solved it in his trilogy on railways in southern England. Following "The Main Lines" and "Secondary and Branch Lines" [I hoped for "Minor Railways" but he concluded the trilogy with] *Independent and Light Railways* (Harper Collins. 1976).

'Searching for other possible definitions . . . the nearest that approached your tentative title was C.J. Gammell's book *The Branch Line Age – the minor railways of the British Isles in memoriam and retrospect* (Moorland Publishing. 1976). This is [primarily] a book of Gammell's photographs [but the brief Preface does include a pertinent sentence: "All minor railways conveyed their passengers with a purposefulness and leisure that belonged to the 19th century – the age of the horse, the years before the all-too-common motor vehicle would infiltrate into every country lane and village"].

'. . . both the Branch Line Society (BLS) and the Industrial Railway Society use the term "minor railways" to mean industrial and preserved (heritage) lines and, in the case of the BLS, narrow-gauge and miniature railways in parks and gardens intended solely for leisure use.'

Tony's reference (but not quoted above) to searching in his own extensive reference library encouraged me to look again at my shelves and I took down *Minor Standard Gauge Railways*. R.W. Kidner, the Oakwood Press. 1971. In his 'Introduction' Kidner does not define 'minor railways' but he does suggest ways in which such railways can be recognised or distinguished from other railways:

'A factor common to most minor standard gauge railways was more or less permanent penury. The reason for this is that undertakings which tapped an ample source of traffic were snapped up by one of the bigger lines, usually before they opened. Often however, the true potential – or lack of it – was not apparent until after traffic began and minor railways were sometimes well-endowed to begin with, at the expense of the shareholders, who later found they had lost their money. The crunch came when this initial equipment began to wear out, and the traffic had not raised the money to pay for new equipment. At this point the purveyors of second-hand engines and carriages came into their own, including of course the larger railways themselves, who were glad to accept £60 for a carriage or £200 for an engine which they had intended to scrap anyway. This stock was usually almost time-expired, and did not last long under its new owners, so that it was laid aside and fresh bargains sought for – thus such lines often had a great deal of stock on their books, little of which was in working order.'

Another of my helpful contacts is Robert Humm, book seller, railway history researcher and author. He shares with Kidner a similar vision of the typical 'minor railway':

'Dear Rob, We all know a minor railway when we see one: usually short, weed-grown track, ancient rolling stock, elderly motive power, lack of traffic, sometimes [in its history] presided over by Colonel Stephens. The problem, as you say, is one of definition.

'The expression is, I suggest, a recent coinage by enthusiasts and authors. Ottley (1966) has no specific titles beginning "minor railways". . . and none of Ottley's alternative categories are suitable definitions. For example:

- Light Railways – The Totton & Fawley branch was built under an LRO but [in the 1920s the largest oil refinery in Britain opened at Fawley and subsequently expanded so] by 1960 the branch was equipped with heavy rail and carried over 1m tons of oil traffic each year.
- Narrow-Gauge Railways – . . . the metre gauge Minas A Vittoria carries 32,000 ton iron ore trains. The Welsh Highland [operates with] Beyer-Garratts and 10-coach, corridor, well filled trains, and brand new stations at both ends.
- Industrial Railways – Same problem. The Port Of London, Manchester Ship Canal (MSC), Corby Steel Works and Quarries were major systems each with 60-70 locomotives. MSC in its heyday carried over 2M tons of freight a year, more than many BR main lines.
- Miniature Railways – I do not think that the Romney, Hythe & Dymchurch Railway would regard itself as a "minor" railway!
- Cliff Railways – Very short but often carrying hundreds of thousands of passengers a year.

'I do not find it surprising that minor railways are not referred to in the Beeching Report because:
(i) The expression was not in general use in 1963;
(ii) Some minor railways, however defined, were deliberately excluded from the Transport Act 1948 (eg. Talyllyn).

'Most of those 'minor railways' acquired by the British Transport Commission (BTC) had already been closed:

- Kent & East Sussex
- Kelvedon & Tollesbury
- Mid-Suffolk Light Railway
- Welshpool & Llanfair
- Rheilffordd Corris

'The principal concern of the BTC in the 1950s (and of Beeching a little later) was "the branch line problem" rather than the minor railway problem. There was a BTC Branch Line Committee to tackle it, which made slow progress.

Why not use the term "lesser railways" instead of minor railways? . . . Robert Humm.'

'Lesser railways' was an interesting suggestion but perhaps not a very marketable title. However, its antithesis of 'greater railways' led me to think of the Great Eastern Railway Company but since it embraced a number of lesser railways I returned to 'minor railways' as a title for this book.

Interest in railways and the Church of England clergy is another coincidence – like Bishop Eric Treacy, Rev 'Teddy' Boston and Rev Wilbert Awdry – which came into my mind while listening to a sermon at York Minster. The preacher was Rev Daniel Jones, Chaplain of St Peter's School, York and Honorary Minor Canon at the Minster. After the service I explained to Daniel that I was researching a book about the minor railways of East Anglia and wondered about a definition for his Minster title? Like my other contacts he responded:

'Hi Rob, I have been doing just a little bit of thinking about this one. I found this definition on the web: "Minor canon – a canon of inferior grade who assists in performing the daily choral service in a cathedral" . . .

'I am not quite sure how this might be linked to railways? Are there such things, I wonder, as superior and inferior grades of railway? Perhaps main lines and branch-lines [or light railways] . . . might be the closest parallel?

'Best wishes, Daniel.'

The Light Railways Act of 1896 did not define a 'light railway' perhaps because the features which distinguish a 'light' from a 'standard' railway – setting aside the gauge – are not in every case the same. Even the differences which these features display are differences of degree rather than of kind so no rigid line of demarcation can be drawn.

It seems reasonable to conclude that a 'light railway' is – having regard to the nature and volume of the traffic to be carried – more cheaply constructed and equipped, less stringently bound by safety regulations, and more economically worked than a 'standard' line.

Distinguishing features may be gauge; curves; gradients; permitted speeds; maximum axle weights; weight of rail, sleepers, ballast; details of fencing and gates; station arrangements, staffing, signalling, etc. So there seems to be no straight forward definition of a 'minor railway'. I intend, therefore, that the paragraph quoted above from Kidner's *Minor Standard Gauge Railways* (page 14) which begins: 'A factor common to most minor standard gauge railways was more or less permanent penury . . '. is the touchstone around which the stories in this book will be told. It satisfies my pedantry and is a word-picture that can be enhanced by some of the illustrations which follow.

Fig 7: Mixed train at Haughley Junction, Mid-Suffolk Light Railway, 28 July 1915.

CHAPTER 3

GREAT EASTERN RAILWAY – AN EAST ANGLIAN MONOPOLY?

Although long before the Beeching Report, the creation of the Great Eastern Railway (GER) was an example of the sort of 'major amalgamations' to which Beeching referred. The Great Eastern Railway Act of 7 August 1862 brought together the Eastern Counties, East Anglian, Newmarket & Chesterford, Eastern Union and Norfolk railway companies as the GER. Two genuine Beeching-type major amalgamations followed. In the Grouping of 1923, GER became LNER and in 1948 LNER became part of the nationalised British Railways.

Fig 8 is a sketch plan of the GER/LNER (copied with thanks from the LNER Encyclopaedia online) with a number of what I consider to be minor railways highlighted in green.

Although the **Fig 8** map seems to indicate that GER was a monopoly operator in East Anglia, there were

Fig 8: The GER lines are shown in red and potential 'minor railways' are in green. The thin black line from Spalding eastwards via King's Lynn to Great Yarmouth marks the Midland & Gt. Northern Railway [M&GNR].

several independent railways not shown on the map. One was the Southwold Railway, added in green as a minor railway, and the Mid-Suffolk Light Railway (MSLR) which was a black non-GER line on the original map and has been over-coloured in green as another minor railway.

The most significant non-GER line was the Midland & Great Northern Joint Railway (M&GNR) marked on the original map as a thin black line and over-coloured on **Fig 8** in green east and south of Fakenham. The M&GNR was an east-west line connecting the Midlands with North Norfolk. On 9 June 1893 a number of smaller and independent railway companies, in most cases sponsored and operated by the Great Northern or Midland companies, finally came together as the M&GNR, jointly owned by the Midland and the Great Northern. The GER had long been opposed to this invasion of 'their' territory by two rival railway companies but finally could not resist, so over 100 miles of Joint railway offered significant competition throughout North Norfolk. **Fig 9** illustrates the blue GER lines and the red M&GNR lines in Norfolk. The main M&GNR line was west-east and ultimately south-eastwards to Great Yarmouth. At Melton Constable, which was the head-quarters and principal workshops of the Railway, a northerly spur served the popular resorts of Sheringham and Cromer and a southern spur led to the M&GNR's station at Norwich City.

It may be argued that GER was the principal railway in East Anglia from 1862 so the M&GN Joint Railway, 31 years later, was not a wholly minor railway. The **Fig 9** map shows that M&GNR served a considerable area of Norfolk so was a successful competitor for many years and sometimes, as at Fakenham, Cromer, North Walsham and Norwich, developed a rival station too (**Fig 10**). But some M&GNR branches have minor railway qualities so – like the Cromer branch – they appear later in the book.

Their hope for the future is to uncover all the railway-related elements of the site and turn it into a memorial garden.

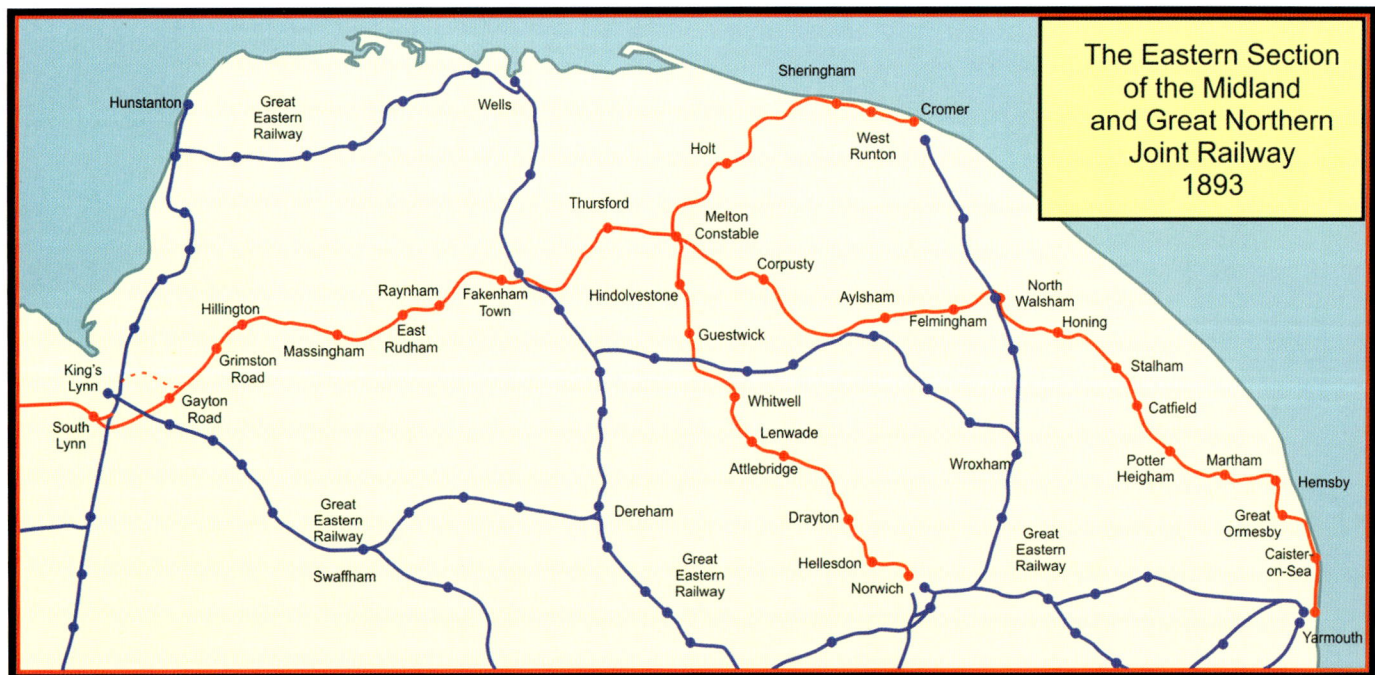

Fig 9 (above): Map (from Wikipedia) illustrating the competition for passenger and goods business between the Great Eastern Railway (in blue) and the Midland & Great Northern Joint Railway in red.

Fig 10 (left): A platform face uncovered at Norwich City Station by the Friends of Norwich City Station (FONCS).

CHAPTER 4

INDEPENDENT RAILWAYS DEFY THE GER MONOPOLY?

Chapter 3 explains the competition between the GER and the M&GNJR so the latter could certainly be said to defy the GER monopoly. Several other railways in East Anglia were not absorbed or taken over by GER but remained independent at least until the 1923 Grouping of railways:

Railway	from .... to	Notes
Barrington Light Railway	Foxton Siding (LNER) to Barrington Quarry	Eastwood Cement Company Rugby Cement Group RMC Group CEMEX Opened 1927 Decommissioned 2005 Re-opened by CEMEX 2015 for trains by DB Schenker Rail UK from Willesden, north London, to the cement works site
Colne Valley Railway	Haverhill South (Suffolk) to Chappell & Wakes Colne (Essex)	Part of LNER from 1923 Closed to passengers 1961 Closed to goods 1965
Mid-Suffolk Light Railway	Haughley Junction to Laxfield	Part of LNER from 1924 Closed to all traffic 1952
Port of King's Lynn	Harbour Junction along Harbour Branch to South Quay King's Lynn Junction along the King's Lynn Docks and Railway Company's to Alexandra and Bentinck Docks and Fisher Fleet	Harbour Branch opened 1846 Part of LNER from 1923 Dock Estate railway closed May 1993 Both GER and M&GNJR had an interest in King's Lynn Harbour but GER was the principal operator in the Harbour
Southwold Railway	Halesworth to Southwold – Junction to Harbour (1914 - 1929)	Opened 1879. closed 1929
Wissington Railway	Junction off Stoke Ferry branch near Abbey Station to serve a 7,000 acres Fenland Estate initially owned by Arthur Keeble. From 1925, in conjunction with LNER, the railway served a new Sugar Beet Factory and was extended by branches to other cultivated fens in the area.	Opened 1906 Lines beyond Beet Factory closed 1957 Remainder closed 1982 Beet Factory served by road transport

Fig 11

Only the Southwold Railway remained a fully independent company until closure in 1929. It liaised with GER/LNER at Halesworth but because the Southwold was not standard gauge, a physical connection and through running were not possible.

The two industrial railways – Barrington and Wissington – worked with LNER/BR because they, and all the other railways in the table above, were standard gauge so connected with the national railway system.

Likewise, the branch lines in East Anglia made physical junctions with the main line railways from which they branched away to Aldeburgh, Benwick, Eye, Hadleigh, Mildenhall, Ramsey, Stoke Ferry, Thaxted and Upwell. Many branches retained an operational independence of spirit and staffing which endeared them to their local users but they were never truly 'independent' in governance, finance, or strategic planning for long-term development.

PART 2

DEVELOPMENT

Part 1, Definitions, explains the geographical and railway context for this book but I cannot precisely define a 'minor railway'.

Fig 12 (below) is a map of the minor railway geography which will be the framework for the remainder of the book. I have looked again at a definition of branch lines – a secondary route from a terminus which acts as a feeder to the main trunk line – and adopted that definition for this map. The heavy black lines are the main trunk lines, or primary routes, to and from London and the green lines are the secondary lines which I am describing, illustrating and exploring as minor railways.

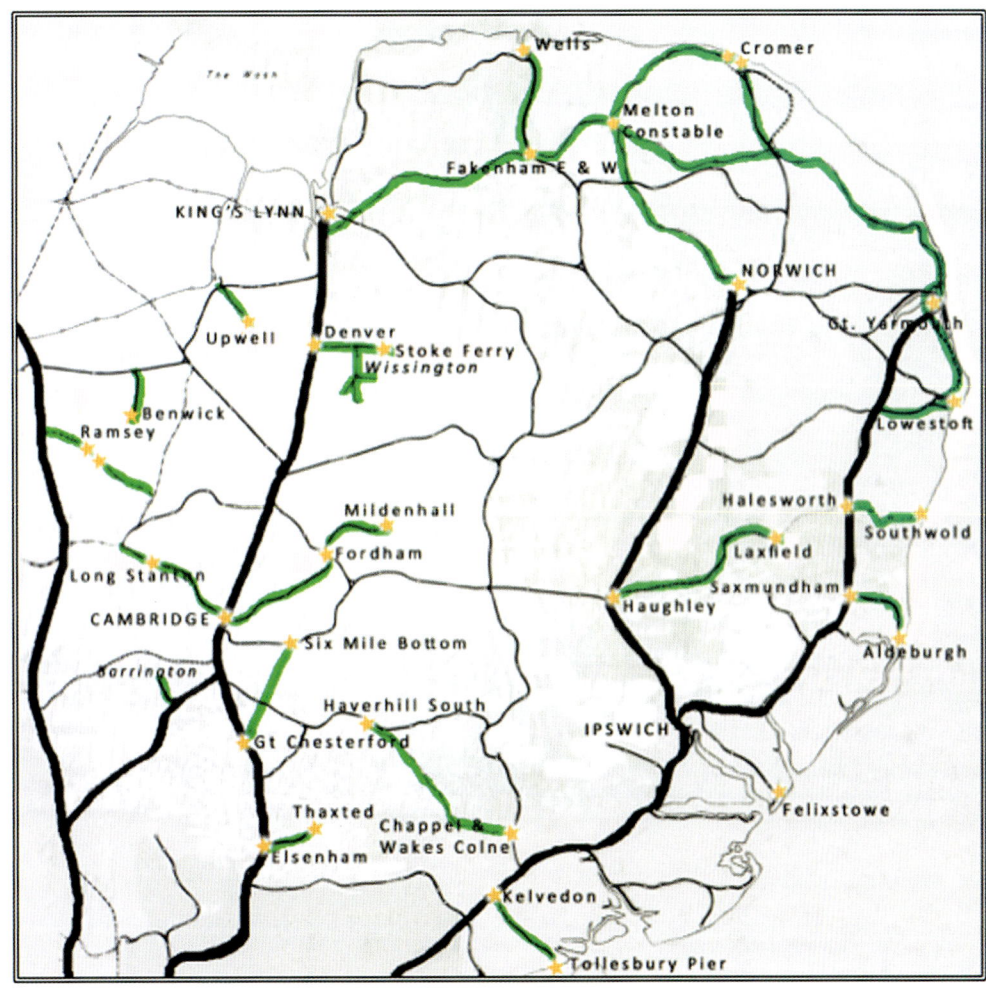

Fig 12: A visual summary of the minor railways – in green – chosen for this book.

Railways for maritime produce and perhaps for tourists . . . .

O Captain! my Captain! our fearful trip is done,
The ship has weathered every rack, the prize we sought is won.
The port is near, the bells I hear, the people all exulting.
Walt Whitman 1819-1892

To find a safe harbour after a stormy voyage must always be a relief to crew, passengers, ship owners and, perhaps, the Harbour Master because a ship entering his harbour will pay some harbour dues and charges. Most oceanic harbours were developed where a large river estuary reached the sea, especially if there was a considerable tidal range, a good ebb-tide flow to scour the lower reaches of rivers and an absence of off-shore hazards like rocks and shoals.

Much of East Anglia lacked such estuaries and although there was potential for European coastal trade, access to Atlantic business meant long voyages south and then west through the English Channel before an Atlantic crossing.

Most East Anglian harbours were therefore busiest with UK coastal traffic – coals from Newcastle; European North Sea shipping; timber from Scandinavia and fishing, especially the herring seasons.

I have suggested that railways to these harbours brought tourists but qualified that statement with 'perhaps'. In the popular perception, a working harbour and tourism were not ideal partners so elsewhere in the UK tourist resorts like Blackpool and Rhyl were developed on a large scale to attract great numbers of tourists from the major industrial centres:

> 'Wakes Week holidays became a tradition in northern towns following the Industrial Revolution, so the cotton mills and manufacturing factories could be closed for maintenance. From June to September a different town was on holiday each week — though the workers were not paid.' *Lancashire Telegraph*. 'Bygones'. 17 July 2013.

But East Anglia has no large-scale heavy industry so holiday resorts around the coast, like Hunstanton, Wells, Cromer, Southwold and Aldeburgh, developed on a smaller scale and only Southwold and Blakeney (between Wells and Cromer and not on the **Fig 12** map) have named harbours. The other centres sustained a small-scale fishing industry and are busy today with yachting and pleasure-boating.

The caution on the charts for Blakeney Harbour reflects the maritime complexities of much of the East Anglia coast:

> '**BLAKENEY HARBOUR**: Depths and banks . . . are liable to constant movement which may necessitate alterations to the positions of buoys and markers.
>
> 'The Harbour should be entered with great caution from seaward and only under suitable conditions of sea, tide and visibility.'
> © IMRAY CHARTS. November 2014.

The harbours I am exploring in Chapters 5 and 6 are King's Lynn, Great Yarmouth, Lowestoft, Southwold – which all have river estuaries – and, in Chapter **7**, Tollesbury Pier which had railway company ambitions to facilitate maritime business but was a typical minor railways overly-ambitious project.

I have not included the Port of Felixstowe, named on the **Fig 12** map and in Suffolk, because it is the biggest container port in Europe so outwith a 'minor railways' book.

Harwich International Port and Parkeston Quay in Essex, on the estuary of the River Stour and south of Felixstowe, are also outside the scope of this book because of their size and traffic. Each chapter concludes with the excitements offered in visits to East Anglian harbours by excursion trains:

> '. . . the excursion train made travel easier and, above all, affordable and opened up many more places to day trippers, in turn helping to expand the kind of activities on offer [at resorts] to all but the poorest workers and their families.'
> *Early Victorian Railway Excursions*. Susan Major. Pen & Sword Transport. 2015.

CHAPTER 5

KING'S LYNN PORT RAILWAYS

King's Lynn is a bridging point across the Great Ouse, a market town and a harbour. It developed in the Middle Ages as a member of the Hanseatic League which was a trading confederation of merchant guilds, ports and market towns in north-western, Baltic and central Europe.

At first, Lynn's export trade was dominated by salt (produced locally in copper pans), wool and grain; principal imports were timber, fish and iron. A number of Lynn merchants were based in North Sea and Baltic ports. Foreign merchants had their own businesses in Lynn, and there was also a considerable interchange of skilled work people. The Grade II* listed Marriott's Warehouse still remains in the harbour as one of the few substantial remains of the Hanseatic League surviving in England.

By the sixteenth century, Lynn's links with the Baltic and, the UK, trade in coal from Newcastle to London, wool and corn from the East Anglian hinterland were enhanced by its good nodal position. In the seventeenth and eighteenth centuries, Lynn, like a number of other East Coast ports, suffered from the growth of London and from the increasing importance of trade to ports such as Bristol and Liverpool that were better placed to serve the burgeoning commerce with the Americas and Africa. However, in the nineteenth century, railways provided the impetus for the construction of a dock (**Fig 13**).

The Harbour Branch, named and credited to LNER on the map, opened in 1846. It was a branch off the Lynn & Ely Railway which, via Ely, gave a direct route to London. Initially the Harbour Branch terminated south of the River Nar and served some small wharves on the Nar and the Great Ouse. The need to serve South Quay wharves on the east bank of the Great Ouse was met by an extension over the Nar and Millfleet across swing bridges. In 1862, the Harbour Branch and those lines marked LNER on the map became part of the Great Eastern Railway (and subsequently LNER/BR).

The GER had a near monopoly of railway operation in East Anglia but King's Lynn's railway development illustrates how nineteenth century competition amongst developing railway companies could breach that monopoly. Two companies, the wealthy and powerful Great Northern Railway (GNR) and the Midland Railway (MR), were seeking an East Coast port and access to East Anglia. They were finally, and jointly, successful in 1893 with the Midland and Great Northern Joint Railway which appears on the **Fig 13** map as an west-east railway bridging over the Ouse, the Nar and the GER and heading to Norwich. The M&GNR had a rail link to GER east of South Lynn but, even after the

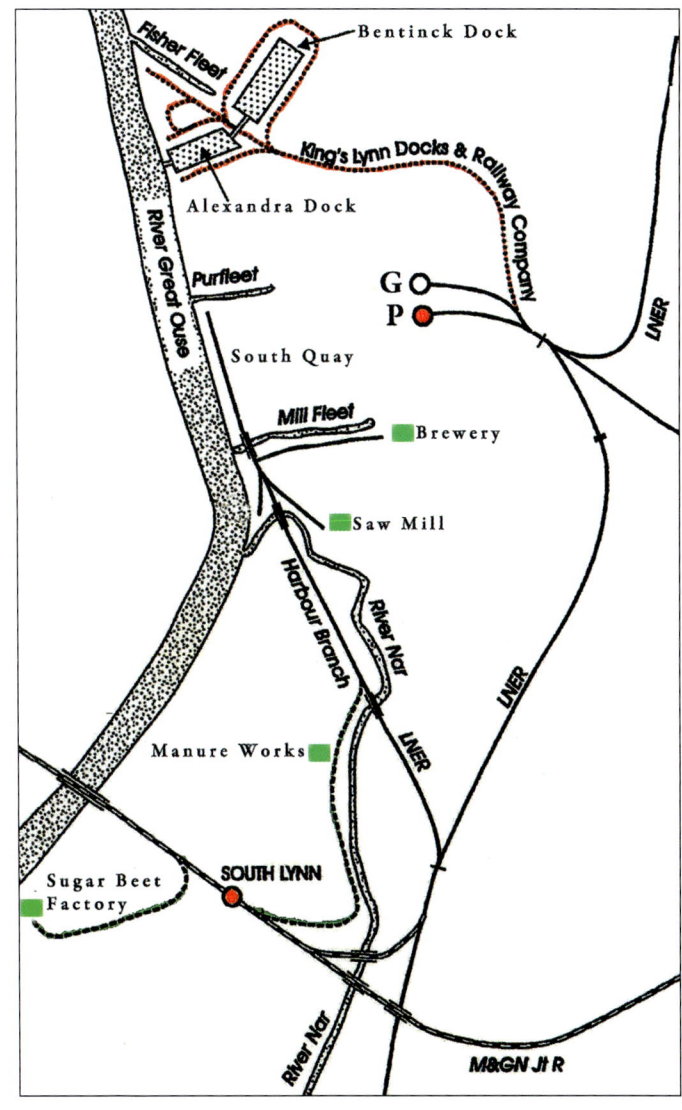

Fig 13: sketch map of railways to and from King's Lynn and those minor railways serving the Harbour and Docks. Based on a drawing by the late Roger Hateley.

Grouping in 1923, LNER and former M&GNR lines were still worked as separate entities. A 1939 Working Timetable stipulates:

'KING'S LYNN HARBOUR BRANCH.
Single Line
Traffic from the M&GN to King's Lynn Harbour must be sent into King's Lynn to be worked by L&NE trips.
'Traffic from King's Lynn Harbour to the M&GN will be worked as follows:
   1.10pm ex Harbour. To detach M&GN traffic at Harbour Branch junction which is [then] to be worked into South Lynn by South Lynn pilot.'

Another glance at the **Fig 13** map shows two independent industrial railways, both principally connected to the M&GN. To the south and west of the map is a line opened in 1927 from the King's Lynn Sugar Beet factory to the M&GN through a west-facing junction. The factory, and the line, became part of the British Sugar Corporation in 1936 and rail traffic ceased in 1993. Outgoing traffic was sugar pulp and molasses; ingoing was machinery, coal, coke, limestone – and sugar beet until 1965. The other line, serving the manure works, was opened in 1872 and connected to M&GN via a west-facing junction near South Lynn and to the Harbour branch. Originally the works and railway was owned by West Norfolk Farmers' Manure & Chemical Co-operative Co Ltd, then by Fisons Ltd from 1965 until rail traffic ceased in 1973; track was removed shortly after.

The largest area of independent minor railways in the King's Lynn area was that shown on the **Fig 13** map as the King's Lynn Docks & Railway Co but its creation was much more convoluted than the railways to the manure works or the sugar beet factory. It is a fascinating story of competition, King's Lynn Corporation's aspirations, and the financial and governance complexities of Victorian railway development.

Fig 14: Illustration from the *Illustrated London News* (1846) showing the first terminus of the Harbour Branch, south of the River Nar at its confluence with the Great Ouse. Two vans are on the railway alongside a two-masted barque; stevedores are loading or transhipping cargo.

A first key to these mysteries is terminology; this chapter refers to King's Lynn port railways, the opening paragraph refers to King's Lynn as a harbour and the **Fig 13** map shows a Harbour Branch and a Docks Railway. My guide for these matters is the two volume *Shorter Oxford English Dictionary*.

'Port: a town or city with a harbour or access to navigable water where ships load or unload.

'Harbour: a place on the coast where ships may moor in shelter, especially one protected from rough water by piers, jetties, and other artificial structures.

'Dock: an enclosed area of water [an artificial structure] for the loading, unloading, and repair of ships.'

The Corporation of King's Lynn was put under pressure by the GNR and MR for railway access to its port, to which GER already had access via the Harbour Branch. A King's Lynn Docks and Railway Company (KLD&R) was sanctioned by the Corporation and their Parliamentary Bill received Royal Assent on 19 June 1865. It was a potential beginning but there were as yet no docks at King's Lynn and the GER had already made public in a special edition of the *Lynn Advertiser* on 21 January 1864 that:

'As a body [GER] had not considered [the Docks proposal] at all and [GER Director, George Bidder] did not think it competent or proper to bring it before [the Corporation] while there appeared to be so much disunion and difference of opinion upon it among the inhabitants of this town.'

These are ingenious weasel words because Bidder knew that GER was proposing a railway to Doncaster and the Yorkshire and North-Eastern coalfields. His Company was already offering transhipment at King's Lynn for coal, and other goods, from Newcastle, which GER would then move swiftly to London by rail. Bidder also made clear to GNR/MR interests that his Company would allow them access to the King's Lynn Harbour wharves via the GER Harbour Branch. So, the GER made plain to the Corporation, investment in the proposed Docks was a matter for them and not for GER.

The Alexandra Dock foundation stone was laid on 9 March 1868 when the excavation for the dock basin was already well in hand; formal opening was on 7 July 1869. For reasons still not ascertained, the dock was built to an outmoded design with sloping sides – technically known as a batter slope – with concrete block facing. The batter meant that vessels could not come alongside so, especially as ships became larger and with a deeper draught, they had to be moored about 30ft off the dockside making cargo handling very difficult.

Fig 15: Coal was big business for the Dock Railway and for Alexandra Dock, illustrated at the north end of the Dock in 1877. The dumb-buffered private owner wagons include some owned by Midlands, North-Eastern and South Yorkshire collieries. Coal was coming by rail to King's Lynn and thence by sea to other East Anglian ports and to London.

The Dock Railway system left the existing GER lines at a junction near King's Lynn passenger and Goods stations and the Dock Company had to provide sufficient sidings near the new junction '. . . so as not to interfere with GER traffic and existing GER lines were not to be used for shunting'. (*An Illustrated History of the Port of King's Lynn and its Railways*. Mike G. Fell OBE. Irwell Press Ltd. 2012.) GER and subsequently LNER and BR worked the Dock Branch from the new junction to Pilot Street crossing and then onto the Docks system. It was, therefore, a truly independent minor railway system which was required to undertake the Dock Company's own operations although, in practice, GER worked the railways.

Despite the difficulties outlined above, Alexandra Dock soon became busy enough to require another dock – Bentinck Dock – which required an Act to authorise this extension, lengthy negotiations on compulsory purchase of the necessary land, and 18 months construction time. The new Dock was opened by William John Arthur Charles James Cavendish-Bentinck, 6th Duke of Portland, on 18 October 1883. Bentinck Dock was built with vertical walls (apart from the north quay with a batter slope) and a water area of 102 acres compared to 72 acres in Alexandra Dock.

The Port became increasingly busy so, for instance, in 1907, 750,705 tons of cargo was handled by the port – of which 450,190 tons was of *exported* coal all arriving by rail. That year there were 210,930 wagon movements on the Dock Railway which demonstrates the value of this minor railway system to the successful operation of the port. After the First World War, motor lorries became more readily available for road transport competing with railways.

The Grouping of the national railway system in 1923 did not affect the KLD&R Company because it did not come under the powers of the Act, but the newly created LNER did become responsible for working the Dock branch and shunting the dock traffic under a revised agreement with the Company. Into the 1930s, dock traffic tended to switch to road vehicles and 24-hour rail traffic was no longer necessary.

In 1948, the Port ownership passed to the British Transport Commission (BTC) until 1962. The Harbour was, and is still, owned by the King's Lynn Conservancy Board but is now bereft of any commercial traffic; the Conservancy Board provides pilotage and towage for the Port. BTC financed a new quay for the Port on the SE side of Alexandra Dock, and a new transit shed, both rail-served, and in 1981 the Docks began to handle deep-sea container traffic for BR Freightliner services. An encouraging development but, as Mike Fell whom I have quoted above explains: 'The Port's railway sidings were not designed with 15-car Freightliner sets in mind . . . [so] three five-car sets were . . . [in turn] . . . brought onto the Dock by a Class 08 diesel-electric shunter . . .'.

In 1963, BTC was succeeded by the British Transport Docks Board. In turn, it was succeeded by Associated British Ports (ABP) in 1986. A new rail business was fostered by a Dutch company offering traffic in steel coils from Ijmuiden but this traffic was short-lived and the last train left the Docks in May 1993.

Mike Fell, who was Assistant Port Manager at King's Lynn from November 1979 to March 1983 and then Manager from July 1984 until April 1987, concludes his excellent book with a paragraph that will serve as a pertinent memorial to many of the minor railways in East Anglia as road competition has overwhelmed one-time busy branch line railway services:

> 'Today (2012) the Port's principal traffics are dry bulk cargoes, forest products, liquid bulks, steel and other metals including scrap. The dry bulks include aggregates, animal feeds, fertilisers, grains and pulses. Three tanker berths are maintained in Bentinck Dock for petroleum products and agricultural chemicals. [There are no railways left on the Dock Estate – see **Fig 17**.]
>
> 'The Port continues to play an important role in the economy of East Anglia. Long may it continue to do so.'

Fig 16: In May 1993 the very last train left the Dock Railways system.

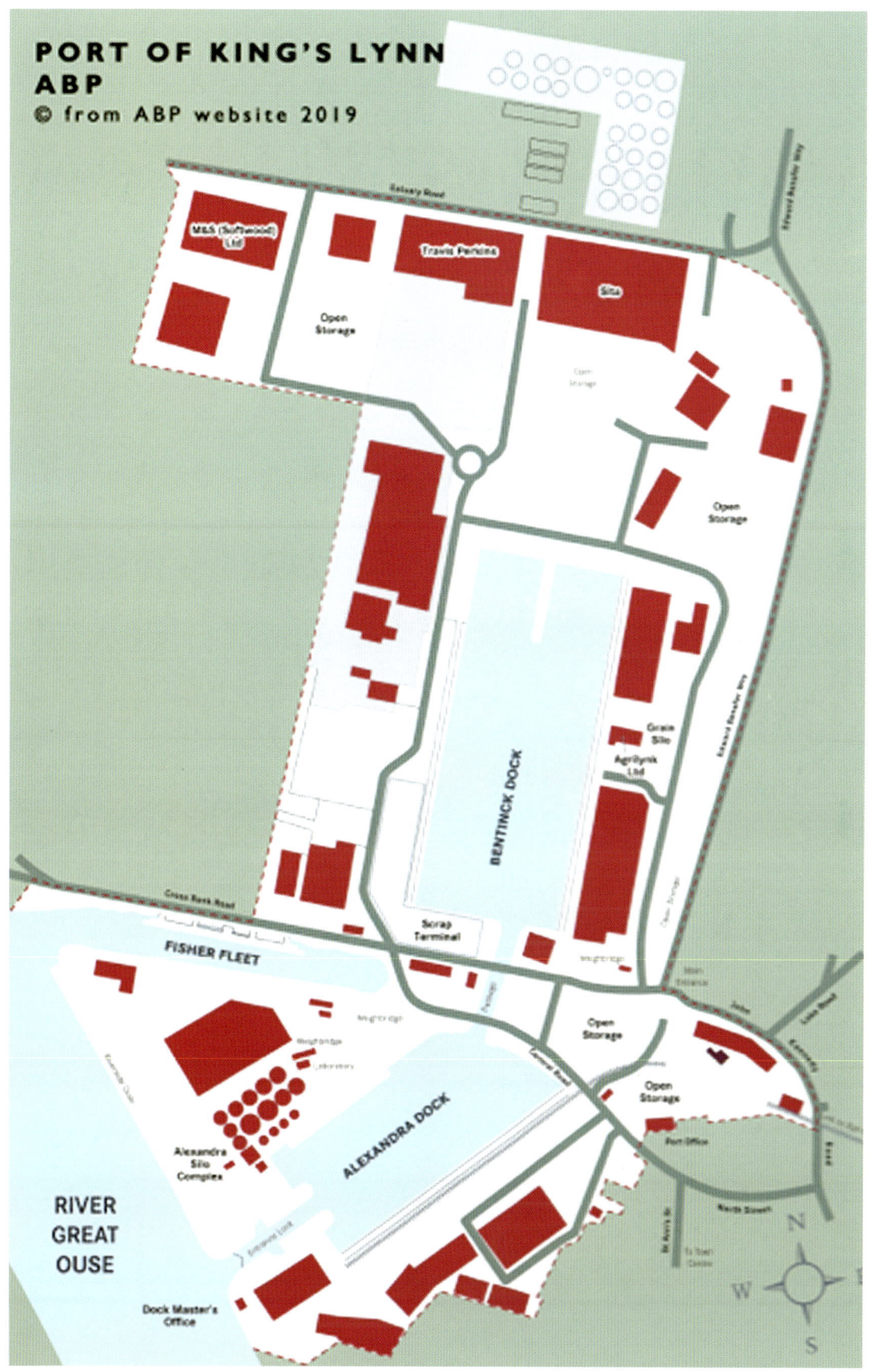

Fig 17: ABP © map of the Port of King's Lynn in 2019 – roads replace railways throughout the Port.

King's Lynn was, and is, a busy Port and it was well served by a network of minor railways on the Port estate but was it, is it, a tourist resort that was promoted by railways? **Fig 18** proves that the LNER promoted the town but, as **Fig 12** illustrates, this promotion was by a main-line railway from London so I must not be side-tracked. However, the LNER poster does include a slightly fanciful impression of the Harbour on the Great Ouse so, because tourism will prove to be an important market for Great Yarmouth and Lowestoft in Chapter **6** it must not be ignored here.

In his *The Companion Guide to East Anglia* (Collins 1970), John Seymour begins Chapter 11, *King's Lynn and the Great Ouse* thus – and the emphases are in the original:

'The most romantic town in England is **King's Lynn**.

'Few towns have been as single-minded as Lynn and Lynn's mind has always been firmly fixed on *trade*.

. . . It is no way a *'show town'* or *tourist resort*, trading consciously on its antique character. Its *modern flavour* is given by . . . merchant sailors – British and foreign – who come roaming off the ships in its modern docks, and by merchants who are the very descendants of the ones who built so much of the Lynn we see, back in the Middle Ages.'

The map of King's Lynn in Seymour's Chapter 11 shows the Harbour and the modern Port and includes all the minor railways which used to serve them and King's Lynn main-line station. Seymour the tourist, visiting and eulogising about Lynn, devotes several pages to descriptions of maritime Lynn Harbour, the modern Port and Lynn fishermen catching shell fish.

Ironically, however, Seymour makes no reference to railways and by 1970 the LNER poster would have been part of King's Lynn history. Seymour maintains that, 'The proper way to approach a seaport is from the sea – in the case of Lynn from the Wash and up the Great Ouse' so we can leave him there but remember his emphasis on trade as one promoter for tourism when we move to Great Yarmouth and Lowestoft which aspire to be tourist resorts.

Fig 18: LNER poster promoting King's Lynn.

CHAPTER 6

GREAT YARMOUTH AND LOWESTOFT DOCKS RAILWAYS AND SOUTHWOLD HARBOUR

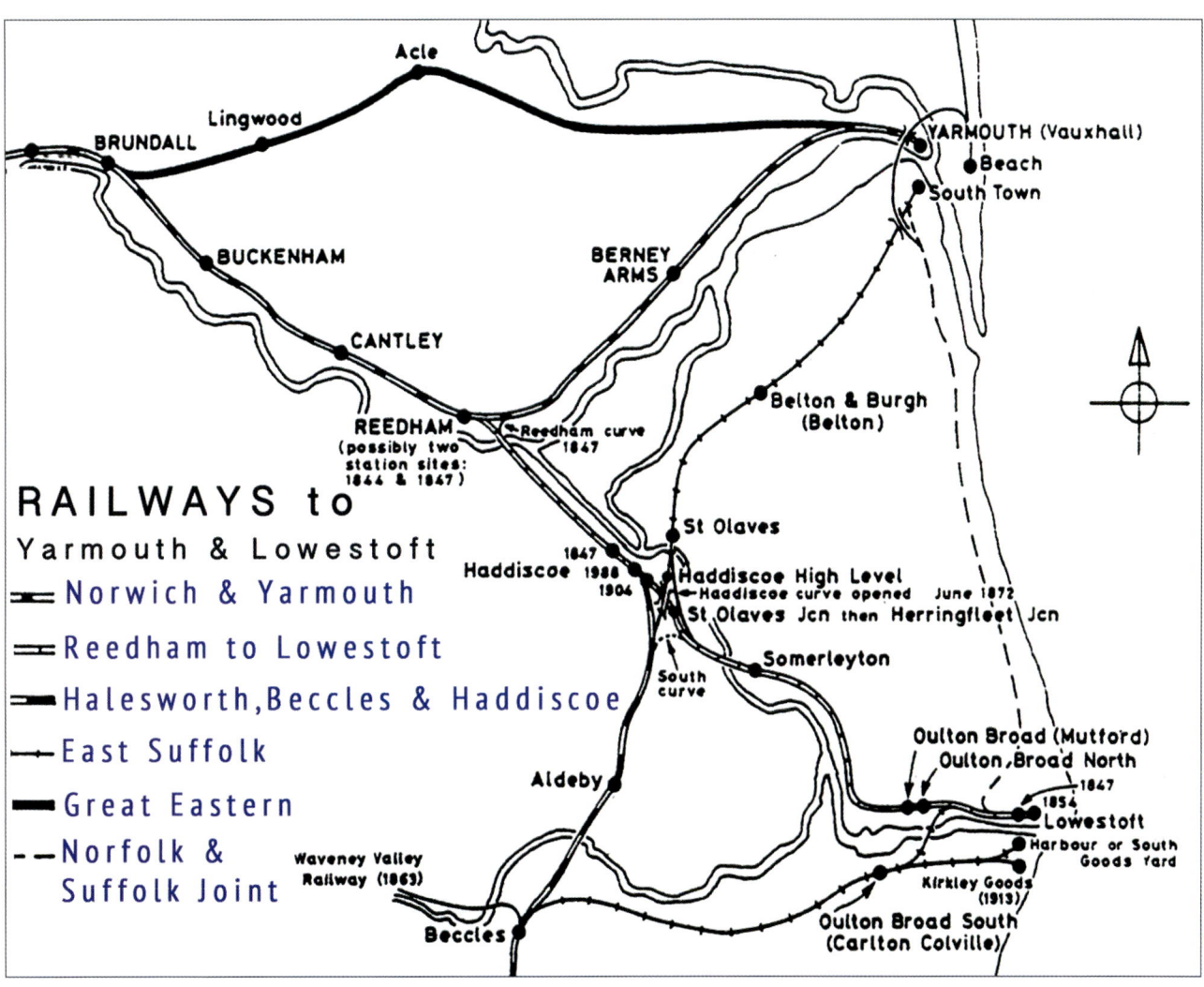

Fig 19: An historical map of the railways serving Yarmouth and Lowestoft.

A reference again to the **Fig 12** map (page 21) is a reminder that Yarmouth South Town (closed to passengers from May 1970) was opened in June 1859 as an extension of the East Suffolk Railway from Haddiscoe, enabling through trains from London Liverpool Street to reach Yarmouth via a main-line link. An even earlier station in Yarmouth was Yarmouth Vauxhall, opened in 1844 as the eastern terminus of the Yarmouth and Norwich Railway.

A first glance at the map in **Fig 19** appears to show that Lowestoft was initially by-passed but Lowestoft

Station – now Lowestoft Central Station – opened in 1847 as the terminus of the East Suffolk Railway from London and Ipswich.

The railway complications implicit in the last two paragraphs and illustrated in the **Fig 19** map echo the competition between Yarmouth and Lowestoft as ports and, especially before the coming of the railways, the competition for Norwich river-borne traffic. For many centuries, Norwich considered itself to be the second city of England – although York has long proclaimed a similar historic status – and it was an important river port. Before the railway age it would have been quicker for a Norwich man to have travelled by water to Antwerp or Rotterdam than to have made a road journey to any major English city.

Once the railways came, Norwich became another London main line destination (see the **Fig 12** map) but it had at least one minor railway connection – and to a separate station – as did Yarmouth and Lowestoft. The battle between them for Norwich traffic before the railways came can be explained by geography and the end of the Ice Age when glacial melt-water changed the topography and the drainage pattern of eastern Norfolk.

Fig 20 (courtesy of Google maps) shows the post-glacial course of the River Waveney which might have been supposed to flow eastwards to Lowestoft but now flows north-eastward and then northwards to Yarmouth. Knowledgeable geographers will detect that Lowestoft on this map should be about 10 miles further south but that can be taken as read. **Fig 21** represents the Rivers Waveney, Yare and Wensum as well as the man-made diversions which allowed Lowestoft to steal Norwich traffic from Yarmouth.

The **Fig 21** map also shows that the sea approach to the Port of Great Yarmouth is difficult, up the narrowing estuary of the River Bure whereas Lowestoft is more straight forward into Lake Lothing, which forms the harbour and thence into Oulton Broad and thence to the River Waveney. However, both Yarmouth and Lowestoft harbours suffer from long-shore drifting, as does Southwold south of Lowestoft, which can block the harbour entrances at low tide and sometimes block them completely even at high tide.

The geography above provides a context for the minor railway history which follows, first in Yarmouth and then in Lowestoft. The **Fig 22** sketch map below illustrates the competitive complexity of the railways to Yarmouth and Lowestoft.

In both Yarmouth and Lowestoft the minor railways, serving the Port wharves and industries in the two towns, became an increasing hazard, or cause of delay, to road users as motor transport replaced the railways.

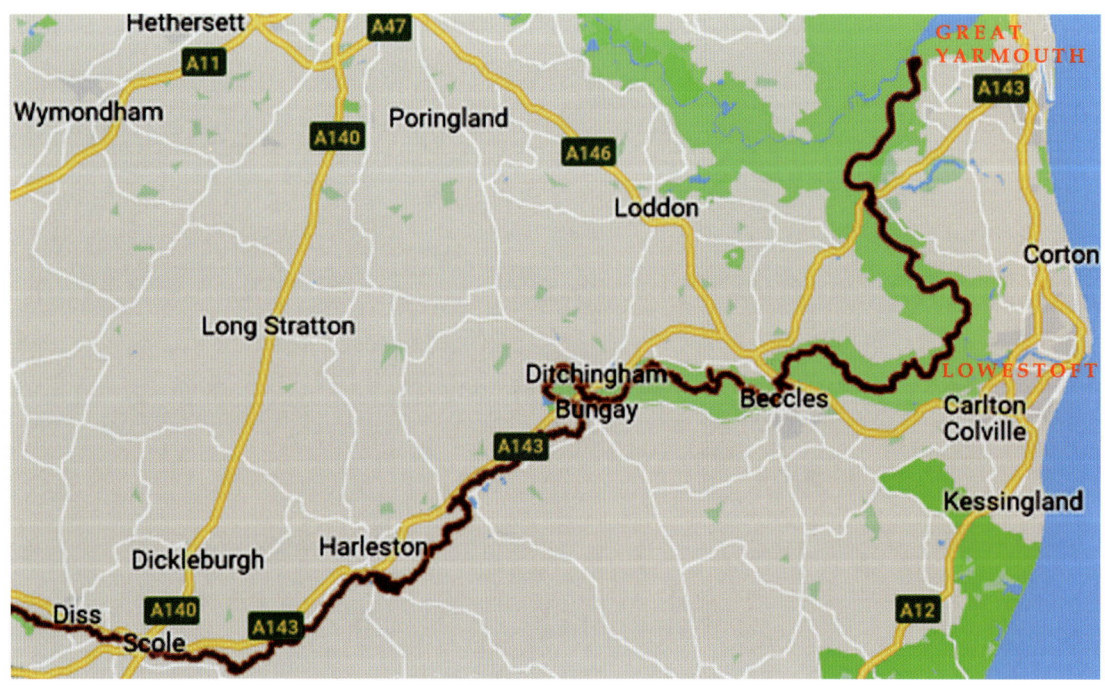

Fig 20: Google map – course of River Waveney is highlighted.

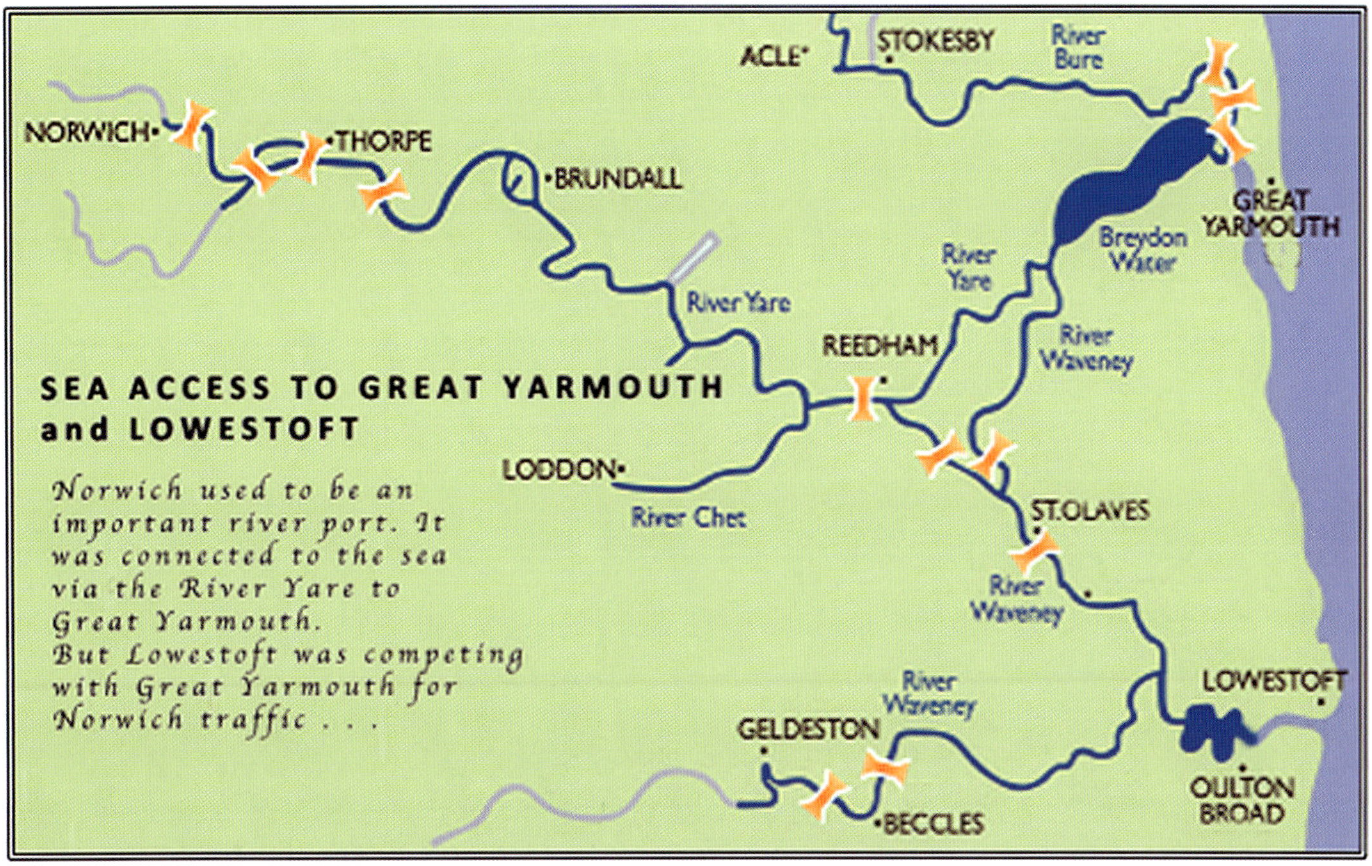

GREAT YARMOUTH AND LOWESTOFT DOCKS RAILWAYS AND SOUTHWOLD HARBOUR • 31

SEA ACCESS TO GREAT YARMOUTH and LOWESTOFT

Norwich used to be an important river port. It was connected to the sea via the River Yare to Great Yarmouth. But Lowestoft was competing with Great Yarmouth for Norwich traffic . . .

Fig 21: Man-made navigational aids – like Oulton Broad and the Haddiscoe Cut from St Olaves to Reedham – join the meandering River Waveney to the River Yare. The Cut, excavated in the nineteenth century, provides a direct route between Lowestoft Docks and Norwich.

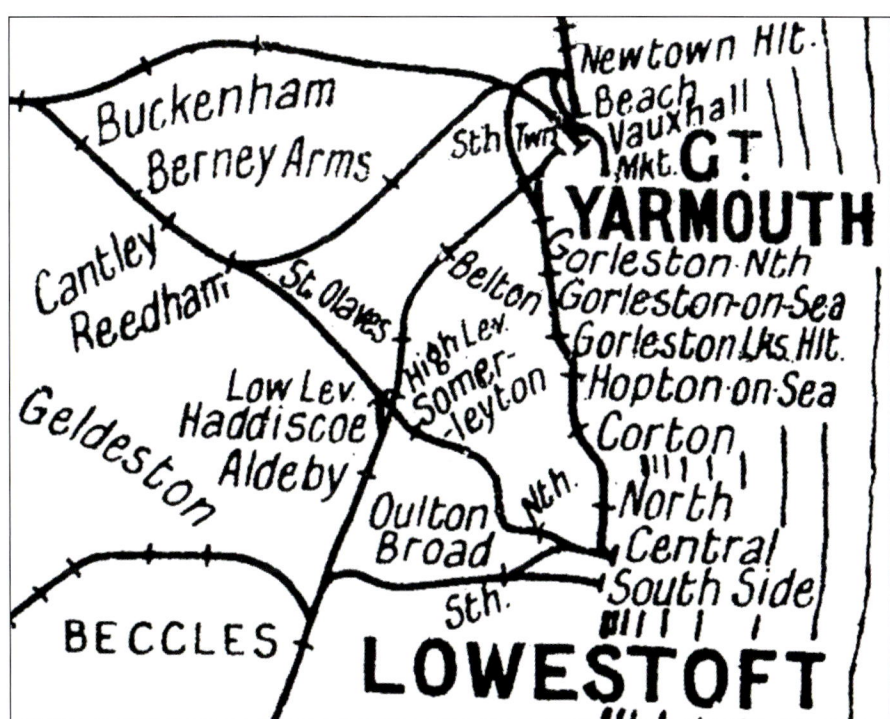

Fig 22: Map extract from Railway Executive – Eastern Region. Civil Engineer. March 1950.

Even more effectively than the **Fig 23** picture, the **Fig 24** map shows the close interconnection between minor railways and urban roads in a port town like Yarmouth. The station marked is Yarmouth Vauxhall and the bus in **Fig 23** is near the 'Q' of Quay [Street] on the map; the 'Brewery' on Quay Street is the large building

Fig 23 (left): Yarmouth near Vauxhall Station, July 1969 – see **Fig 24** 6-inch OS map.

Fig 24 (below): extract from © 6-inch OS map. Norfolk LXVI.SE ca1946.

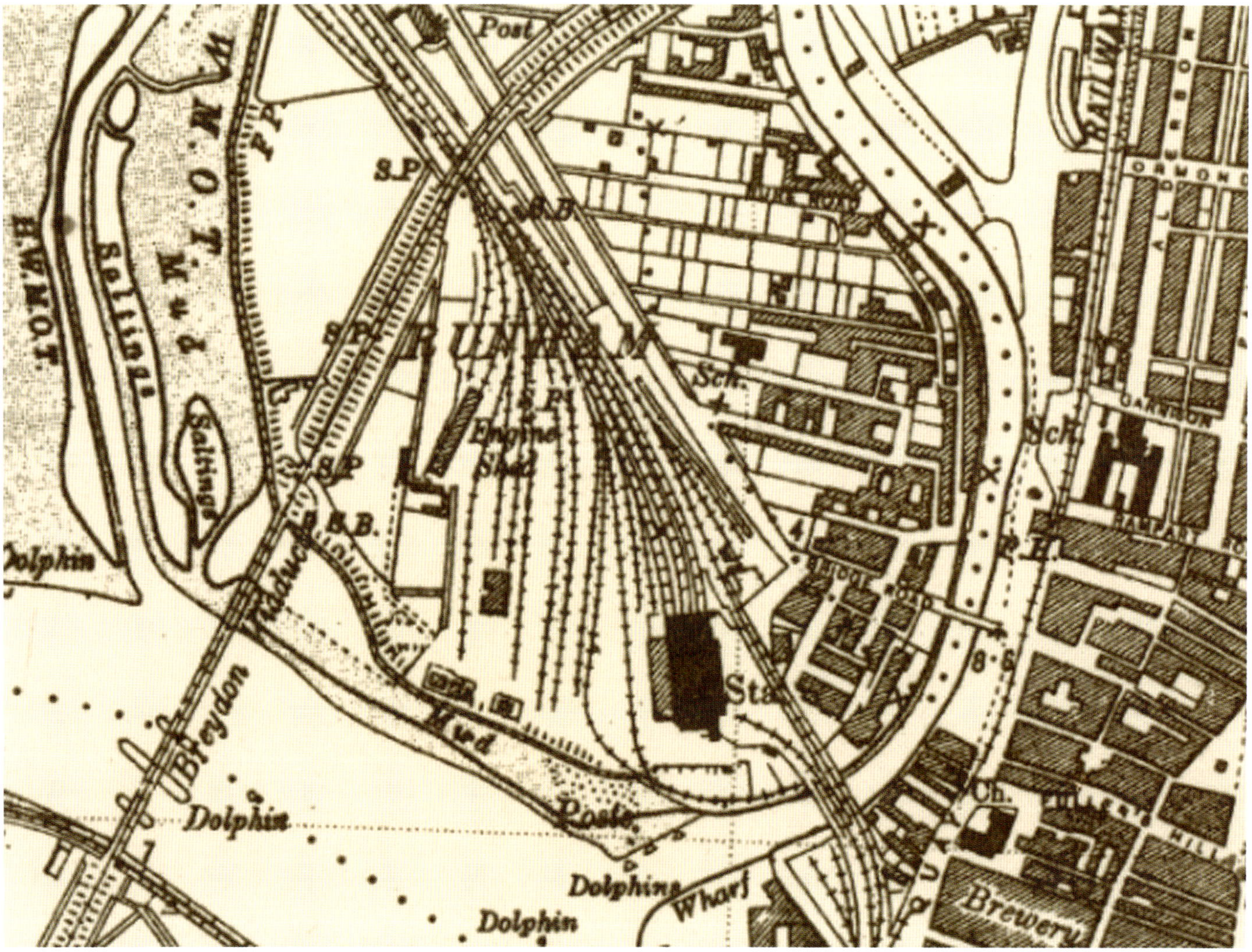

Fig 25: a railcar at Yarmouth.

to the right of the bus. Unfortunately, Yarmouth falls on an OS division of 6-inch maps so it has not been possible to show the whole of the town but its North-South extent can be envisaged from **Figs 21** and **22** and, on **Fig 22**, the 3 passenger stations – 'South Town', 'Vauxhall', 'Beach' – and the Goods Station – 'Market' are all named.

I have already quoted from John Seymour's *The Companion Guide to East Anglia* (Collins 1970), and his robust style is pertinent for Yarmouth too because he cites the town as both a busy port and a tourist resort:

> 'Yarmouth is supposed by many people to be nothing but fat cockney women in funny paper hats jostling each other along the crowded prom. It is that, but many other things too . . . Yarmouth still flourishes as a trading port . . . and is becoming [1970] an oil boom town . . . as a base for drilling operations in the North Sea.'

Seymour's reference to '. . . funny paper hats . . ' is a useful reminder that Yarmouth is not only a tourist resort but also a port offering extensive beaches, two piers, a promenade, special day-return fares from London and a different sort of minor railway in **Fig 25**.

Main line railways sought to bring tourists to Yarmouth as the early twentieth century GER postcard illustrates in **Fig 26**. And 'special offers' were continued into BR days as in the **Fig 27** flyer from 1957:

Fig 26

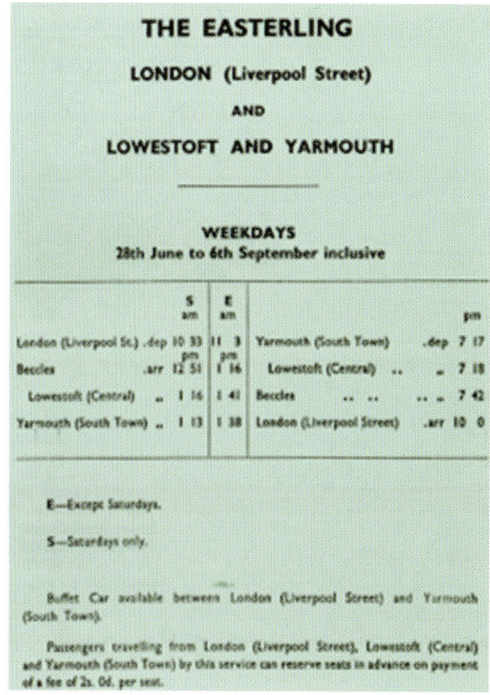

Fig 27

The Easterling was an express train through, with only one stop at Beccles, to Yarmouth South Town station. It was, in the context of this book's categories of East Anglian railways (see **Fig 12**), a main line service but today there are no through trains from London to Yarmouth and Yarmouth South Town station closed in 1970.

This flyer is therefore a useful segue from Yarmouth to Lowestoft which was a port and resort competitor with Yarmouth for several centuries and never had a main-line connection with London for regular through trains.

Ironically, in the light of the history already reviewed in this Chapter, there is today no direct London connection with either Yarmouth or Lowestoft and the best route involving only one change is via Norwich. So that powerful medieval city triumphs again over the coastal ports, not least as a much-visited tourist resort.

So to minor railways again and the port, and resort, of Lowestoft. **Fig 20** showed that the pre-glacial River Waveney very probably reached the sea in the vicinity of what is now Lowestoft but post-glacial changes, including medieval peat-cutting, created Lake Lothing which is now Port Lowestoft.

Fig 28, six-inch OS map extract, shows the Inner and Outer Harbour which together form the Port of Lowestoft and the network of minor railways which serve it and the town's passenger station (**Fig 29**).

Yarmouth, and Norwich which depended on it, were riverine harbours and suffered the sort of problems of silting that were common to many riverine harbours. Yarmouth, as **Fig 21** illustrates, also had a difficult sea entrance, north up an extended and relatively narrow estuary and then a 130° south-westerly turn into Breydon Water.

The economic origins of Lowestoft Harbour can be traced back to the mid-nineteenth century energy, skills and determination of Sir Samuel Morton Peto (1809-89) which brought prosperity to the fishing industry and to the town. Peto was an engineer, a very successful railway contractor and, for over twenty years, an MP for Norwich, then Finsbury, then Bristol. He was a speculative entrepreneur who, in partnerships with Grisell, then Petts, and then Brassey

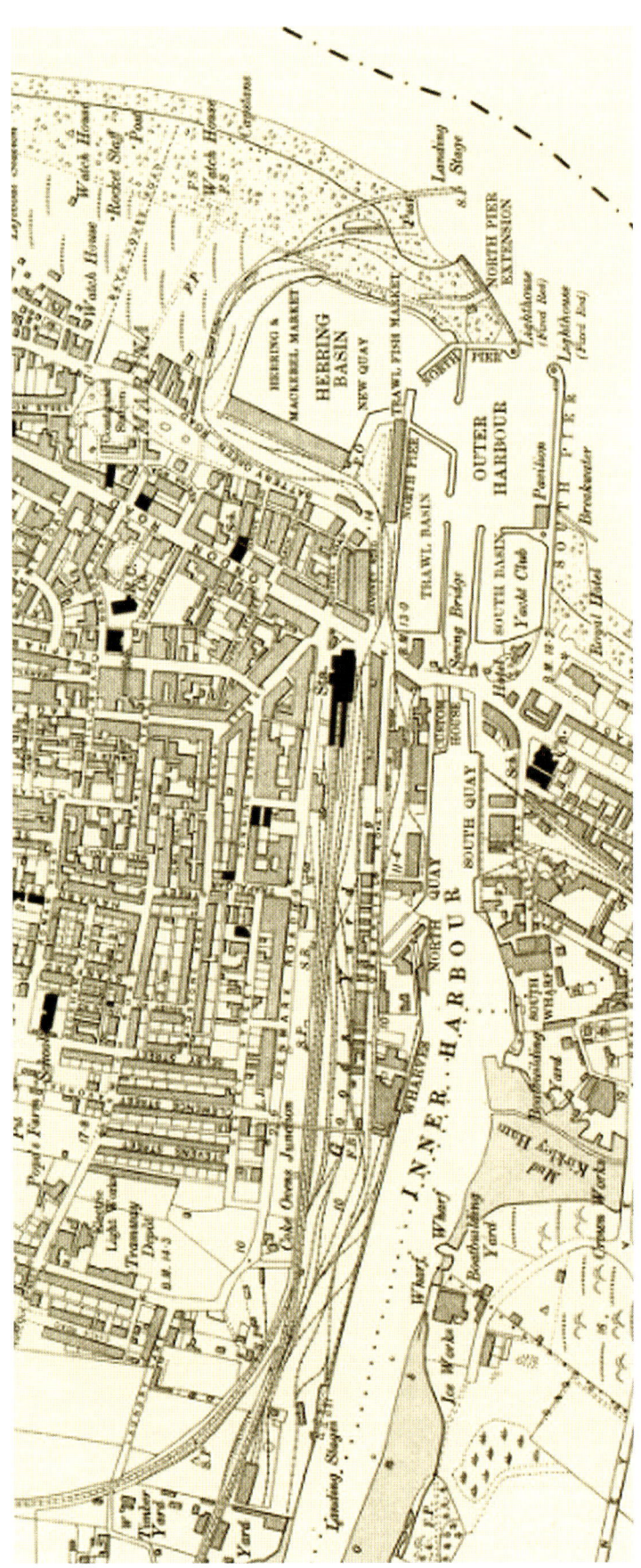

Fig 28: Suffolk X.NE [Lowestoft] 1906. OS Six-inch-to-the mile map.

Fig 29: Lowestoft Central Station in the 1950s.

successfully undertook a variety of major building works and railway contracts. He had no family links in East Anglia but, through his many contacts, he had 'a good eye for the main chance' and in the early 1840s he was building the Eastern Counties Railway. In 1844, he purchased the Norwich & Lowestoft Navigation Company which included Lowestoft harbour. The Company had already undertaken the man-made cuts described earlier which connected Oulton Broad to the River Waveney and thence via the Haddiscoe Cut from St Olaves to Reedham to the River Yare and Norwich (see **Fig 21**).

However, the Lowestoft Harbour was insufficient for the traffic which Peto planned to develop. In 1845, he created the Lowestoft Railway & Harbour Company (LR&HC), and within a year improvements to the harbour had begun. By 1847, contractors Grissell & Peto had built for the Company the Lowestoft to Reedham Railway and thence, via Brundall, to the Norfolk Railway and Norwich (see **Fig 19**). This Lowestoft railway link was immediately leased to the Norfolk Railway, of which Peto was chairman. Lowestoft was now in railway contact with London and the rest of the country.

Peto added an Outer Harbour (see **Fig 28**) entered between two piers; the 1,800ft long North Pier was for fish markets and South Pier provided a 'beautiful and healthful promenade' because Peto also intended that Lowestoft should be a resort. Further inland, on the north bank of the Inner Harbour, about 30 acres of land was levelled for a number of industries and a bank of 83 coke ovens which supplied fuel for Norfolk Railway locomotives. At this time, Peto leased the LR&HC and the Norfolk Railway to the ECR and subsequently to the monopolistic GER so Lowestoft became a railway port.

Peto encouraged substantial capital investment in the Harbour by developing the growth of the herring industry and encouraging the import of cattle and timber from Northern Europe. The North of Europe Steam Navigation Company (NESNC) provided steam packets for this trade and needed maintenance facilities for their vessels. A 260ft dry dock was constructed in

1849 on North Quay off the Inner Harbour, followed in 1852 by a set of huge sheer legs for the removal and installation of ship's boilers and masts. A year later came the range of quayside ironworks that formed part of the Harbour Works, the engineering works where the harbour's plant, machinery and infrastructure were maintained (see **Fig 29**).

NESNC went into liquidation in 1858 so in August 1859 ECR took over their ironworks, dry dock, sheer legs and cattle sheds for £3,350; ownership passed to GER in 1862. The ironworks were part of what was developed as the Harbour Works, an integral part of both harbour and railway, since both were in common ownership. As the railway company was responsible for the harbour, it became involved with various marine activities such as maintaining a fleet of vessels including tugs, dredgers and pile-drivers. The dredgers fought an almost continuous battle to keep the harbour mouth clear from drifting sand and shingle, though the railway company was able to make good use of the sand and shingle by selling it for ship's ballast. The Harbour Works were served by a network of minor railways shown on **Figs 28** and **29**. On the north side of the site were sawmills and a creosote treatment plant because the import of Scandinavian timber for railway sleepers had made Lowestoft one of the largest sleeper depots in the country. The creosote was a by-product of Peto's coke ovens on North Quay.

GER continued to invest in the harbour, and trading conditions showed a general all-round improvement for Lowestoft. An interesting commercial venture was the distribution by rail of sea water. Loaded into casks, it went to inland towns for Sea Water Public Baths and for occasional specialist customers like the penguins and polar bears in London Zoo.

In 1883, Waveney Dock was excavated – labelled as Herring Basin on the **Fig 28** 1906 OS map. This Dock encouraged a build-up of enormous shoals of sand and gravel on the North Beach which, like the sea water, offered commercial possibilities for use and/or sale as ships' ballast. A network of sidings was extended across the shoals, terminating at the high water mark, and a wagon was positioned on each siding into which shingle was shovelled.

Dock enlargement was continued by GER as the herring fishery business grew so a northern extension to Waveney Dock opened in 1906 as Hamilton Dock – named after Lord Claud Hamilton, GER Chairman –providing 300 more berths for drifters. The East Anglian herring fishery was approaching its peak but contraction began during the First World War and ended in the 1920s. GER ownership was succeeded by LNER ownership in 1923 and drifters were replaced by trawlers for more extensive deep-sea fishing.

In 1938, the LNER set about harvesting its crop of shingle on a more-industrial scale. A vast screening plant, known locally as the 'Shingle Mill' or 'Pebble Mill', appeared on the North Beach skyline, built using massive timbers and standing fifty feet high, astride what had become a small marshalling yard, with sidings running out over the beach on jetties. The Mill sorted the shingle into various sizes, ranging from grains of sand to large stones. One of the duties allotted to the Harbour Works' departmental locomotive was to run out to the Mill with a supply of empty mineral wagons, which were shunted and exchanged for full ones to be taken back to the Harbour Works for processing at the newly opened pre-cast concrete plant there.

The Concrete Works on the north side of the Harbour was another railway development in 1938, covering 22 acres and employing 100 men. Inspector H. Twiddy ran the plant; he had worked at the M&GN's pioneering

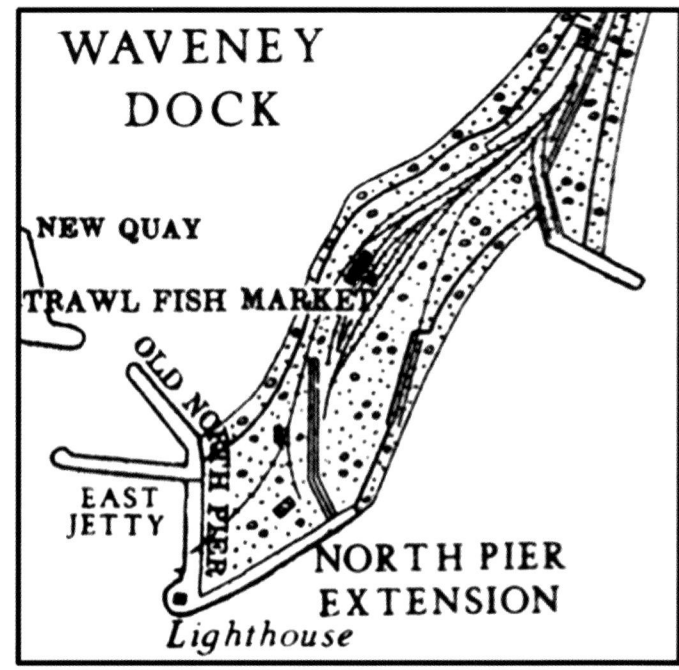

Fig 30: North Pier and the Shingle Mill – just north of 'ET' of 'MARKET' with its network of sidings. OS 6-inch map extract from sheet X.NE 1951.

concrete works at Melton Constable and brought with him some useful moulds, a few of the employees and a lot of experience. Lowestoft Harbour plant manufactured concrete products for use throughout the LNER, including bridge sections, fence and gate posts, cable conduits, drainage and telephone ducts, building blocks, platform slabs and edging. The output of the Concrete Works was 4-5,000 items per week.

The Harbour Works employed outdoor gangs who were responsible for sorting out problems including virtually anything broken on LNER property. One such problem occurred on 15 August 1950 when Somerleyton Bridge failed at 11.50; Harbour Works engineers left Lowestoft by taxi and found one of the hydraulic jacks damaged. While platelayers hand-jacked the bridge to receive rail traffic, the damaged jack and pipe were brought back to the Harbour Works by taxi, repaired, returned by lorry, and fitted and tested by 20.00 the same day.

Lowestoft Harbour was an unheralded triumph of minor railway operation and **Fig 31** illustrates the business which the railways served.

In January 1963, the British Transport Commission handed over control of Lowestoft Harbour to the British Transport Docks Board, freeing the railway of the responsibility after 118 years. The Sleeper Depot was closed in May 1964; supervision of the Harbour Works and Concrete Plant was switched to York and the Concrete Works closed in 1985. The little railway traffic which remained was carried out on hard-standing by shunting tractors and in September 1970 all locomotive working ceased.

On 3 July 1988, the historic Harbour Works was closed and so ended the career of a little-known railway works that had survived for 135 years. All that has survived of former railway property on the North Quay side of the Harbour is the dry dock, now a private operation.

Fig 31 shows the Harbour-related industries in South Lowestoft but the development of the seaward side of south town – adjoining South Beach – was primarily by Sir Morton Peto, who bought the land south of the Harbour bridge for just £200. It is said – and reported in Robert Malster's book, *Lowestoft East Coast Port* (Terence Dalton Ltd. Lavenham, Suffolk. 1982), – that Peto:

'. . . invited the Improvement Commissioners, appointed by Act of Parliament "for better paving, lighting, cleansing, watching and otherwise improving the Town of Lowestoft" to lunch at [his Suffolk home] Somerleyton Hall. During the meal, [he] asked them to sell him the land lying along the back of [South] beach to the south of the Harbour.

'They were so [surprised] by the idea that there should be any value in waste land that they invited

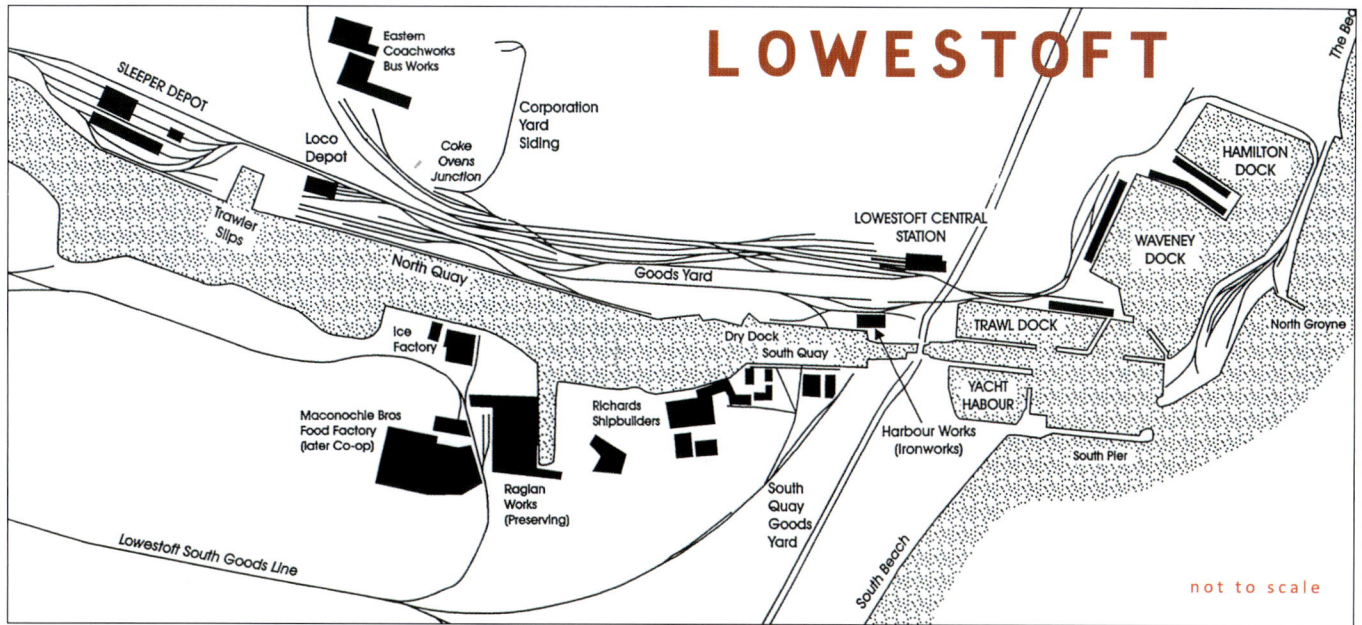

Fig 31: sketch map of Lowestoft Harbour in the 1960s showing the network of minor railways serving the Harbour and industries around it as well as the passenger station – Lowestoft Central.

Fig 32: The landward end of South Pier and The Royal Hotel opened in 1849. An 1869 Guidebook reports that '. . . the bathing establishment is on the best principle, the baths being supplied with salt or fresh water by a steam engine, which also supplies water for other purposes'.

Peto to name his own price and eagerly accepted what they considered to be his magnificent offer of £200. History does not record their feelings when, after lunch, Peto took his guests into the library and showed them the plans already drawn up for the Esplanade, the Marine Parade and the Wellington Gardens. Peto . . . laid out this new suburb in excellent taste.'

The principal contractors were a local firm, Lucas Brothers, who had already worked with and for Peto. About 300 bricklayers, labourers and joiners worked on the Lowestoft contract, building many new houses, churches, schools and a new railway station on the same site as Peto's original Lowestoft terminus but now called Lowestoft Central. Lucas Brothers also built the 80-bedroom Royal Hotel (**Fig 32**).

As roller-skating became popular in the 1870s, an indoor rink was opened followed by an outdoor rink and then, on the same site, the Marina Theatre which is still open to visitors today. Its advertising claims that, 'With a mixture of live entertainment and great

Fig 33: a rather time-worn plaque celebrating the 19th century roller skating rink.

cinema the Marina Theatre is at the cultural heart of the community.'

Fig 34: South Pier – a Family Entertainment Centre with fish and chips conveniently to hand next door.

The Royal Hotel closed in the 1960s and was derelict for several years until demolished in 1970 but the South Pier survives and is still an attraction today.

By the middle of the twentieth century, Lowestoft was still a busy port but also a seaside resort attracting thousands of trippers who came by rail from Norwich, Ipswich, and further afield, for a stay or as day visitors on Bank Holidays. In 2020, it has sustained that relative prosperity; trains still bring in visitors from Norwich and Ipswich, there are attractions, a long south beach and the Port is now owned by Associated British Ports (ABP) and their website confirms that:

'The Port of Lowestoft serves the busy sea routes between the UK, Europe, Scandinavia, and the Baltic States. The Port is linked by A-roads to the M11 and M1 and has quayside rail links. So the minor railways are still doing some business.'

And finally in this chapter, the Port of Southwold, about 10 miles south of Lowestoft and developed in the estuary of the River Blyth. It is another riverine port, with a relatively narrow estuary, but it has a relevant story to tell in this book because the trials and tribulations of its development and sustainability are similar to Yarmouth and Lowestoft and it was served by a minor railway harbour branch.

This story is a shortened version of that told in *The Southwold Railway 1879-1929. A Tale of a Suffolk Byway* (David Lee, Alan Taylor & Rob Shorland-Ball. Pen & Sword Transport. Feb 2019).

'Southwold Harbour is the only reasonably accessible haven between Harwich and Lowestoft and is increasingly frequented by fishing and other small craft . . . It is considered, that the closing of the Harbour would cause considerable hardship to small craft on the East Coast.'

Memo from the Cruising Association to the Ministry of Agriculture and Fisheries, 1949.

Quoted from: *Southwold Harbour and the Blyth Marshes*. Mackesey P.J., Private manuscript.

Southwold obtained an Act of Parliament in 1746: 'To open, cleanse, scour, widen, deepen, repair and improve our Haven' and a body of Harbour Commissioners was appointed with powers to levy charges on vessels using the harbour. The necessary improvements were set in hand but, at first, with little understanding of the natural conditions involved. The Blyth was originally tidal to

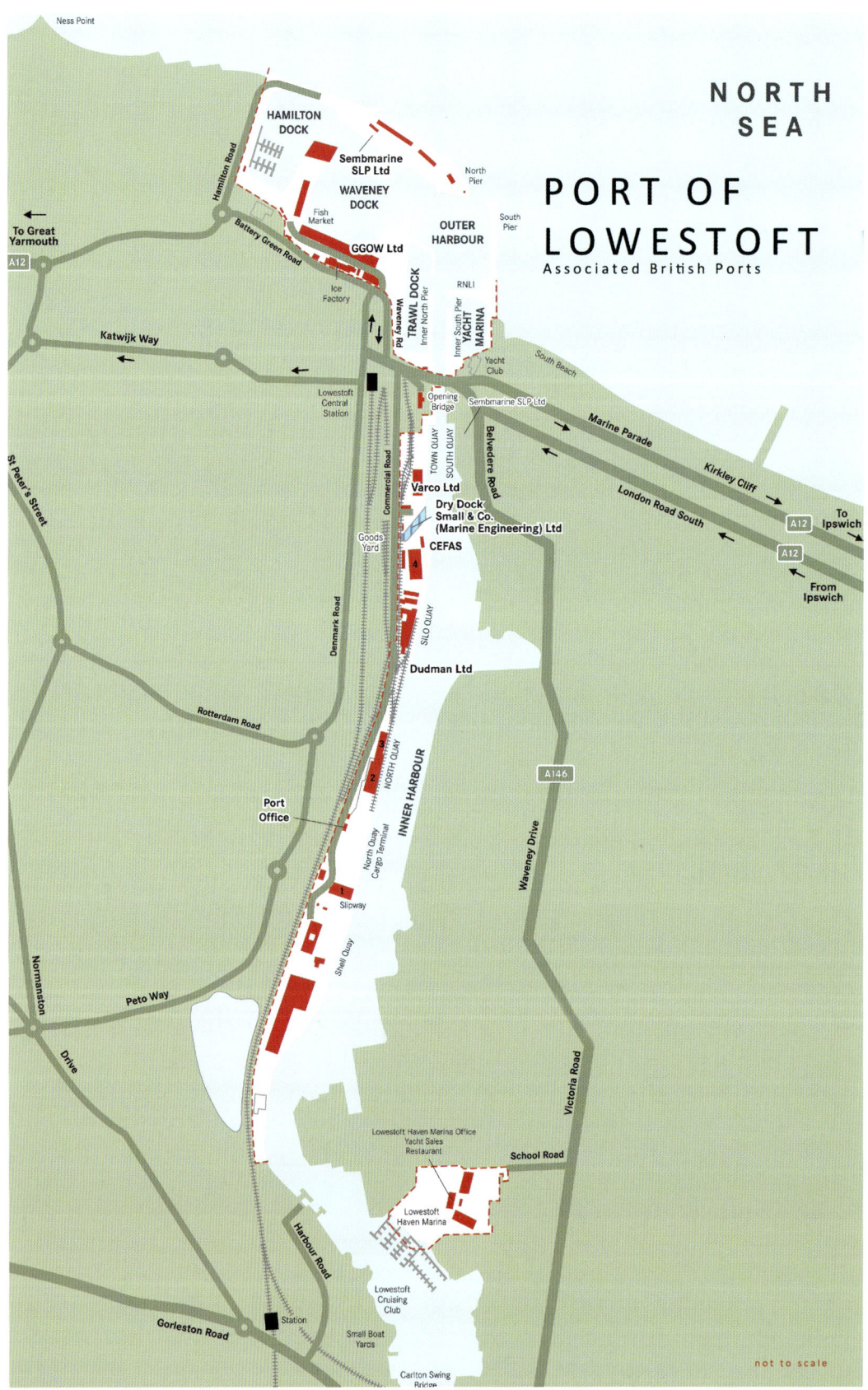

Fig 35: Plan of the Port of Lowestoft, edited from ABP Website 2019.

Halesworth and flowed over the lower part of its course through a large area of mud flats which flooded at high tide (**see Fig 36**). These flats acted as a reservoir, greatly augmenting the normal flow of the river on every ebb tide and thus providing a considerable scour over the Harbour bar. By 1761, work had been completed to make the Blyth a Navigation from Southwold to Halesworth for the mutual benefit of both towns. Four locks were necessary and the tidal extent of the Blyth was reduced by more than half. Furthermore, local landowners, noting the fertility of the tidal mud flats, began to enclose them with embankments. By 1845, 2,704 acres had been so enclosed and the scour of approximately 950,500,000 gallons of water was lost on every ebb tide.

The irony of the situation was that most of the landowners – the wealthy local gentry – had been made Harbour Commissioners under the 1746 Act. Their original enclosures of the tidal flats had doubtless been made in ignorance of their possible effects on the harbour but their ignorance was short-lived. Rapid and serious silting occurred and it soon became obvious to the Commissioners that their interests in their land and in the harbour they administered were directly at variance. To ensure that their interests in the land were not endangered, they succeeded in maintaining the Board of Commissioners as almost wholly gentry and landowners under four further Harbour Acts (of 1756, 1789, 1809, l830). Attempts were made to improve the harbour by dredging but the Commissioners were as nicely on the horns of a dilemma as any men could be and inevitably their actions met with little lasting success.

The Tidal Harbours Commission – 'appointed by Your Majesty to inquire into the state and condition of the Tidal and other Harbours . . . of Great Britain and Ireland . . .' – gave an unbiased assessment of their findings in 1845. On Southwold they stated:

> 'Commissioners have manifested great want of vigilant control and the landed, and fishing, and Corporation interests have often been preferred to the rights of the merchants and ship-owners and to the general interests of navigation. These interests having been so powerful as to occasion a dry bar, a deserted port and all but ruin of the ship owner and merchant.
>
> 'It appears in evidence that, with the exception of two, the Southwold Harbour Trustees are self-elected; they consist of land proprietors, merchants, etc., but only a single Southwold representative.'

The 'dry bar' to which the Tidal Harbour Commissioners referred was already well known to Southwold folk and merchants trying to use the harbour. In 1839 a bar had formed across the harbour mouth wide enough and dry enough to drive a carriage across and a number of vessels were impounded. Many of these belonged to a wealthy Halesworth Maltster, Patrick Stead, and he called for:

> '. . . . a better Harbour and a new Bill. Unless a new Act of Parliament be obtained so as not to exclude from the Commission practical and nautical men, I submit that the confidence of the public and parties interested cannot be supported.'

Application was made for a new Bill but the Commissioners attempted to introduce clauses making legal their claims to the lands they had embanked. In 1845, however, the passing of the General Enclosure Act gave them all they required; they abandoned the new Harbour Bill and virtually abandoned the Harbour. It rapidly decayed as shown in the account of a visit made in 1882:

> 'The piers are tumbling to pieces and the great worn capstans which are used for hauling vessels through the shingle [and over the bar] looked almost past use. All around are speaking evidences of its decay as a port: rotting barges, disused smacks and desolate wharves.'

The last wherry worked up the Blyth Navigation in 1908. A short-lived attempt was made to cleanse and overhaul the whole Navigation passage but failed, largely because the Southwold Railway was operating an efficient through service to Halesworth.

In 1891, the Harbour Commissioners attempted to have the harbour taken over by a public organisation with a view to improvements being made. An approach was to be made to the General Manager of the GER at a meeting on the 5 June 1891 but it was subsequently reported that the GER had declined to take on the harbour because they claimed not to have powers to raise funds.

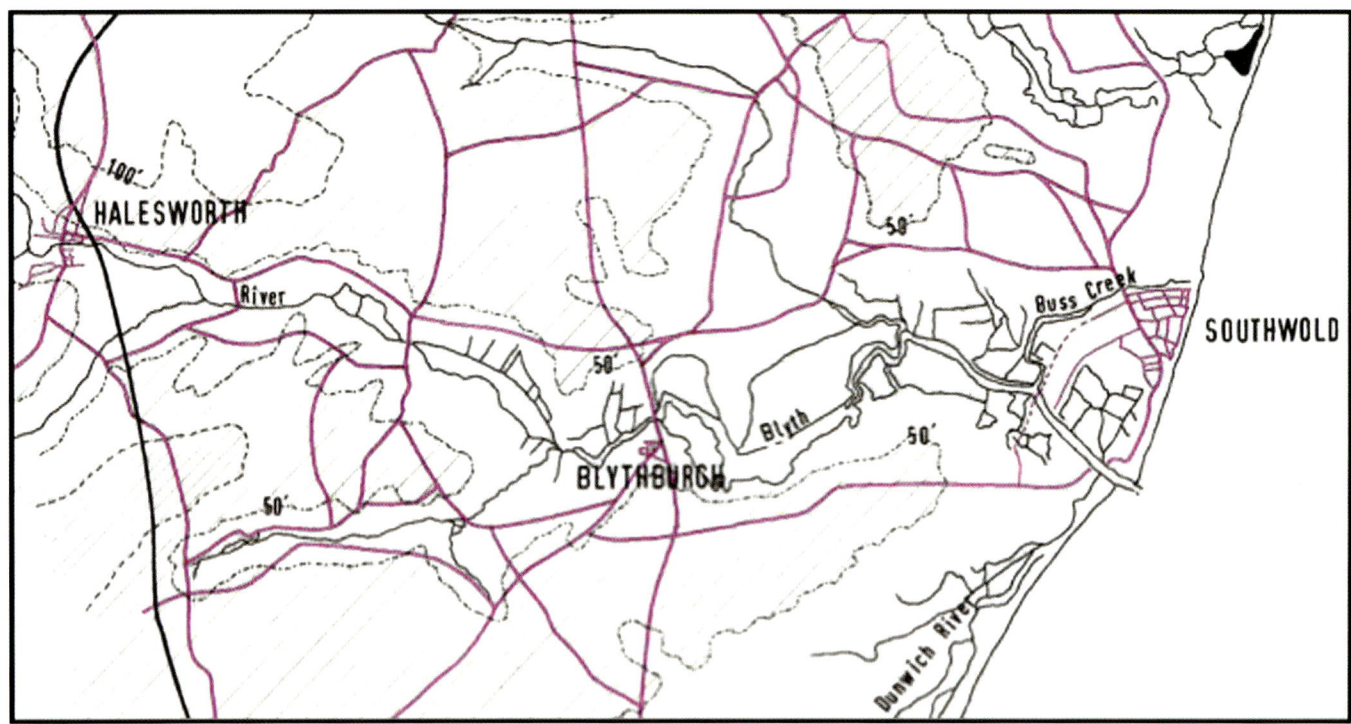

Fig 36: 1960 sketch map showing the River Blyth, winding its way to the North Sea through extensive tidal salt marshes. From 1879 to 1929 the Southwold Railway followed the Blyth valley from Halesworth to Southwold.

Nevertheless, development of the harbour was important to Southwold Corporation so in 1898 they successfully dissolved the Harbour Commission by Act of Parliament. At this time, Lowestoft and Great Yarmouth were thriving fishing ports and were packed to capacity, suggesting an opportunity to transform Southwold Harbour into a commercial undertaking.

The Corporation now owned their harbour and evolved an improvement scheme with the BoT and a London contractor, W. Fasey & Son of Leytonstone. Fasey had done work for the GER at Lowestoft to develop a fishery harbour to relieve the congestion at Great Yarmouth and Lowestoft. Southwold Harbour Company was created and a BoT-approved scheme gained a Government grant of £21,500 subject to the Harbour and several acres of adjoining land being freely conveyed to Messrs Fasey.

Work started in 1906 and was completed by late October 1907 but too late for that year's herring season. **Fig 37** is a map extract edited from OS County Series 1:2,500 for 1927 which illustrates the layout of the Harbour including the 'Kipperdrome' – a local nickname for the fish market – and the eastern end of the Harbour Branch railway.

Fasey rebuilt the harbour piers with a SE sweep giving sheltered water in the Harbour even during onshore gales. A 1,200ft fish quay was constructed on dry land on the Southwold bank of the river then the sand on the waterside was removed by the Dutch dredger *Zealand* which also dredged the harbour bottom to give a maximum high water depth of 18ft 6ins.

Gutting areas – staffed by many Scottish women who travelled to Southwold for the autumn herring season – curing houses, the Kipperdrome fish-market and a multi-gauge weighbridge were erected. On the Walberswick side, a spending beach absorbed waves which travelled up the harbour.

The first commercial cargo landed in the 'new' harbour was 272 tons of granite in April 1908 off the SS *Commandant* from Guernsey. The peak year for fish landings and general cargo was 1909 including a visit by two Royal Navy torpedo boats but business declined gradually year by year to 1913; in 1914 the outbreak of the First World War ended all commercial shipping until 1919.

The Kipperdrome survived into the 1920s, but the herring fishing trade never recovered in Southwold as Lowestoft and Yarmouth developed deep-sea trawling

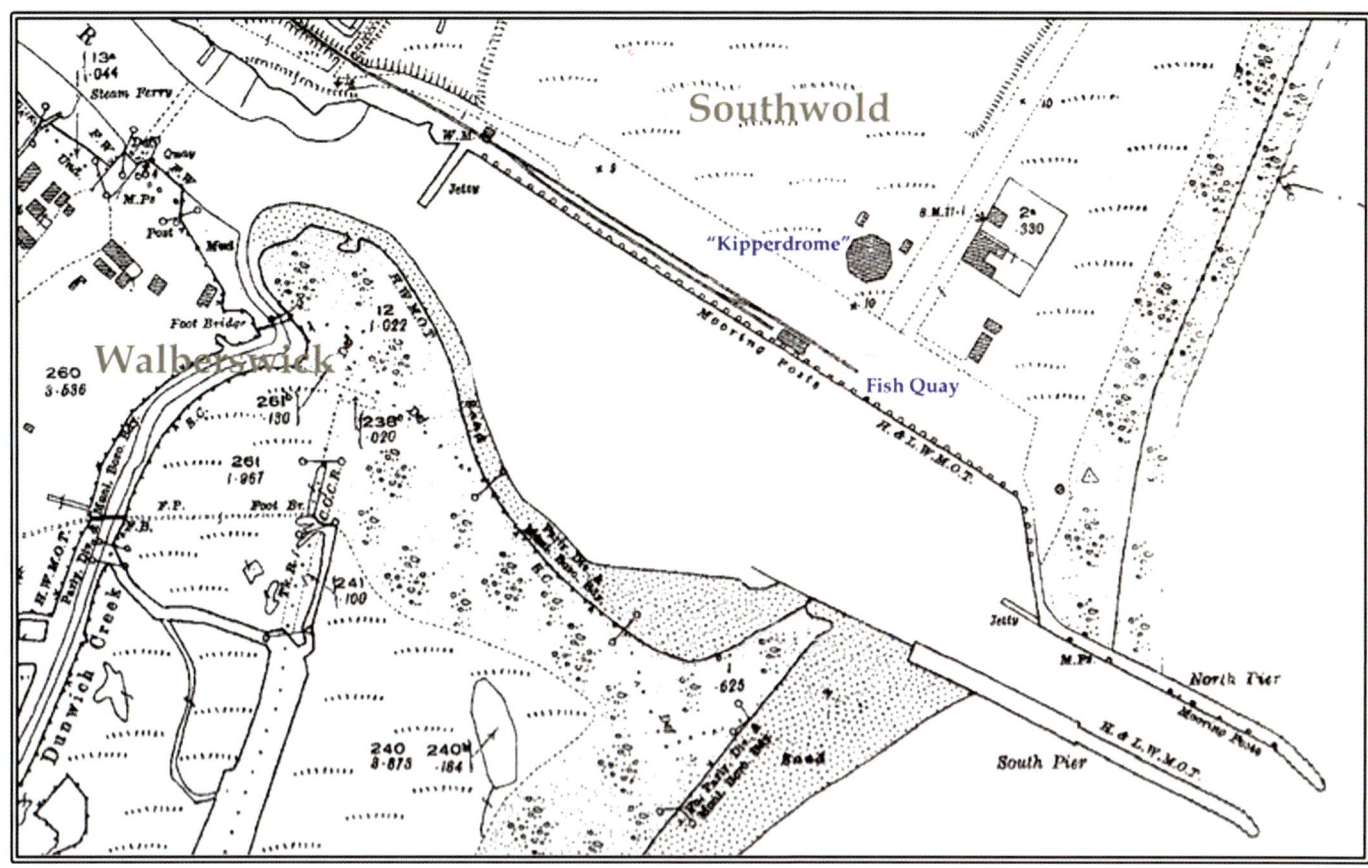

Fig 37: Southwold Harbour on map extract edited from OS County Series 1:2,500 for 1927.

and there was no standard gauge railway from Southwold Harbour. The 1927 map does show the seaward end of the Harbour Branch but it, like the harbour it was intended to serve, did not last long and it seems likely that the 1927 map is based on earlier surveys which had not been updated. Another important factor in the herring industry which the SR Directors seemed never to have considered is that, before the First World War, more than 80 per cent of the herrings landed were then exported to Germany, Russia and Norway. Some were first gutted, cured or salted but, once ice was readily available, many went as fresh fish to Northern Europe. Some business for Southwold Harbour but very little for the Southwold Railway.

Nevertheless, in July 1910, the Harbour Grants Committee of the Board of Trade, '. . . expressed the opinion that [a Southwold Harbour Branch] line is all important for the development of the fishing industry and in fact is the key to the situation'. The Southwold Railway Directors met in September 1910 but they could not agree how to proceed. Should Fasey build the Branch and operate it? Should the Southwold Railway Company build and operate the branch, allowing Fasey 1d per ton carried? Should it be a Light Railway (which Southwold Railway was not) so requiring BoT approval? Should it be 3ft gauge, like the Southwold Railway, or standard gauge which would mean re-gauging the whole railway to Halesworth? Discussions, negotiations, fund-raising, approval by the BoT all took time so the 3ft gauge branch did not open for goods and mineral traffic until 1915, thus missing the 1914 herring season. **Fig 38,** showing the Harbour Branch weighbridge in the early 1920s, reflects the lack of decision which plagued the Harbour Branch. Then the weighbridge was boarded-up and, like the Branch, was no longer in use.

Southwold Railway Harbour Branch was an expensive misjudgement by a minor railway which otherwise provided a passenger and goods service for fifty years until closure in April 1929. It is the only minor railway considered in this book which was narrow-gauge and therein lies one reason for the closure. Through trains to Southwold were not possible and transhipment at Halesworth was a time-consuming business (**Fig 39**).

Fig 38: Southwold Railway mixed gauge weighbridge on the Harbour Fish Quay.

Fig 39: Halesworth GER standard gauge station on the left and Southwold Railway goods shed and transhipment platform centre and right. Standard gauge wagons are on the track in the centre but the narrow-gauge tracks are empty, possibly because of a shortage of SR wagons that may be awaiting emptying at one of the SR stations.

Passengers could tranship themselves but goods transhipment, especially coal shovelled from standard gauge to narrow-gauge wagons, was a slow and laborious task for SR's one transhipment porter. Nevertheless, this minor railway was relatively successful for fifty years and created memories still recalled today. It may, yet, be recreated by two charitable institutions based, appropriately, at the two termini – Halesworth and Southwold. When the SR closed in 1929, the whole railway remained almost complete but moribund until 1941 when Second World War demands for scrap destroyed most of the physical remains but left the trackbed almost entire. These were not the times for groups of enthusiasts to purchase and restore a closed railway so for many years, much of the trackbed has been accessible to walkers, as in Fig 40.

Fig 40: List's Cutting, looking towards Blythburgh and Southwold, 2013.

But from the mid-twentieth century, and now in the twenty-first century, heritage railways are an important source of pleasure and well-being for the volunteers who operate them and the visitors who ride on them.

In Southwold, the Southwold Railway Trust has created a visitor site 'Southwold Railway Steamworks' as near as now possible to the course of the Railway and the Station.

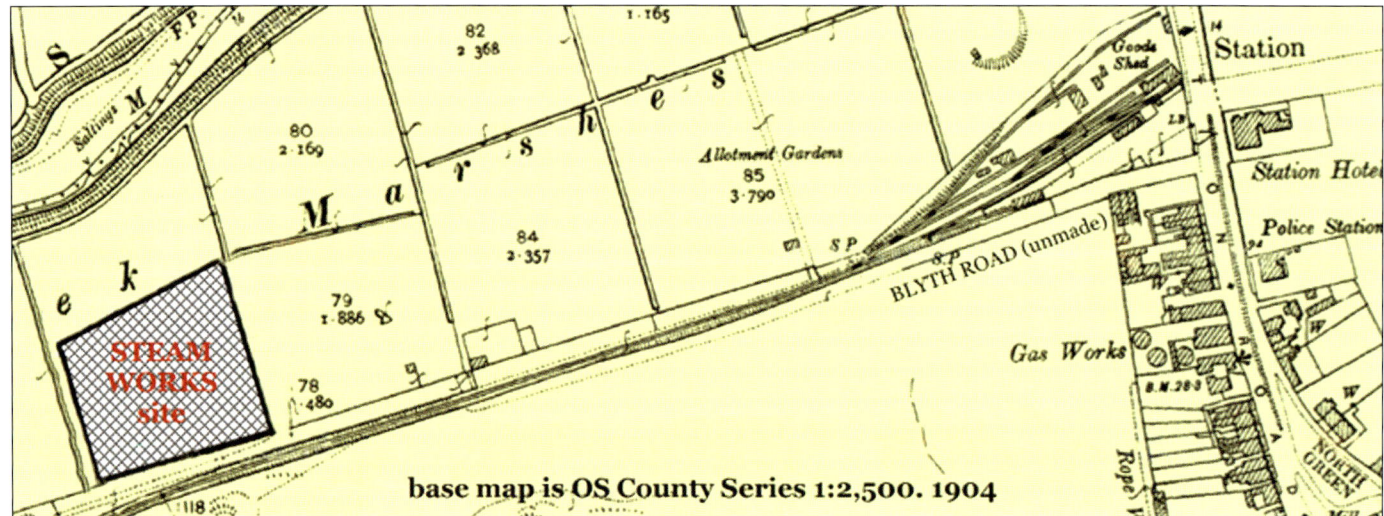

Fig 41: SR Steamworks development on Blyth Road, Southwold, superimposed on a 1904 OS map which shows the course of the Railway and Southwold Station.

CHAPTER 7

KELVEDON, TIPTREE AND TOLLESBURY (PIER) LIGHT RAILWAY

I decided to include this minor railway because it has an intriguing name and used to serve an area I have visited. A number of the pictures I have collected suggest a memorable minor railway – as in **Fig 43**.

'Memorable' indeed for passengers waiting for a train on a winter Essex evening with cold winds blowing across the adjoining marshes. The only light was one gas-lamp on the end of the platform, the Waiting Room was unheated and there were no facilities. The Railway terminated, after an extension in 1907, at a Pier so it seemed the promoters had holiday traffic in mind.

The Railway crossed a rich farming area and the produce, principally fruit, vegetables, peas and potatoes, was very saleable in the London area only 40 miles away but the nearest railway was the GER at Maldon, to the west or Kelvedon to the north. Fishermen working the Blackwater Estuary were experiencing similar transport difficulties because fish, especially, needed to be fresh in the London markets to sell at all.

Several deputations of business people approached the GER throughout the later-nineteenth century to encourage the building of a branch line but to little avail. It was not until the passing of the Light Railways Act, 1896, '. . . to alleviate

Fig 42 (left): Extract from OS 1-inch New Popular Edition, 1945-1947. The map has been tilted to the right to encompass the whole of the Railway from Kelvedon Station (GER and then LNER) to Tollesbury Pier projecting into the River Blackwater. Compass North follows the grid lines.

Fig 43 (below): Tolleshunt Knights Station – 1951.

the distress of agricultural depression', that this Essex minor railway became possible. In May 1897, a group of local 'undertakers' applied for a Light Railway Order for a Railway nine miles, six furlongs, seven chains in length from Kelvedon to a terminus on the shore of the River Blackwater. In October 1898, an Enquiry was held at Kelvedon to consider the application. A local landowner and one of the undertakers of the railway project, Sir William Abdy, outlined the project proposals.

A standard gauge railway, nine-and-a-quarter-miles long, was proposed to be operated by steam traction. It was to follow a route via the villages of Inworth, Tiptree, Tolleshunt Knights, Tollesbury and thence to Mill Creek on the River Blackwater. At that point, the Blackwater estuary was over one-and-a-half miles wide and the Railway would terminate at a pier to be over a quarter mile long.

Sir William reported that in May 1898 the Lands Commission of the Treasury had agreed to provide a grant of £16,000 on completion of the line, on condition that all the required land must be donated by landowners and GER was to operate the line. Maximum line speed was to be 25mph. Total cost was estimated at £45,000.

Mixed trains were permitted and continuous brakes were not required. There were to be five gated crossings, with crossing-keepers over highways and fourteen ungated crossings.

Finally, a Light Railway Order of 29 January 1901 was confirmed on 27 February 1901 with a 10mph speed limit only to apply within 300 yards of level crossings. Construction began in November 1902 and opening was scheduled for summer 1904 but exceptionally wet weather delayed work. On 1 October 1904, and in pouring rain, 120 guests met at Kelvedon for the first run to Tollesbury. On 15 May 1907, Tollesbury Pier was complete so a small group gathered at the pier head for an opening ceremony. The original plans of the undertakers had been to develop the land around the pier with bungalows, houses and a nearby yachting station which would doubtless be called a 'Marina' today. It was also intended to create a continental packet station and to encourage weekend yachting and trips across the Channel to France, Belgium and Holland. The Pier Station, when opened, suggested the importance of this site – **Fig 44**.

None of the dreams was realised. The Pier itself was only a long jetty, albeit extending for 1,770ft (**Fig 45**).

Fig 44: Tollesbury Pier Station c1907; Station Master, Jack Gallant, from Tollesbury is at the Waiting Room door. When necessary, he rode down on the train to carry out duties here as there was no permanent employee.

Fig 45: Tollesbury Pier.

The Pier, as a potential invasion stepping-stone, was guarded during the First World War and although rail services were restored to the Pier Station for a few years, it was on an 'as and when required' basis. Very few passengers, and no freight, 'required' to travel to the Pier so the railway extension to the Pier Station closed in 1921 and the wooden pier was not maintained. It was taken over by the War Department in the Second World War and a section was blown up. It was finally demolished in 1951 and whatever remained was swept away by the 1953 East Coast floods.

After the First World War, and then the 1923 Grouping, the branch services continued to Tollesbury but road transport was developing and several local merchants bought lorries – sometimes redundant military stock – and a bus company – Osbourne's – developed services in competition with the Railway. A further deterrent for would-be travellers or freight consigners was an unofficial rail strike in January 1924 and then the General Strike in 1926. On both occasions, services were curtailed or cancelled.

The Depression of the 1930s and the Second World War did not help branch-line traffic but, ironically, it was the Railway's growing reputation for elderly rolling-stock, especially the carriages of the Wisbech & Upwell Tramway from 1928 and the Stoke Ferry branch from 1930, which attracted railway historians and enthusiasts. Several elderly GER tank locomotives worked on the Railway and some light-weight tender engines too – **Fig 46**.

Fig 46: LNER/BR 68616 J67/1 0-6-0T shunting a mixed train at Kelvedon. 29 July 1950. The three passenger vehicles are bogie tram carriage E60461, brake thirds E62262 and E62261.

The locomotive in **Fig 46** was built at GER Stratford Works in 1901 and was cut up there in 1959. The first carriage was originally on the Wisbech & Upwell Tramway as GER No 7 and has ornate end balconies and side steps to accommodate the low platforms on both the tramway and the KT&TLR. The two brake thirds are 6-wheel carriages from the Stoke Ferry branch, in poor condition when that branch closed in 1930 but 'resurrected' at Stratford for additional service on the KT&TLR.

Operating a loss-making working museum was not appealing to the Railway Executive so announcements were made in July 1950 of likely closure for passenger traffic 'subject to further investigation'. Whatever any 'further investigation' revealed did not save the railway; closure for passenger traffic was announced by BR in April 1951 and was effective from 7 May. Tom Driberg, MP for Maldon, made a plea in the House of Commons for preserving 'an authentic Edwardian curiosity' which he thought, 'might attract a number of summer visitors'.

Freight traffic continued but, south of Tiptree, business was poor so BR announced that as and from 29 October 1951, all freight facilities south of Tudwick Siding, Tiptree, would be withdrawn. After that, the bulk of inward goods traffic annually was to coal merchants Frost & Garwood – about 2,000 tons – and the outgoing freight was almost exclusively from Wilkin & Sons' jam and preserves factory in Tiptree. In 1961, BR claimed that keeping the railway open for this traffic was costing £600 per year so total closure was on and from 1 October 1962.

It is appropriate to end this chapter with Wilkin & Sons, a name known to many and still in business – though using road transport. I have edited a short section from their current (2018) Website:

'The "Tiptree" jam-making story began around the early 1700s with Trewlands, the farm that was later to become the main site for jam-making in the Essex village of Tiptree. The Wilkin family moved from arable to fruit farming in 1865.

'Fruit farming in Tiptree involved growing the fruit, then taking it by horse and cart to Kelvedon railway station and from thence on to London for sale at the markets. When Prime Minister Gladstone commended fruit preserving to the population at large, Arthur Charles Wilkin leapt on this idea as a way to finally make a success of farming in Tiptree. In 1885, The Britannia Fruit Preserving Company was formed and the very first "Tiptree" preserves were made, all sold to a merchant who shipped them to Australia. Within 10 years, more than 200 tons of fruit was being produced, half of that used for making jam.

'The opening of a rail link between Kelvedon and Tollesbury via Tiptree did much to help the business and also encouraged population growth as travel became more accessible. Over the years, Wilkin & Sons bought and farmed much of the land surrounding the village; today, the "Tiptree" estate includes farms in Tiptree, Tollesbury and Goldhanger.

'By 1906, the Company owned 800 acres of land yielding some 300 tons of fruit each season, and it has continued to grow and to prosper.'

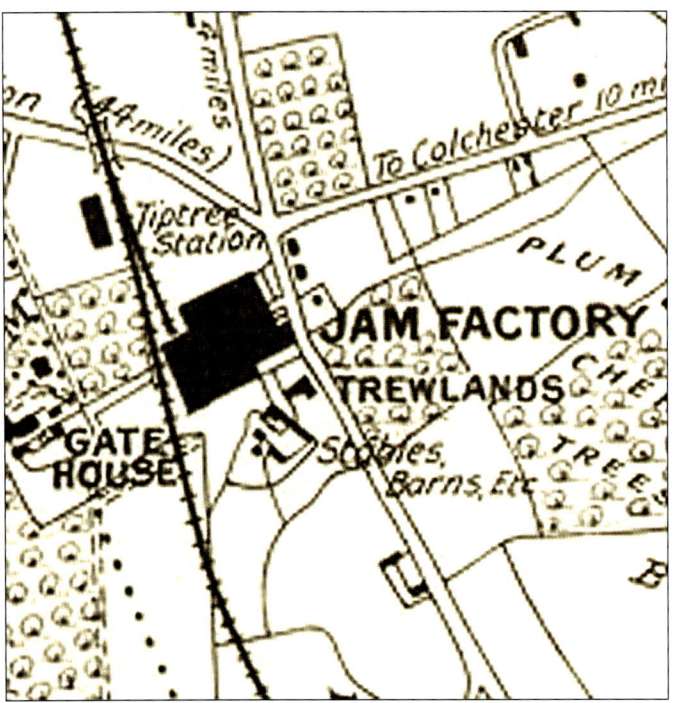

Fig 47: Map of Wilkin & Sons Jam Factory in Tiptree showing the railway siding. © Wilkin & Sons from the Company website.

Fig 48: 'An Edwardian curiosity' near Kelvedon on 31 March 1910.

Railways for agricultural produce and passengers . . . .

A reader who has concentrated on the book thus far may be confused by the section heading above. The Kelvedon, Tiptree and Tollesbury Pier Light Railway, at the end of the last section, seemed principally to carry agricultural produce – especially fruit – and some passengers but very little maritime produce or tourists so has it been misplaced?

A purist might argue that it has but, as with many minor railways in East Anglia, it had great ambitions – a long pier was an attraction in itself, with delicate ironwork and exotic lighting. And around the landward end there were plans for a Blackwater Estuary Yacht Harbour . . . .

The physical geography (as illustrated in **Fig 49**) was low-lying, marshy and neither attractive for agriculture nor seaside living. So that previous chapter segues into this section and into the Three Horseshoes to Benwick branch which is the best example I know in East Anglia of a minor railway built to serve fenland agriculture.

Fig 49: Tollesbury Pier Station and potential development facilities.

CHAPTER 8

THREE HORSESHOES TO BENWICK BRANCH

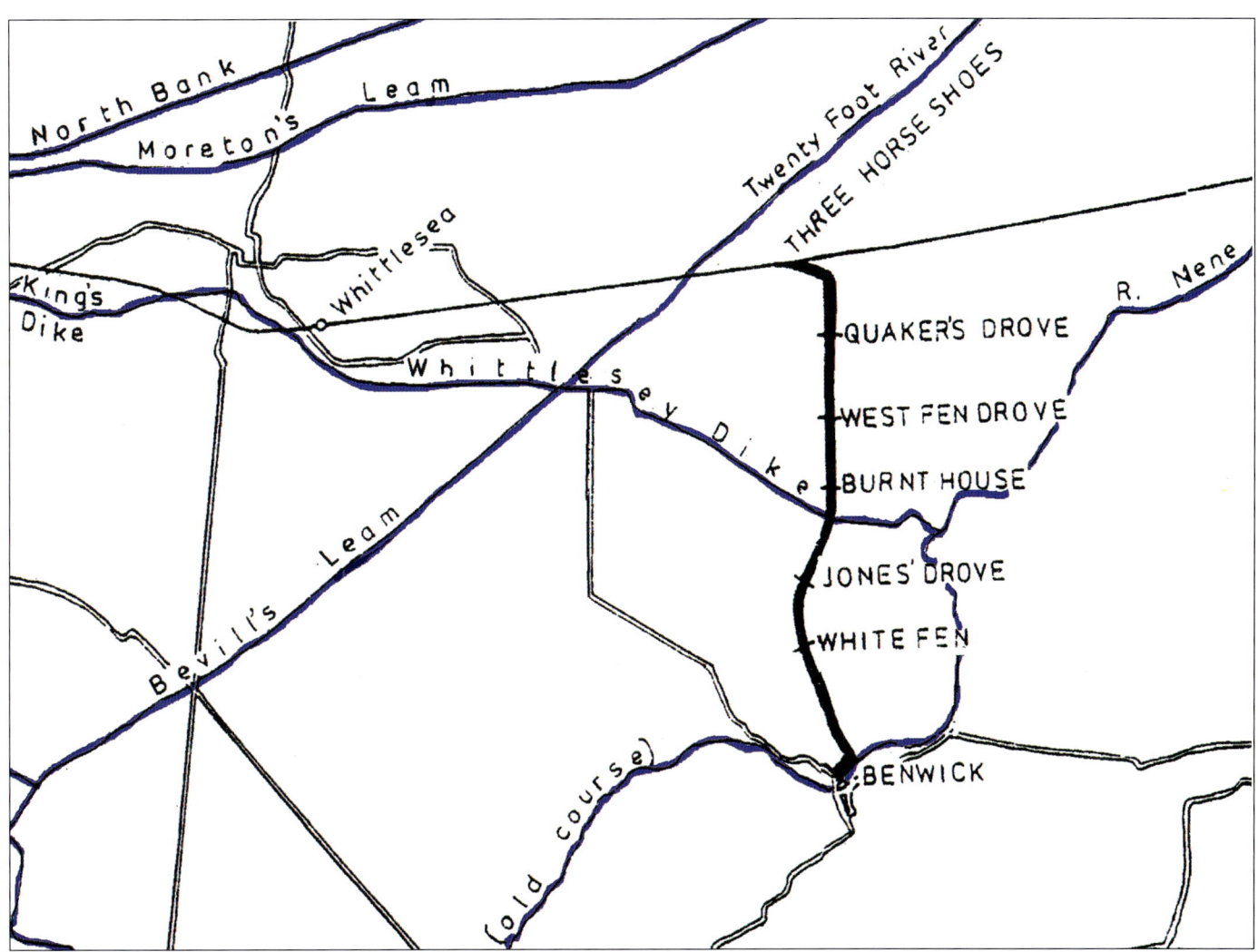

Fig 50: Map of the Benwick Branch edited from a larger version (otherwise unacknowledged) in *The Benwick Branch*, Peter Paye, John Masters. 1998.

When I was exploring fenland railways on a bicycle in the early 1950s I found an earlier but similar version of the map in **Fig 50**. I was fascinated by a recorded railway that appeared to have halts at a number of fen features – 'droves' – which are channels for irrigation or drainage. A little more research established that Benwick was, and is, a small fenland village but, perhaps not surprisingly, the railway was a single-track freight-only line opened in 1898 and closed in 1966.

The new line served an area of rich fenland soils, especially good for potatoes, carrots, mangold wurzels and other root crops and for livestock movements, for which there was a ready market in London and the Midlands. From the mid-19th century groups of fenland farmers petitioned GER but initially made no progress. Other GER railways were already at work in the Benwick area. For instance the village of Stonea (population 250), 10 miles NE of Benwick, on the Ely-March line was generating annual traffic returns in excess of 11,000 tons.

Once the branch was underway, freight traffic grew and the railway was an effective outlet for local produce: barley, wheat, oats, hay, straw, root crops mentioned above plus onions, swedes, parsnips, turnips and, from the 1920s, sugar beet went to local markets at March, Cambridge, King's Lynn, Peterborough and Wisbech and the London markets at Spitalfields and Covent Garden. Imports included fertilisers, seed potatoes, coal and coke.

By the late 1950s, most of this traffic had transferred to road haulage for direct delivery from farm to market or factory. Coal traffic, albeit in decreasing tonnages, continued from a variety of smaller collieries until the Benwick Branch closed in the 1960s.

The fenland dike is the old course of the River Nene, adjoining the 'B' of the name Benwick on the **Fig 50** map. The Branch line promoters and GER constructed a wharf here – now obscured by debris and bushes – so that fenland lighters could transfer material to and from water to rail. So this is a truly 'minor' railway, worked as a siding from Three Horseshoes signal box, carrying no passengers (officially) and, for many years, providing a loyal and appreciated service to the nearby fenland farmers.

Fig 51 (above): terminus of the Benwick Branch – early 1920s. Motor lorries working with the railway here but, as motor lorries became larger and more sophisticated, the double-handling implicit here was replaced by farm-to-market journeys and the railway was cut out.

Fig 52 (left): is a view to the right of the earlier picture, taken from the motor road in **Fig 51** in the summer of 2018.

CHAPTER 9

ST IVES LOOP AND LONG STANTON STATION

With permission from Michael Blakemore, Editor of *BackTrack*, I am grateful to be able to draw on several of the excellent railway history articles published in the magazine. For this chapter I have used material from Stanford Jacobs' article: 'The Loop: Cambridge-St Ives-March' from *BackTrack* Volume 9, Number 7, July 1995.

And, for the details of Long Stanton Station, my own experience working there as a cut-flower clerk in the 1960s; memories of Graham Burling who also worked there in the 1960s; and the excellent records of the Great Eastern Railway Society, of which I am a member.

As with most railway developments in East Anglia, the Loop came together piecemeal but by 1862 most of the lines relevant to this Chapter and the map (**Fig 53**) were owned by the Great Eastern Railway whose monopoly over most of East Anglia was comprehensive. However, the Great Northern had a

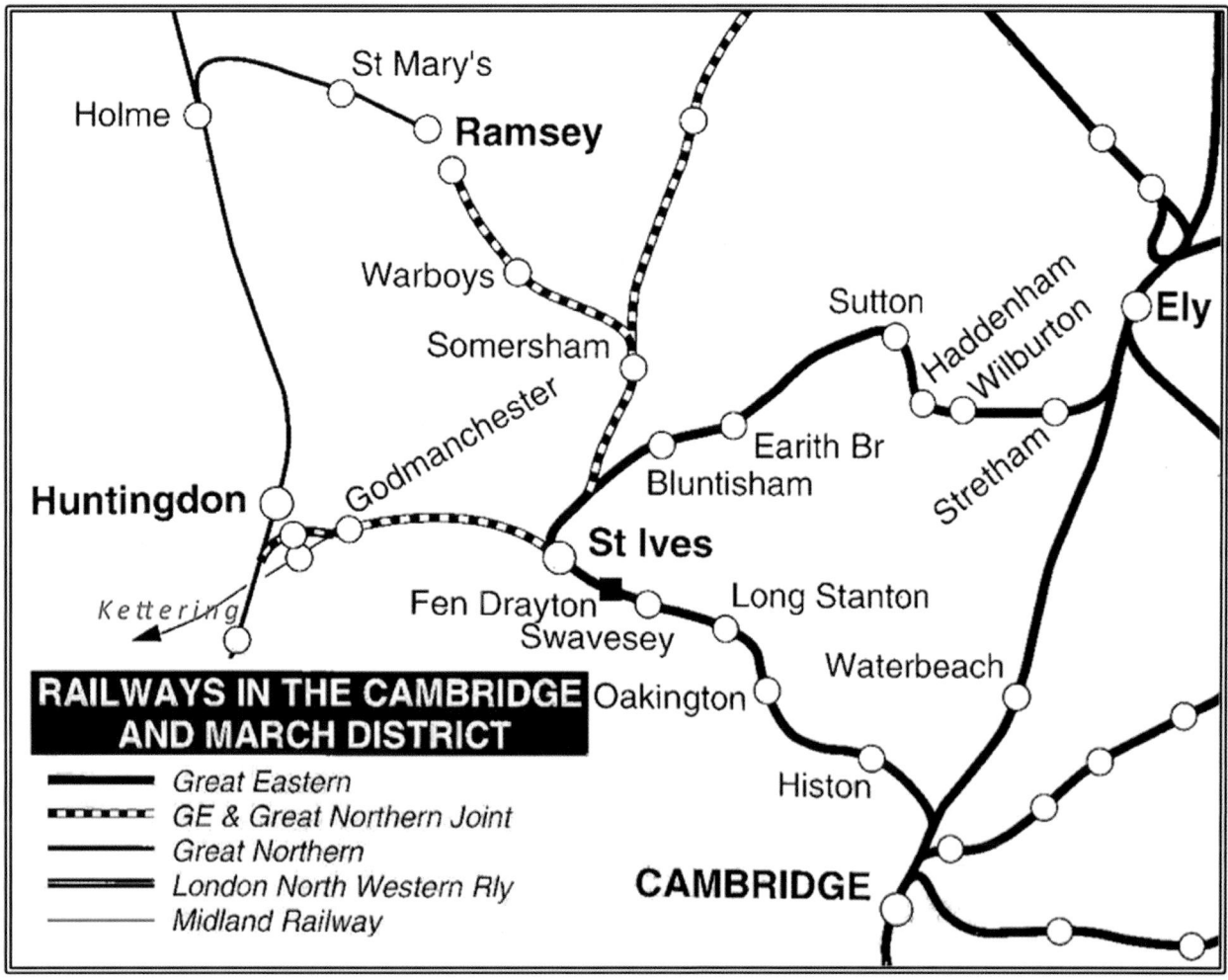

Fig 53: A cropped map illustrating some of the network of minor railways around Cambridge, St Ives, Ely and March. 'The Loop,' always so-called by local railway men, was between Cambridge, St Ives, Somersham, Chatteris (not named on this map) and March.

competitive interest in the coal traffic from the north and east and the agricultural freight from East Anglia to Midlands and Northern markets. So, from 1882, several lines west and north of St Ives were jointly worked as the GN&GE Joint line.

As far as was operationally practical, most of the heavy freight traffic travelled via the Loop. Cambridge used to work trains of up to 100 loose-coupled empties round the Loop at night.

I have already acknowledged the information I have gleaned from Stanford Jacobs but I am pleased to explain that I worked on the Loop at Long Stanton station as a cut-flower clerk each summer season from 1962 to 1965. I can therefore write with a little knowledge of the daily operation of one of the Loop stations.

The Station site did not change much over the years but **Fig 56**, taken from the same UP home signal as in **Fig 54** in 1947, relates helpfully to the details of the 1903 OS map, particularly the cattle dock which is just out-of-camera to the left. Note, too, that 'SB' – Signal Box – on the OS map appears to be midway along the UP platform but the labelling has been displaced by 'Railway Cottages'. Another dated conventional sign on the map is 'LB' – Letter Box – which was often found at rural stations in East Anglia; where else to post a letter than a well-known and named location where the 24/7 presence of a Station Master in the Station House afforded a degree of security for Royal Mail when the box was emptied?

When I came to Long Stanton in 1962 on a summer short-term contract, I had a busy 8-10 weeks. I had not previously seen the station except by occasionally travelling through to St Ives and Peterborough. But research for this book has revealed a busy rural station, especially during the East Anglian fruit and flower season, with many pick-up freight trains calling and a number of through trains signalled via the Loop to free other lines for passenger traffic. **Fig 57** of the Station Goods Yard in the early 1920s shows a busy scene with local growers using horse-drawn carts and wagons for delivery and collection. The Station Master is clearly 'in charge' and nearly all of the men at work are farm labourers and not station staff.

My job at Long Stanton was as a cut-flower clerk. My principal task was to record daily in a large BR ledger:

- Names of growers delivering boxes of cut flowers to the Station Yard
- Numbers of boxes each grower delivered

Fig 54: A view of Long Stanton Station, looking DOWN towards St Ives and taken by the author from the UP home signal which is shown as 'SP' on the **Fig 55** OS record of the site in 1903.

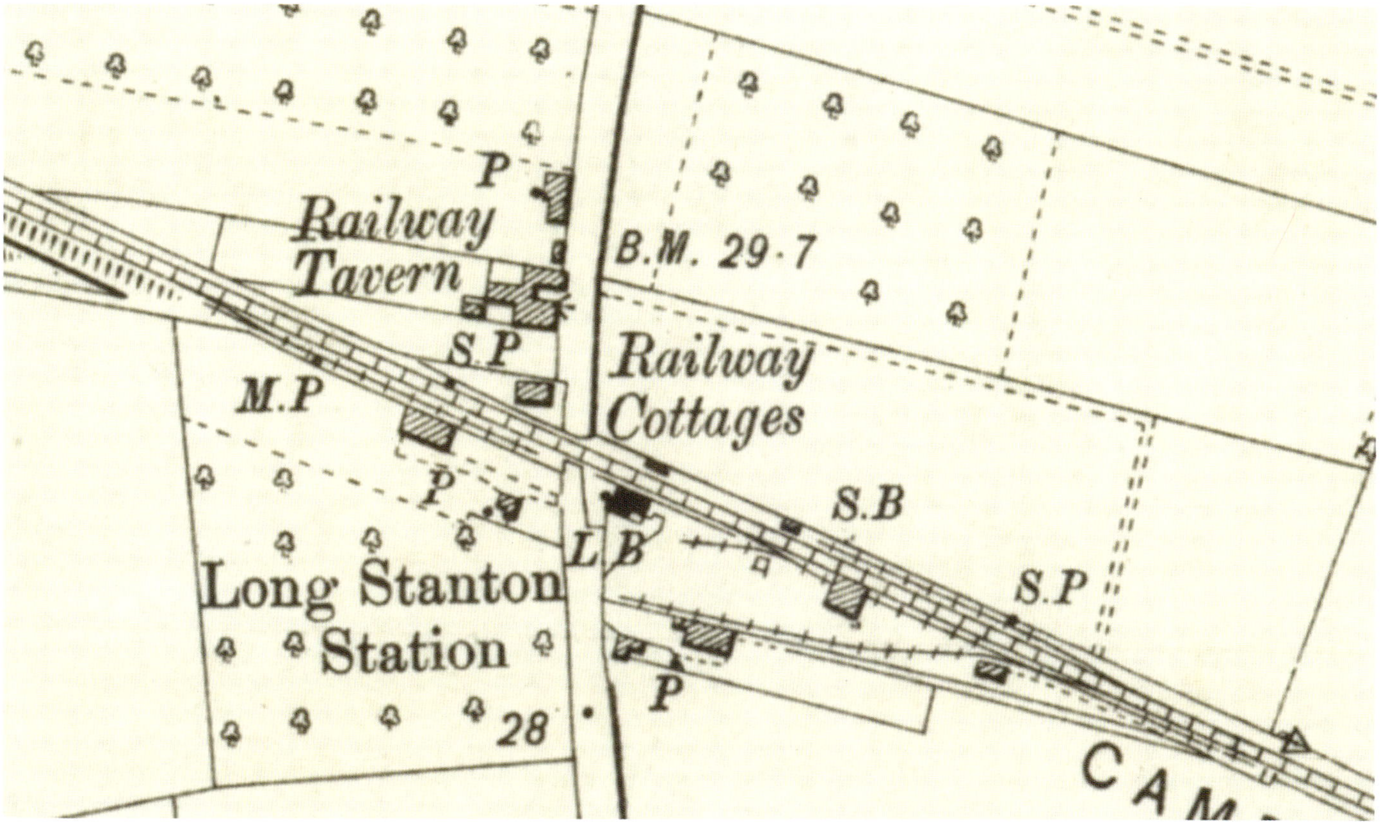

ST IVES LOOP AND LONG STANTON STATION • 57

Fig 55: taken from OS 6 inch 1903 map – Cambridgeshire XXXIII.SE.

Fig 56: Another useful reference view of Long Stanton Station from the UP home signal – in 1947.

Fig 57: The Goods Yard at Long Stanton in the very early 1920s during the East Anglian fruit season.

- Flower Market destinations for each box; some growers were supplying to several Agents at the Flower Markets
- Receiving Agent's details including names and addresses. The Agents and the Flower Markets were across the UK and fresh-cut flowers required next-day delivery:
    - Bull Ring Market, Birmingham
    - Old Flower Market, Bristol
    - Cardiff Market
    - Old Fruitmarket, Glasgow
    - Kirkgate Market, Leeds
    - Covent Garden, London
    - Piccadilly Flower Market, Manchester
    - Grainger Market, Newcastle

I then worked out the cost-per-grower at the BR fast-freight rate and prepared the information for Invoices. We had one battery-powered calculator in the office!

Each day, 20-25 Vanfits were filled with boxes of cut flowers, moved to Whitemoor Marshalling Yard by the late-afternoon pick-up goods, then despatched by fully-fitted express goods trains to destinations all over the UK for the next morning's flower markets.

When I started in 1962 the Station Master (SM) was Charles Moulton who lived on site with his family and had ready access to the station office through a private door from the station house (**Fig 58**).

The staff included two clerks – plus me in summer – five shift goods porters, three shift signalmen and one BR cartage motor driver based in Cambridge collecting and delivering to growers without their own transport.

Once I had learned the clerical job, Mr Moulton gave me a number of other tasks as time and need required, including:

- assisting the BR cartage motor driver collecting boxes from growers, loading them on his lorry, unloading into Vanfits in the Station Yard and checking destinations on flower boxes and wagon labels.
- assisting in the Long Stanton station office with ticket sales, telephone messages and general station office work.

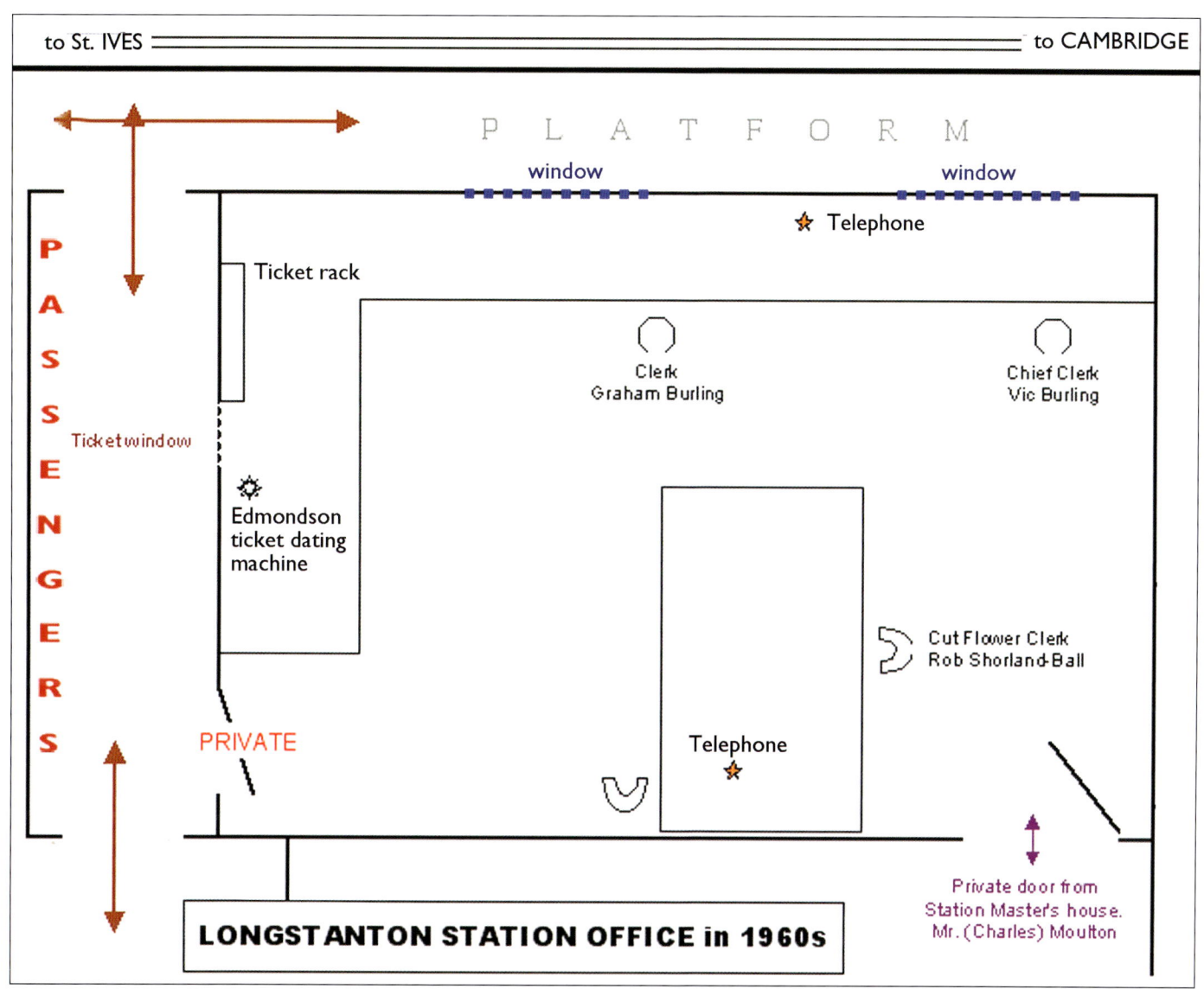

Fig 58: Interior of the station office.

- with all the available clerical and manual staff, pushing wagons – like horseboxes – specially ordered, delivered from Cambridge attached to a DMU, detached at Long Stanton, and pushed into the Cattle Dock siding as is the horsebox in **Fig 54**.
- Changing signal lamps on signals, including those 'out in the country' but still controlled by Long Stanton Signal box.

I enjoyed my time at Long Stanton and learned a lot about a working station on a minor railway before the Beeching report *The Reshaping of British Railways* was published on 27 March 1963. Mr Moulton was a skilful, politically-savvy and hard-working SM who spent time away from the station marketing the services BR could offer to growers, farmers and local businessmen. He was very aware of the Beeching report and I remember, as soon as he managed to get hold of a pre-publication draft copy, he brought it into the office to show it to us. He said, 'Keep this to yourselves lads; it is not yet published for general circulation and only relatively senior officers have yet seen a copy. We are cautioned, subject to dismissal, if we discuss it with our staff or the general public. I am afraid it is the end of the Railway we have enjoyed serving'.

Fig 59: Clerical and Manual Staff at Long Stanton 1962. From left: Charlie Grumbley (Porter); Graham Burling (Clerk); Albert (Alby) Cousins (Goods Porter & Shunter); Victor Burling (Chief Clerk); Charlie Ingle (Porter). Picture by Rob Shorland-Ball (Cut-Flower Clerk).

I have kept in touch with Graham Burling and am grateful for his memories for this book because he knew the Station throughout the year.

'I moved from Bartlow to Long Stanton in 1962. The staffing at the time was a Station Master, Charles Moulton, later replaced by Thomas Edlington. Two clerks, Vic Burling (no relation) and me, working early and late turns. Early turn started at 07.00 and involved catching the 06.30 from Cambridge. There was always a heady mix of smells as there were still steam engines on the Cambridge Shed but the passenger trains on the loop were normally DMUs and the early ones had fresh wet fish in a tray in the guard's compartment. Diesel fumes, paraffin, fish and smoke!

We finished about 16.00 and late turn started about 10.00 and finished about 18.00 so neither desperately early or late. This was for six days a week. We both sold tickets, charged parcels and dealt with all the other associated activities. Additionally the senior clerk had responsibility for freight charging and accounts. Freight accounts were centralised at the Traffic Manager's Office in Cambridge but there was still some work to do locally. As the more junior clerk I dealt with passenger accounts which were still done locally including chasing and recording payments. The staffing was augmented in the summer during the fruit and flower season by the addition of another clerk.

'Signal Box was open continuously from 06.00 Monday until 06.00 Sunday and manned by three signalmen working turns. There was a rest-day relief signalman and a variety of General Purpose relief men who worked the box. It wasn't very busy and to keep occupied the signalmen kept the place in immaculate condition. The brasses on the instruments were polished, the wooden footboard at the edge of the frame was scrubbed white, the lever tops were oiled and polished and the lino floor was polished too. It was very cosy. There was a coal fire with a chimney which was stoked up until the chimney glowed red hot, a comforting sight for the passengers outside freezing on the platforms! It was also a place where underworked clerks could creep up and scrounge a cup of tea then have a go at signalling trains – answering and sending codes on the block instruments; turning the wheel to close the crossing gates; pulling off the signals. Highly irregular but one or two of us became very proficient.

'We had a Cambridge-based BR Cartage lorry driver who would come from Cambridge in the morning with any freight stuff for delivery in our area and he would pick up any parcels we had for delivery. He would also collect parcels from the villages we served. He had a busier role in the summer as Rob has mentioned above.

'Passenger traffic was relatively light but because Long Stanton was the station used by RAF Oakington we would get a reasonable amount of warrant traffic and reduced-rate tickets for the airmen.

'There was a trickle of general parcels traffic, in and out, augmented significantly by RAF Oakington who sent and received quite a lot of packages to and from other bases. In those days, to show the parcel had been consigned and paid for correctly it was necessary to glue a ledger label to the parcel positioned slightly over the label to prevent fraud. There were seven types of ledger labels plus a cash label – LL1 was general traffic delivery-paid; LL3 was station-to-station; LL6 an agreed flat rate and LL7 was military traffic.

'General freight traffic was wagons of coal, some full loads for the RAF, and wagons of seed potatoes in the autumn. Mostly small freight traffic items from Long Stanton were taken by lorry to Cambridge to be sent on from there so we were progressively loosing pick-up freight business and, statistically, our freight business was declining. Just the sort of 'evidence' that Beeching was looking for.

'Our main freight business was the fruit and flower traffic in the summer – hundreds of stout cardboard boxes containing cut flowers and wooden boxes of fruit.'

Fig 60: Cut flower boxes. SMs Moulton then Edlington would probably have been critical of stacking in this scene. But the picture shows the style and size – say 4ft to 5ft long – of the corrugated cardboard boxes we handled.

Some of this traffic was sent by passenger train but mostly it was loaded into VanFits in the Goods Yard and sent all over the UK via express freight trains from Whitemoor to arrive in time for market on the following morning.

'Some of the larger growers brought their own produce to load directly, some smaller ones used agents and some had their stuff collected by the BR lorry. For us BR staff at the Station it was "all hands to the pump" to get the produce loaded before the pick-up goods was scheduled to depart. Overtime was on offer for the early turn staff to help in the yard. Free samples of fruit were handed out from time to time and very gratefully received.

'The ticket office had a rack of Edmundson card tickets [see **Fig 62**] which were pre-printed for popular destinations. They had to be dated, as sold, with the Edmundson ticket printing press which was a familiar part of every railway ticket office at that time [Fig 61].

'Every day we had to balance ticket sales and other various business with the cash-in-hand. We would send cash to bank on the train to St Ives. It was placed in a leather bag, tied tight with string and a wax seal stamped over the knot. The cash bag was signed for by the train guard at the sending station and by station staff at the destination.

'In the summer there was no booked Sunday passenger service but there were occasional excursion trains to Skegness. Unfortunately the ticket office had to be open before these trains to sell tickets then closed and cashed-up afterwards.

'The only way for me to get there on a Sunday was to cycle the 14 miles out and the same back just to get in a three hour Sunday turn. Fortunately this was quite lucrative as Sundays were paid at time and three quarters!

'However, the first of these excursion trains I booked was quite frantic. It was very popular but we didn't have any pre-printed tickets so I had to hand-write every one and keep a quick note on a scrap of paper so that I could record and balance it later.

'A final memory of Long Stanton office work was labelling empty private-owner coal wagons for return to their colliery.'

Fig 61 (left): Edmundson ticket dating press.

Fig 62 (below): Pre-printed Edmundson ticket showing destination with ticket number on face and Edmundson press date on back.

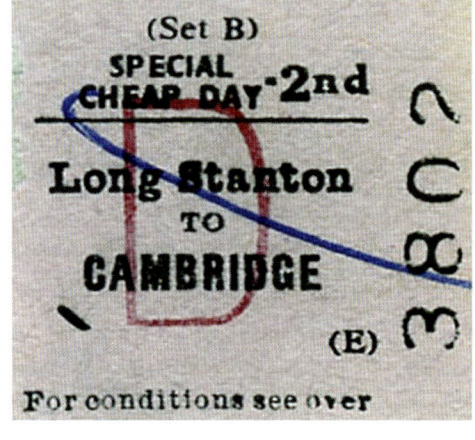

ticket face

ticket back

I am ending this story of the Loop with a brief account and more memories of the next Station down from Long Stanton, Swavesey.

I am including Swavesey as I visited the village by train on several occasions because a friend who was at school with me in Cambridge lived there. He had to travel to and from every weekday, as did a number of other children, because the nearest large schools and the biggest local grammar school were in Cambridge.

While researching this book I met Peter Wakefield whose father was SM at Swavesey and he sent me some detailed memories of 'living over the shop' in the Swavesey Station house from 1958 to 1962. I have added an edited version of his memories to complement what has already been told about Long Stanton. A useful introduction is the aerial picture, **Fig 65**, which can be compared for layout with the map:

Peter recalls:

'My brother and I lived in Station House. Our bedrooms overlooked the signal box, just over the level crossing, and goods yard respectively. A constant back-drop in the early morning was the thud of the Edmundson ticket dating press as dozens of tickets were issued each early morning. A different night-time background noise was the continual dropping with a clatter of the down starter GE-style lower quadrant semaphore signal . . . plus the brief rattle of signal wires and then the rumble of a heavily laden goods train on its way to Cambridge yards, Temple Mills in London, or north to Whitemoor and beyond. Coal was the major traffic as were the returning coal empties; vital to the economy was getting the empties

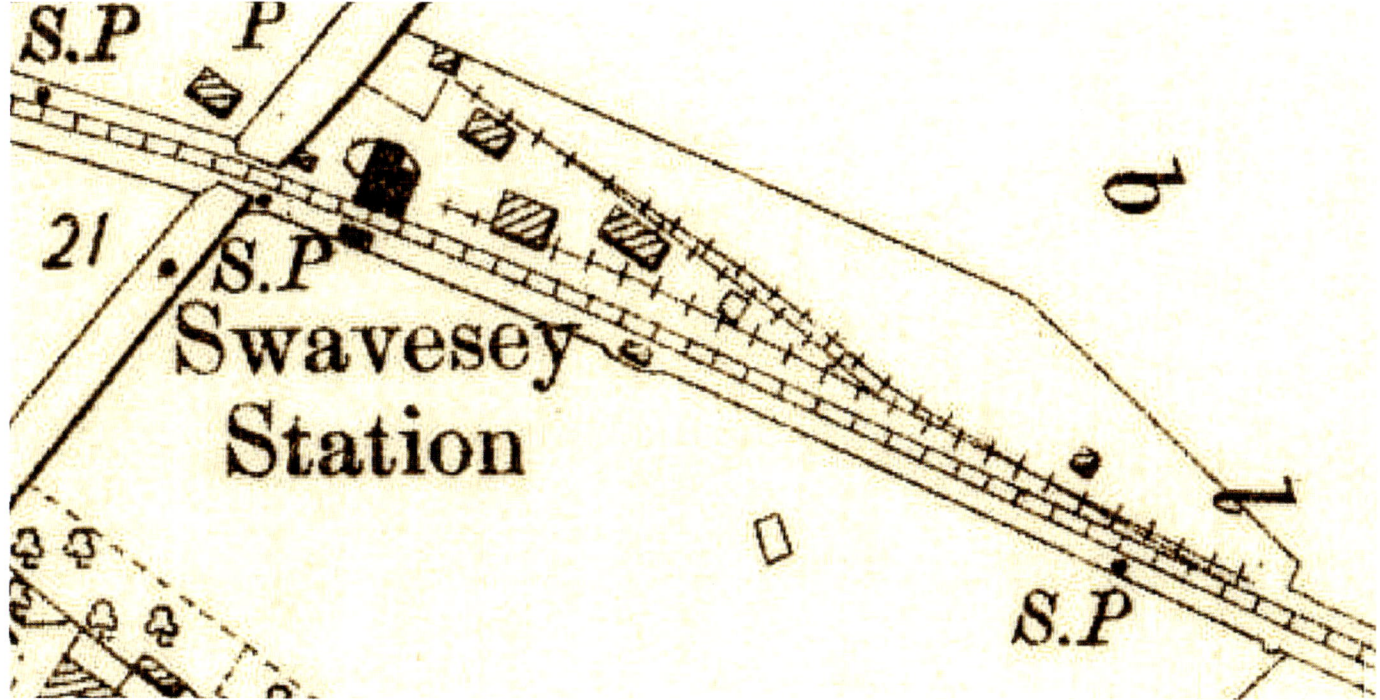

Fig 63 (above): LNER Empty Wagon direction label.

Fig 64 (below): taken from OS 6 inch 1903 map – Huntingdonshire XXXIII.NE.

Fig 65: an aerial view of Swavesey Station during the 1947 floods.

back to the collieries. The power stations and gas works in Cambridge, the Lea Valley and London needed immense quantities of coal . . . as did every home in the country.

'In those days the signalmen opened and shut the level crossing gates at Swavesey. At night they generally left the gates across the road as there was little road traffic about.

'The Loop was mainly about running local and long distance freight trains but Swavesey Station also had high passenger numbers too. The first two trains to Cambridge were very busy as were all the late afternoon return journeys. The first up train carried many women to work at Histon Chivers Factory – well over 50 for there alone. There were also a few London seasons on the first two trains. Unlike today there were no peak fares but very cheap workmen tickets were sold, allowed on the 07.30 both to Histon and Cambridge; it was a busy train.

'Over 100 passengers joined the 07.59 Up. Many had Cambridge season tickets – for instance the Cambridgeshire High School for Boys; Cambridgeshire High School for Girls [both nicknamed 'County' schools]; the Central Technical School; St Mary's Convent School; with some day-pupils to the principal Public Schools like Perse and Leys; office workers; medical staff for Addenbrookes Hospital. Journey time to Cambridge was only 22 minutes which is unbeatable today!

'Local freight traffic or 'goods' as it was called then, was very heavy, especially in Spring and early Summer. All the passenger trains carried substantial amounts of parcels of all sizes – known as 'sundries traffic' – that needed unloading and loading such as small loads of flower boxes and fruit in chip baskets, endless amounts of tyres from Barwell Remoulds, who had a factory in the village. The railway cartage lorry brought in full loads of individually addressed large cardboard boxes of new luggage produced by Papworth (Hospital) Industries. These went all over the country.

'The freight day started early with the first passenger train arriving at about 06.30, on its way to Kettering via Huntingdon. It was met by the Swavesey and Over village newsagents who received huge quantities of daily papers, magazines and sorted them out on the platforms. Wet fish also arrived on this service in wooden fish boxes.

'Around about 10.00 the up local goods to Histon arrived from St Ives yard. On a daily basis this train brought in several loads of coal for the local coal merchants as well as all sorts of wagon loads for local growers and farmers, including basic slag fertiliser in bags from the steel works at Haverton Hill on Teeside, the all important 'returned empties', which were the wooden re-usable flower boxes, crates for plums, apples chip baskets for fruit and so on. Seed potatoes arrived in winter in dozens of wagon loads from Scotland. In the fruit and flower seasons it also brought in the vital empty wagons to be loaded out during the afternoon. This goods train also had traffic for Long Stanton and was usually very long.

'My brother and I used to look out particularly for the Express Full-load freight trains of newly made Ford cars from Thamesside; sometimes several trains a day. About 18.00 we were on the look-out again for the newly-introduced Enterprise Express freight train, name board and all – the 'Lea Valley Enterprise'. This started at Tottenham Hale Yard and filled up at various other stations in NE London and then ran fast to Whitemoor. It was so successful it loaded up to 80 wagons drawn by two of the new Brush Type 2 diesel locos – the only time we saw double-headers on the Loop. Another Enterprise Express service was 'Fenland Enterprise' that ran from Wisbech via King's Lynn, St Ives, Ely, Cambridge and on to Bristol and Cardiff.

'This busy station was manned by the Station Master (dad), a clerk, and two porters. They all worked the platforms getting the trains away as quickly as possible and the latter two were very busy in the goods yard too.'

So the Loop was a minor railway which was thriving in the 1960s but Beeching showed a small loss and closure came – partly because much of the van-load traffic was costly for BR and big growers were buying and using modern large-capacity diesel lorries for door-to-door delivery. But, as Chapter 26 illustrates, a minor railway converted to a Busway can be successful . . .

CHAPTER 10

ELSENHAM TO THAXTED LIGHT RAILWAY

I recall seeing glimpses of this railway and its rustic coaches when my parents took me to London Liverpool Street in the early 1950s. I was only nine years old but already very interested in East Anglian railways and my father pointed out this survivor as '. . . the Gin & Toffee line'.

The 'toffee' I learned later was a Thaxted product by George Lee's company; he and Gilbey were generous local entrepreneurs who made the line possible but it was a struggle. It was the last 'traditional' branch line built in East Anglia, originally sanctioned as a narrow-gauge line but not supported by GER until the plans

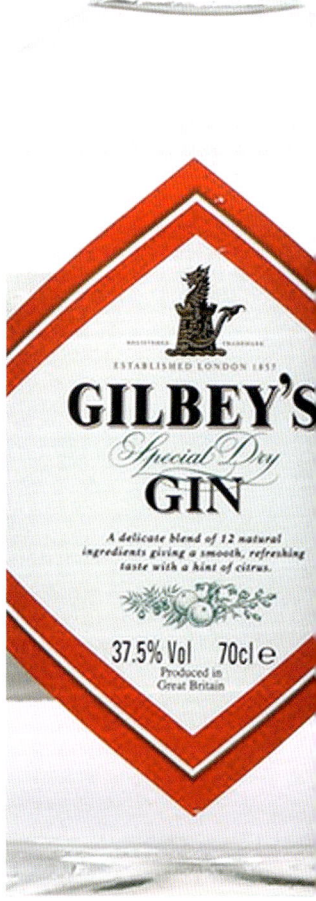

Fig 66 (above): Elsenham – 08.55 train (drawn by LNER 68530 Class J69/1 0-6-0T) departs for Thaxted on 14 July 1951, fourteen months before closure. Behind the train is the back of the wooden waiting shelter on the LNER UP platform and the brick building ahead of the train is the Booking Office.

Fig 67 (right): Sir William Gilbey – whose UK-made gin was highly regarded in the 1900s – lived at Elsenham Hall.

were changed to a standard gauge light railway; it opened in April 1913.

The single-track railway was built throughout with strict economy in mind. There was only one intermediate station – Sibleys for Chickney and Broxted – and the three other Halts were not very well-placed in relation to the places they were intended to serve. Cutler's Green Halt is almost unique in the UK because it could only be accessed by footpaths. An idyllic concept, perhaps, on a mid-summer's day but hardly practical for business people intending to reach London Liverpool Street which was only 36 miles south of Elsenham.

The greatest construction economy was illustrated by the position of Thaxted Station in relation to the town as illustrated in **Fig 68**.

The Station was about one mile from the centre of Thaxted and did not even serve utilities like the Gas Works which required frequent coal supplies.

The economy which led to Thaxted Station's position 'in the country' was the decision to avoid earthworks, brick-built abutments and a steel-framed bridge over

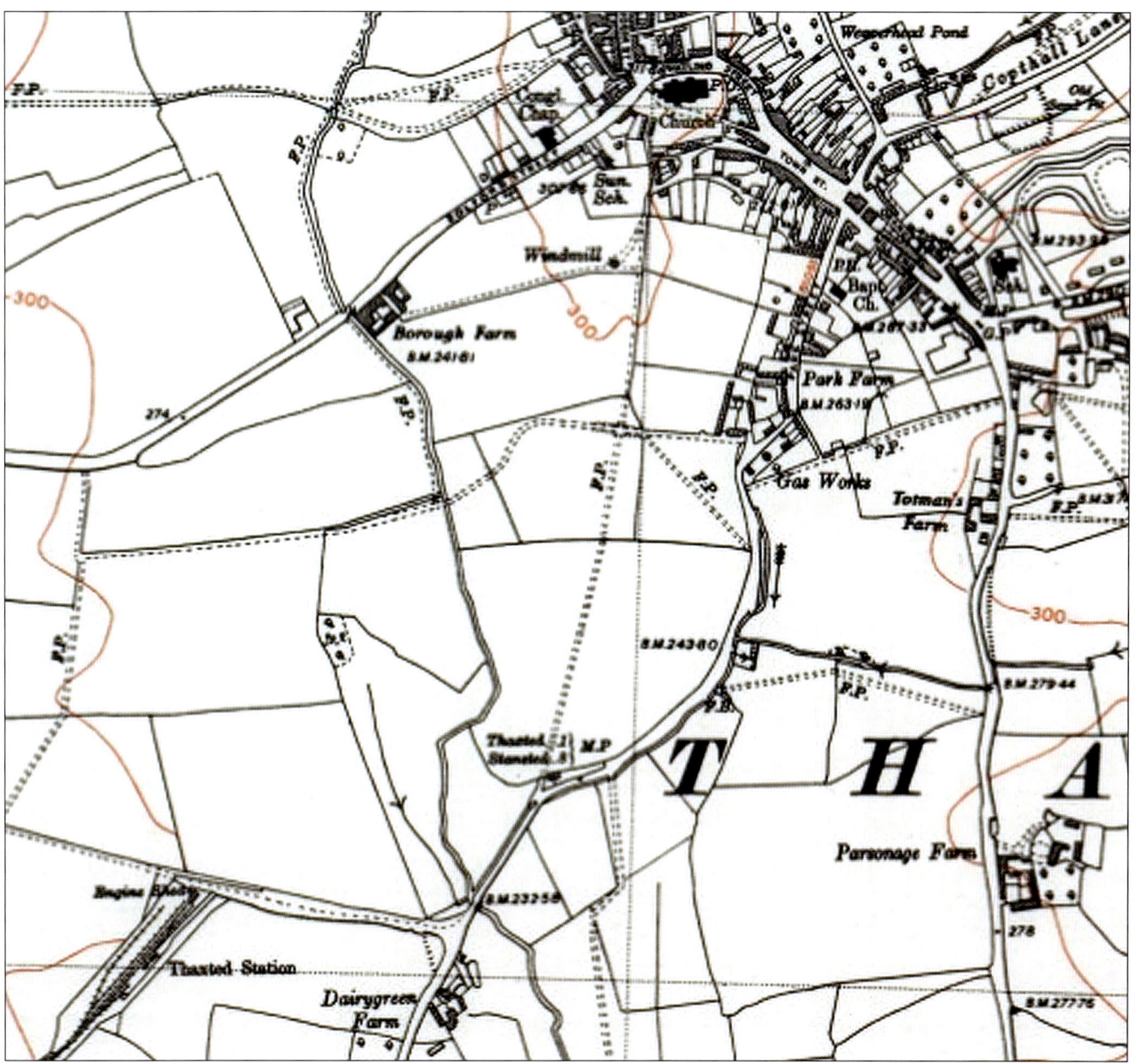

Fig 68: OS 6-inch map 1951 – Essex nXXIV Thaxted.

the River Chelmer but it proved to be a false economy. The station plan – and the passenger facilities shown in **Fig 69** – suggest a well-built terminus for a five-and-a-half mile railway if shown in **Fig 70** out of the context of the **Fig 68** map.

For the first twenty-five years the railway did quite well because there was no competing bus service, but a turning point in its fortunes was the outbreak of the Second World War. Passenger services were cut back to two per day so people made alternative arrangements which they continued after the war and the average daily passenger usage was about fifty. Freight revenue, too, suffered because motor lorries were favoured by many businesses to avoid trans-shipment.

Curiously, for a surviving historic railway relatively near to London, few railway enthusiasts visited or

Fig 69: Thaxted Station shortly after opening in 1913.

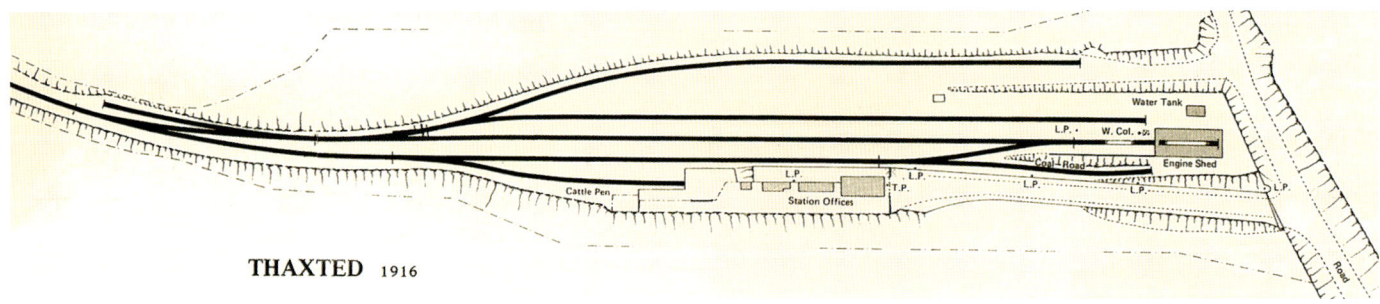

THAXTED 1916

Fig 70: An apparently well-equipped terminus station, including a brick-built Engine Shed which housed the one engine in steam that worked the Light Railway. Thaxted was a sub-shed of Cambridge Shed and the usual practice was to change the engine each weekend. The out going engine went north to Cambridge on Saturday evening and the replacement arrived on Monday morning. There were no Sunday services.

recorded a visit. One of the few reports to appear in the contemporary railway press was in the March 1951 issue of the *Railway Observer*:

'. . . on 10 February 1951, J68 No.8645 was working the branch with coaches E61471 and E62450. A third coach – E62461 - was on standby. The three coaches were bogie corridors which had arrived on the branch only a few years previously; they were ex-World War One ambulance coaches – one a ward car, one a pharmacy car and the other an "infectious" car. For use on the Thaxted branch they were specially fitted with steps which was necessary because of the low height of the branch platforms.'

In Spring 1951, BR announced the proposed withdrawal of passenger services and the final passenger train ran in 1952. Eastern National Omnibus Company provided a substitute bus service from Bishop's Stortford via Elsenham to Thaxted. Freight services were continued until one train every Wednesday was sufficient for the demand so the line closed entirely from 1 June 1953; track lifting followed soon after.

Fig 71: Mill Road Halt in the early 1950s. A truly 'economical' Halt. The low platform – accessed from the trains by steps attached to the coaches – is barely longer than the passenger waiting room.

CHAPTER 11

DOWNHAM & STOKE FERRY RAILWAY (D&SFR) & WISSINGTON LIGHT RAILWAY

I am very pleased to give credit where it is due so, for these two inter-connected railways, the credit is with: Roger Darsley and the Industrial Railway Society [IRS] for *The Wissington Railway – A Fenland Enterprise*, IRS, 1984 and Peter Paye for *The Stoke Ferry Branch*, Oxford Publishing Co, 1982.

Roger Darsley's book inspired this chapter; I have owned it since publication so re-read it recently as part of my research and was fascinated; truly 'A Fenland Enterprise'.

I contacted Roger and he agreed that I might quote his text and use some of his maps and pictures; he also confirmed that I had similar permission from IRS so thank you both.

Location, natural resources and significant entrepreneurs, seem good starting points. **Fig 72** is a not-to-scale and diagrammatic representation of the location of the D&SFR.

The natural resources lay in the rich soils of a low-lying area of fenland to the north of Ely known as the Black

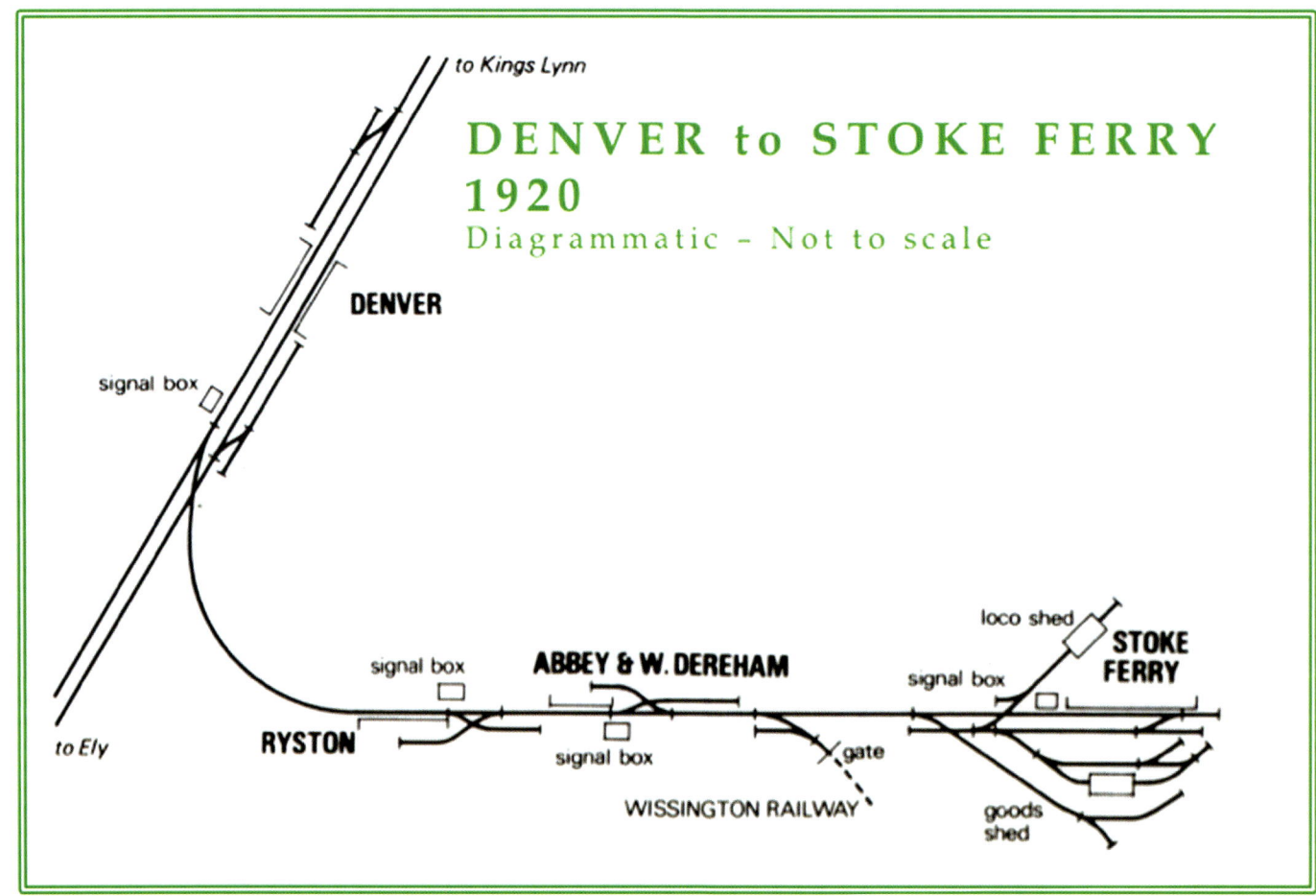

Fig 72: an edited map from the IRS book; the branch to Stoke Ferry was just over seven miles in length.

Fen. Arthur Young in his *General View of the Agriculture of the County of Norfolk* (1804 – from County Reports to the Board of Agriculture in England) describes:

> '. . . a vast area of no less than 12,000 acres . . . a very great common Fen but situated at such a distance that many people who would otherwise use it could not do so except for fuel . . . it [is] one of the richest tracts of grass in Norfolk.'

At this time fenland south of King's Lynn and east of the Great Ouse was not stocked regularly with cattle and the land under cultivation diminished. However, a decrease in grain production was accompanied by a great increase in grazing so farming became more profitable and the rents of the rich and fertile fens of Marshland and Spalding rose sharply. Small farmers in the area began to look around for similar but cheaper land and in so doing moved further east – to the Black Fen.

Arthur Young's observation about access to Black Fen – 'situated at such a distance' – was one of the drivers for railway contact and the Downham and Stoke Ferry Railway was promoted as a 'farmers' line' although GER support was lukewarm. However, 24 July 1879 saw the incorporation of the Downham & Stoke Ferry Railway Company (D&SFR). Its line ran from Denver on the Lynn & Ely Railway through the villages of Fordham, Ryston and West Dereham (whose station was known as Abbey to distinguish it from East Dereham some fifteen miles away!) and ended at a point just south of the small market town of Stoke Ferry.

The promoters of the D&SFR agreed with GER that D&SFR would finance their new railway and construct it to a standard acceptable to GER. In return GER would work and staff the line for 50 per cent of gross receipts and allow running powers to Downham Market. On 1 January 1898 GER absorbed the D&SFR.

The branch was complete and working; for a time it offered reasonable returns on freight and useful passenger services. The two key people in this story, the wealthy and strong-minded entrepreneurs, were Arthur James Keeble (1856 – 1922) and William Abel Tower (1895-1961).

From an early age Keeble had a great interest in chemistry and the application of science to agriculture. While still a young man, he and his elder brother George moved to Peterborough where they built up a very large corn and hay merchants business in the name of Keeble Brothers Ltd. It had branches at Woolwich, Nottingham, Manchester and Liverpool, with at one time an annual turnover of £250,000. The brothers participated in a number of industrial and real-estate promotions from the 1880s and were involved in 'Fletton' brick making through the Peterborough Brick Co Ltd (incorporated in July 1896 and becoming the New Peterborough Brick Co Ltd in 1897) and the Saxon Brick Co Ltd (incorporated in February 1898). The New Peterborough Brickworks had a capacity of up to 90 million bricks a year and was second only to the London Brickworks (104 million) in Peterborough at this time.

Keeble and his brother were Peterborough city councillors and, at various times, he was a member of the Huntingdonshire County Council and the Soke of Peterborough County Council. In 1903, he ceased to take an active part in the corn and hay business and turned his attention to farming. By 1904, he was living in Denver, Norfolk, farming at Middle Drove. Having come to the Black Fen, he decided to take advantage of the need for smallholdings and bought a large estate of fenland south of the River Wissey from the Duchy of Lancaster. His estate of Crown fenland, given by Deed of Grant from Edward VII on 29 September 1904, extended to over 7,000 acres. At this time the principal crop was hay which went to a forage factory at Littleport and then on to London to feed the horses working the trams and hackney carriages there. However, in the Norfolk tradition of experimental farming, Keeble decided to grow celery, potatoes, carrots and other market crops. Other experiments were being tried in the area, tobacco being one of the least profitable, though a group of fruit farmers met with more success. The fenland peat proved to be very high in nitrogen and Keeble hoped to develop an industry for producing ammonia from it: he also experimented in collecting marsh gas to use as a household fuel.

However, the most important element to this railway story was that Keeble's land had no hard roads so he decided to build a private railway to connect with the GER's Stoke Ferry branch near Abbey station. All the land on which the railway was built was private so no Act of Parliament or Light Railway Order was required. The construction of his railway was described by W.H. Barrett, a well-known fenland writer:

> '. . . in one of the most isolated spots in the Norfolk Fens was a place called Five Mile, just a few scattered cottages close to the banks of the River Wissey. This river, choked

with weeds, carried no traffic to spoil the carpet of yellow and white lilies that stretched from bank to bank but change was at hand; already looking northward one could see gangs laying down a railway track to cross the river and snake across the Fen. The new landlord . . . made plans whereby he hoped to extract much wealth from the water-logged Fens he had purchased. . . .'

The first stage of the Wissington Railway opened on 30 November 1905. The terminus, known to Keeble as Wissington Station, was at Poppylot where the Railway met the Feltwell to Southery road, the only hard surfaced highway in the district. At Cross Roads, in the middle of the estate, were a railway office and store with blacksmith's and carpenter's shops. At least one train each way was to be run, if necessary each day except Sundays; the charge per ton was 1s 3d (currently £6.65).

GER provided wagons and vans but charged no demurrage until after seven days. Traffic at this time comprised seed, fertiliser and market-garden produce to and from the smallholdings, although large quantities of trussed hay were carried until the decline in the use of horses after the First World War. After the arrival of the morning goods from Stoke Ferry, the Wissington train of about 15 to 20 wagons went down the fen from Abbey at about 08.00 delivering newspapers on the way as well as empty wagons, and returned in time to connect with the 15.33 GER goods to Downham. No records of any privately owned wagons at this time have come to light but there was a passenger carriage, believed to be an ex-GER four-wheeled carriage, which was used on Tuesdays and Fridays (market days at King's Lynn and Downham Market respectively) and enabled people to catch a GER train from Abbey into Downham Market. A platform was built at Abbey sidings and passengers had to walk the short distance from there to Abbey GER station. The carriage had gone by 1916, by which time passengers travelled in the wagons or on the engine.

Although Keeble had moved to the district and farmed some of the land, he expected the real return on his investment to come from his Eley Ammonia Factory adjoining Five Mile Farm on the south bank of the River Wissey. The Factory destructively distilled peat from the fen by heating it in an oven in the absence of oxygen. Under such conditions, the nitrogen content is converted into ammonia and various organic and gaseous products are produced. The ammonia could then have been combined with sulphuric acid to produce the fertiliser ammonium sulphate which was the end-product of Keeble's Factory.

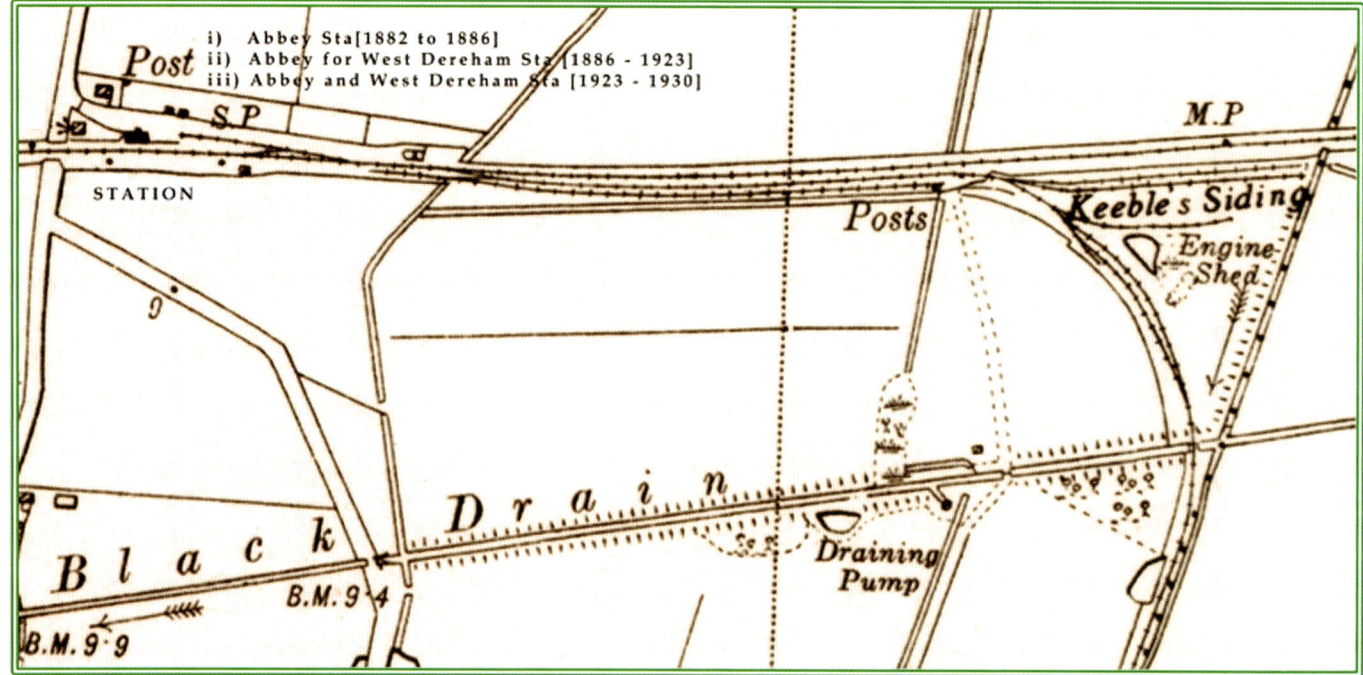

Fig 73: Abbey Station – OS 6-inch map –Norfolk LXIX.SE. Note 'Keeble's Sidings' which was the start of the independent Wissington Railway.

Alas, Keeble's enthusiasm outran his financial resources. He had arranged a loan of £380,000 with the Stamford, Spalding & Boston Bank (SSBB) who had taken a mortgage on the estate's peat resources which were valued at £4m. Fearing that they might not recover all their monies, the SSBB, on 24 May 1912, appointed John Kirby Rodwell as Receiver. On 23 January 1913, Mr Justice Warington ordered Keeble to give up all the Wissington lands to the Receiver. Warrington felt that Keeble's financial state was not good enough to merit leaving him in charge. This was the beginning of the end for Keeble; the ammonia factory struggled on until Keeble's death in 1922 when it was closed and dismantled.

However, another wealthy entrepreneur, William Abel Towler, who knew Keeble, lived nearby, bought substantial areas of fenland and believed that the cultivation and processing of sugar beet was the most cost-effective way to exploit the Black Fen area. Towler also believed in the value of an enlarged Wissington Railway, so he approached LNER and agreed on a secured loan of £2,500, carrying an annual interest rate of 5 per cent for fourteen years, but with an option for the LNER to waive interest charges after seven years. This enabled Towler to extend his railway anticipating that this would open up some 14,000 acres of fenland and provide an annual traffic to the LNER of 28,000 tons. If traffic should exceed 28,000 tons, the interest charge would be reduced to 2.5 per cent and waived altogether if 31,000 tons was reached. On the other hand, the LNER reserved the right to demand repayment of the loan if the tonnage did not reach 28,000. Towler was a business gambler and, for a time, he succeeded. He financed a sugar beet processing factory at Wissington which was completed later in 1925 by Sir Robert McAlpine & Sons for British Sugar Manufacturers Ltd (BSM). Towler sold the 35-acre site of Five Mile Farm to BSM on 16 June 1925 at £40 per acre, and then leased the railway to BSM for ten years at an annual rental of £1,500 with an option for them to purchase it at any time within four years for £30,000. On completion, the land and buildings were valued at £258,741 and the machinery and plant at £260,142. Production began on 1 December 1925 but the early years of operation proved very difficult. The factory was in competition with the three other sugar beet factories already in operation – King's Lynn, Cantley and Ely. Furthermore, Wissington's output was small and the management inexperienced.

At first, the beet for the factory came from farms north of the River Wissey but, as the management became more experienced, Wissington sugar beet factory, which was built to process 600 tons of beet per day, was enlarged to 1,000 tons and later 1,600 tons. Extensions to the Wissington Railway began hurriedly in the factory's third campaign (1927-8) when large contracts for beet from the southern areas of the Black Fen were needed. Quotes were received for second-hand track and sleepers, and for new but untreated fir sleepers. (The fir sleepers only lasted a couple of years!) In the 1930s and '40s the railway served Black Fen as the **Fig 74** map illustrates.

When the farmers had beet or produce to deliver, they contacted the railway and a locomotive took wagons down the line to the nearest loading point. Internal 'Wissington' wagons were used for beet and main line wagons for traffic onto the LNER. There was a daily goods train from all loading sidings during the sugar beet campaign, and a daily service to those points that required it out of season. Loaded wagons were collected by the locomotive, marshalled at Wissington factory and then despatched as required. Contact with the railway office at Poppylot and the factory weighbridge could be made by telephone but there was no system of communication for the railway out on the fen. The only way of determining the location of the locomotive and train was to listen very acutely. Consignment notes were often written on the back of a Woodbine cigarette packet, or the like, which made things difficult for the clerk, who had to record the date, truck number, consigner, and destination.

From 1940, the Second World War intervened in the fate of the Railway. The Ministry of Agriculture agreed to take possession of the railway under the Defence (General) Regulations, 1939, for three years, provided the war did not finish before then, and to review the situation after two years. They took over all lines south of the factory with full running rights to Abbey and estimated that the cost to the Ministry would be £2,000 per year. Wartime food production requirements much increased traffic on the line and, ironically, this was when the railway acquired the title of Wissington Light Railway though under powers of requisition rather than Act of Parliament. Train loads during the war were often very heavy and it was not exceptional for over 100 wagons to be moved with two locomotives at the head and one banking or *vice-versa*.

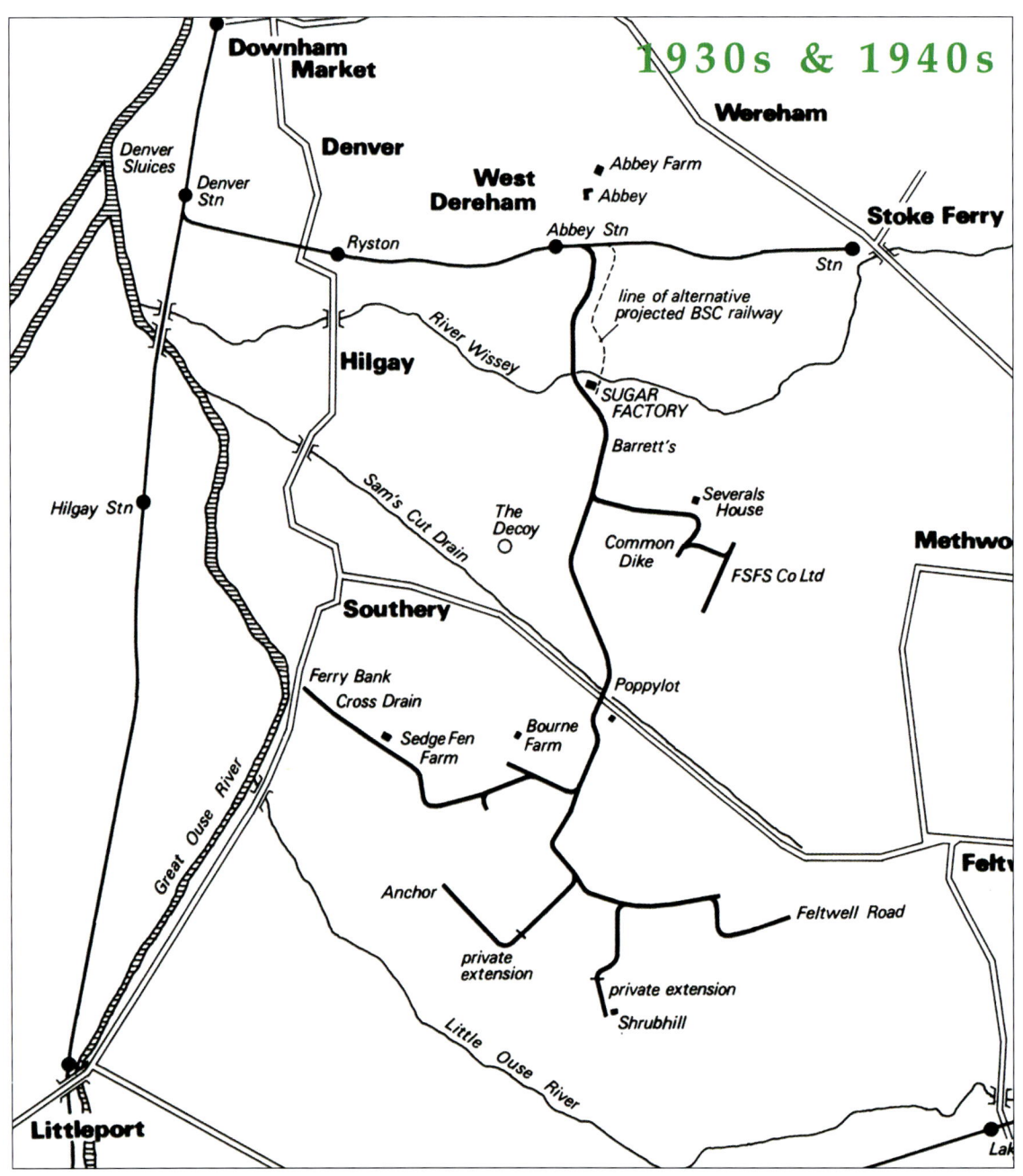

Fig 74: from the IRS book – the extent of the Wissington Railway in the 1930s and 1940s.

The method of working the line during the war remained basically the same as before. Lights were prohibited at night but there was only one collision in the blackout and no injuries. There were no signals and if more than one locomotive was out on the line, the crews would leave a note of their whereabouts on a piece of paper secured to a fence post at each junction. Before proceeding, the driver would make sure that the other locos were out and away.

At the end of the war, the Ministry of Agriculture decided to dispose of the railway under the terms of their requisition. The Ministry bought the railway from Wissington Estate in 1947 and offered it to the Ministry of Transport for inclusion in British Railways under the Transport Act of 1947. The offer was declined but was declined on the grounds that '. . . it was not strictly a railway but was a means of conveyance of agricultural produce from certain growers to the main line'. It seems that the Ministry of Agriculture rather enjoyed owning a railway. An official tour of inspection meant a good day out in the country with the chance of some good shooting on the side.

A memorandum for the Ministry of Agriculture was compiled on 23 March 1955 and reported detailed traffic returns. The railway was used by ninety-five farms, but carried annually less than fifty tons for thirty of them; less than 200 tons for sixty-eight; and over 1,000 tons for only two. Although railway rates were cheaper than the cost of hiring a lorry, the advantage of a lorry was that it could pick up in the afternoon and still be at the London market by 04.00 the next morning, a day earlier than could be accomplished by rail. The end was in sight for this 'Fenland Enterprise' and in 1956 a formal decision was agreed to close the Railway. On 26 June 1956, Sidney Dye, the local MP, asked in the Commons – amid cheers and laughter – that if British Railways were not prepared to take over a railway that had been making a profit, should he not ask the Wissington Light Railway to take over British Railways?

In May 1957, the railway was put up for sale by tender as: '. . . eighteen miles of standard gauge track, 4,785 yards of sidings and rolling stock including an 0-6-0 tank engine . . . built in 1924 . . .' It was purchased *in toto* for scrap by Thos. W. Ward Ltd, Sheffield; by 17 September 1957 no rolling stock remained on the railway and the track had already been broken near the factory. So ended the tenuous life of the Wissington Railway.

Wissington sugar beet plant – British Sugar's largest refinery in the UK and in Europe – is now supplied by bulk road tankers. The 1981-2 campaign was the last one to see the BR railway in use because BSC decided to terminate rail operations at Wissington on 31 January 1983. The last BR freight train on the Abbey branch ran on 21 December 1981 leaving Abbey at 12.17 with 29 loaded Vanfits of beet pulp nuts.

The plant can handle over 10,000 tons of beet per day. In 2007, Wissington was further developed as the UK's first bioethanol power plant, the excess heat from which was used to heat on-site greenhouses that produced 70 million tomatoes each year; in 2017, the greenhouses switched to growing cannabis plants for medicine production.

Fortunately for this record of an unusual 'minor railway', enthusiast photographers began to visit the Stoke Ferry Branch and the Wissington Light Railway in the 1950s so it is appropriate to conclude this Chapter with some memories (**Figs 75, 76, 77, 78**).

Fig 75: Stoke Ferry Station c1910; the terminus of the line was closed to passenger services in September 1930.

Fig 76: 0-6-0ST No 1700 *Wissington* (Hudswell Clarke Foundry. Leeds 1938) picking up a truck of potatoes from a road-side siding. May 1957. Note the very overgrown track and the points to the siding hidden in the verdure.

Fig 77: During the 1956/1957 sugar beet campaign, a loaded train *en route* to the Wissington Factory passes a pick-up siding.

Fig 78: Sedge Fen unsurfaced fenland drove and fragments of the Wissington Railway, early 1960s. The sturdy and newly-built loading platform marks the succession from rail-borne to drove-borne traffic.

Railways for industry . . .

It could be argued that if agriculture is an industry then the previous chapter is misplaced. However, since GER called several of their branch lines 'farmers' lines' I suggest that the Wissington (Light) Railway segues into the next three chapters which are wholly 'industrial'.

CHAPTER 12

LEISTON WORKS RAILWAY

Richard Garrett & Son

Richard Garrett established his works in Leiston on 8 April 1783 by purchasing an existing workshop in the town. As **Fig 79** illustrates, the works grew . . . and grew . . . until Old Works had been complemented by New Works and both had a railway connection with GER/LNER/BR at Leiston Station.

The Leiston Works Railway was completed with the first part of the Aldeburgh branch from Saxmundham Junction to Leiston and opened to the New and Old Works in 1859.

Although the Aldeburgh branch was closed to passengers in 1966 – and the site has now been re-developed – Leiston Station remained as a level-crossing point because of periodic trains to Sizewell B Power Station. In 2010, when I explored the remains of the Leiston Works Railway, it was clear to see where the Works Railway linked with Leiston Station sidings.

Garrett's Old Works finally closed in 1980 but was rescued from demolition and established as the Long Shop Museum. The New Works has been demolished and the site re-developed for housing.

The Works Railway closed in the 1960s, already long out-of-use, and was dismantled in 1968. The trackbed survives and it is planned to recreate the Works Railway.

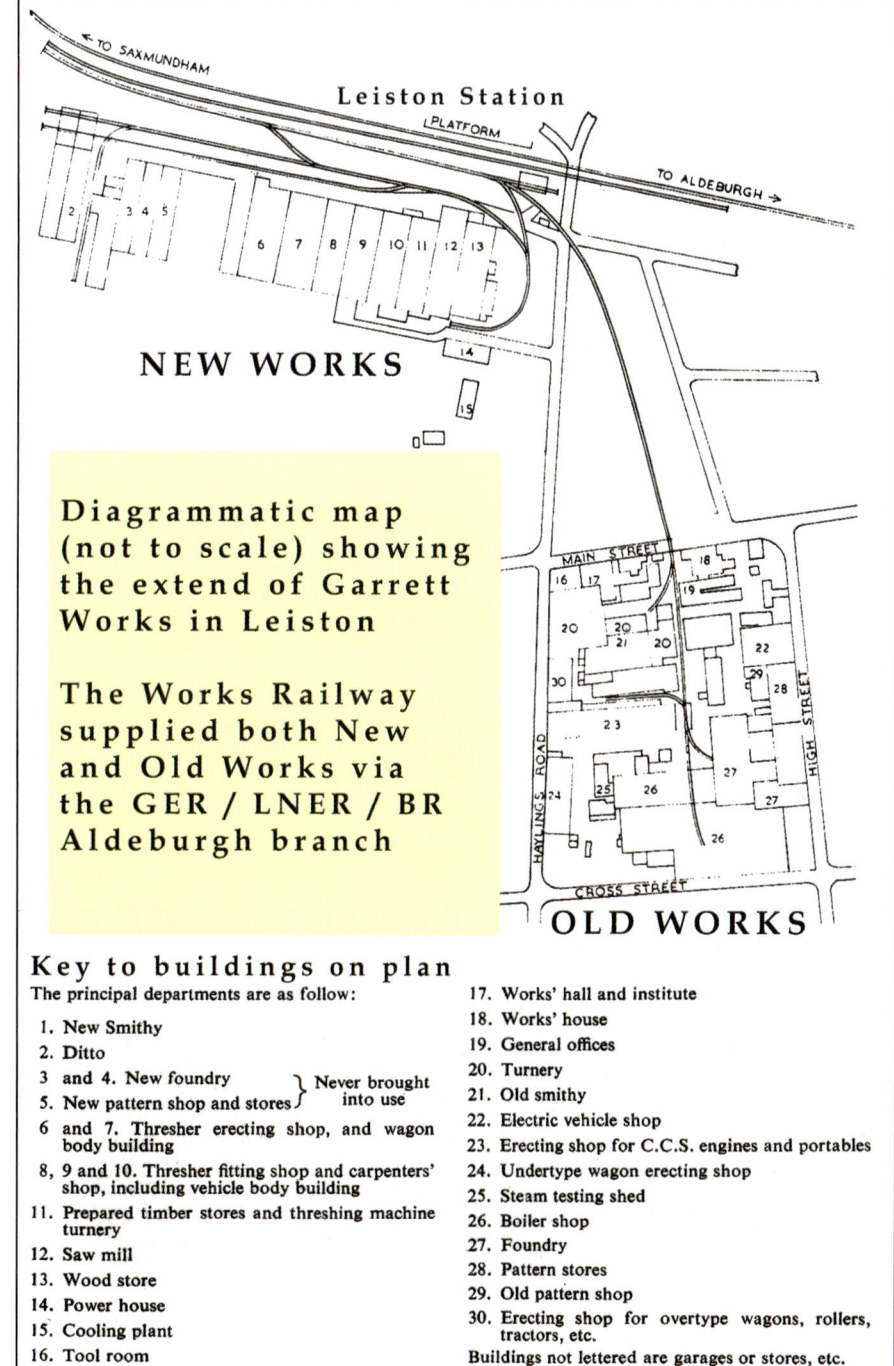

Diagrammatic map (not to scale) showing the extend of Garrett Works in Leiston

The Works Railway supplied both New and Old Works via the GER / LNER / BR Aldeburgh branch

Key to buildings on plan
The principal departments are as follow:

1. New Smithy
2. Ditto
3 and 4. New foundry ⎱ Never brought
5. New pattern shop and stores ⎰ into use
6 and 7. Thresher erecting shop, and wagon body building
8, 9 and 10. Thresher fitting shop and carpenters' shop, including vehicle body building
11. Prepared timber stores and threshing machine turnery
12. Saw mill
13. Wood store
14. Power house
15. Cooling plant
16. Tool room
17. Works' hall and institute
18. Works' house
19. General offices
20. Turnery
21. Old smithy
22. Electric vehicle shop
23. Erecting shop for C.C.S. engines and portables
24. Undertype wagon erecting shop
25. Steam testing shed
26. Boiler shop
27. Foundry
28. Pattern stores
29. Old pattern shop
30. Erecting shop for overtype wagons, rollers, tractors, etc.
Buildings not lettered are garages or stores, etc.

Fig 79: The extent of Garrett Works in the early 1900s.

Fig 80: Crossing point for the Leiston Works Railway into Leiston Station goods yard sidings in 2010.

Fig 81: The surviving track-bed of the Leiston Works Railway in 2010.

Fig 82: Garrett's own loco, SIRAPITE, on the Works Railway.

CHAPTER 13

SNAPE MALTINGS RAILWAY

Newson Garrett (31 July 1812-4 May 1893)

Another Garrett was the entrepreneur behind the building and development of Snape Maltings. In March 1841, Newson Garrett bought the business of Osborne & Fennell, barley and coal merchants, at Snape Bridge. The site began to evolve, using the River Alde to transport barley in Britain on shallow-draught lighters and into Europe on Thames barges. Within three years of his arrival, Garrett was shipping 17,000 quarters of barley a year from Snape Bridge. Much of this barley was destined for breweries, where it had first to be malted. Newson saw an opportunity and in 1854 he began malting at Snape and was soon shipping malt, rather than barley, to the breweries.

Snape Maltings was built adjoining Snape Bridge and the business expanded quickly and thrived as demand from breweries increased. A purpose-built branch of the East Suffolk railway line was built to Snape Maltings to support the business and from 1859 to 1960 up to

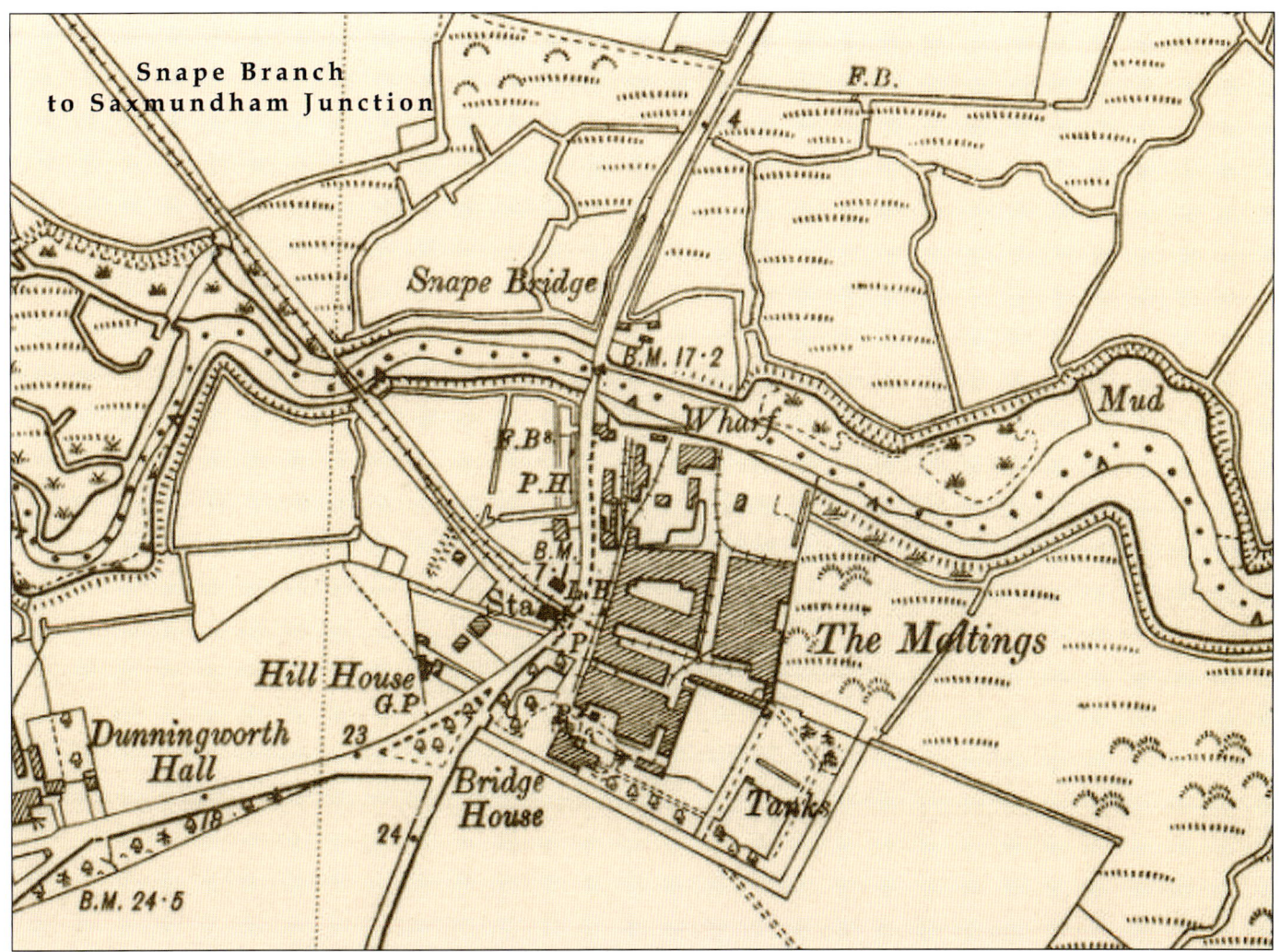

Fig 83: OS 6 inch map – Suffolk LX.SW 1950. Snape Maltings and the industrial railway branch from Saxmundham Junction to Snape Goods Station.

three trains per day ran to and from the Maltings. At full industrial use, Snape Maltings grew to some seven acres of buildings and was one of the largest flat floor maltings in the country.

Any necessary shunting took place in the Station Goods Yard then wagons were moved over to the lines serving the Maltings by shunting horses or by tractors towing or pushing the wagons.

In 1960, after 120 years, the malting of barley ceased. The large complex was no longer an efficient maltings so the site was purchased by Suffolk farmer George Gooderham. By the 1960s, Aldeburgh Music Festival was outgrowing the limited space available in the Jubilee Hall. Benjamin Britten had the vision to see the largest Malthouse, in its magnificent setting overlooking the maltings, as a possible site. Negotiations began with George Gooderham and after little more than a year, Snape Maltings Concert Hall was ready to be opened by the Queen at the start of the 1967 Aldeburgh Festival.

CHAPTER 14

CEMENT WORKS IN CAMBRIDGESHIRE

Norman Cement Works, Cherry Hinton

Barrington Cement Works – Barrington Light Railway

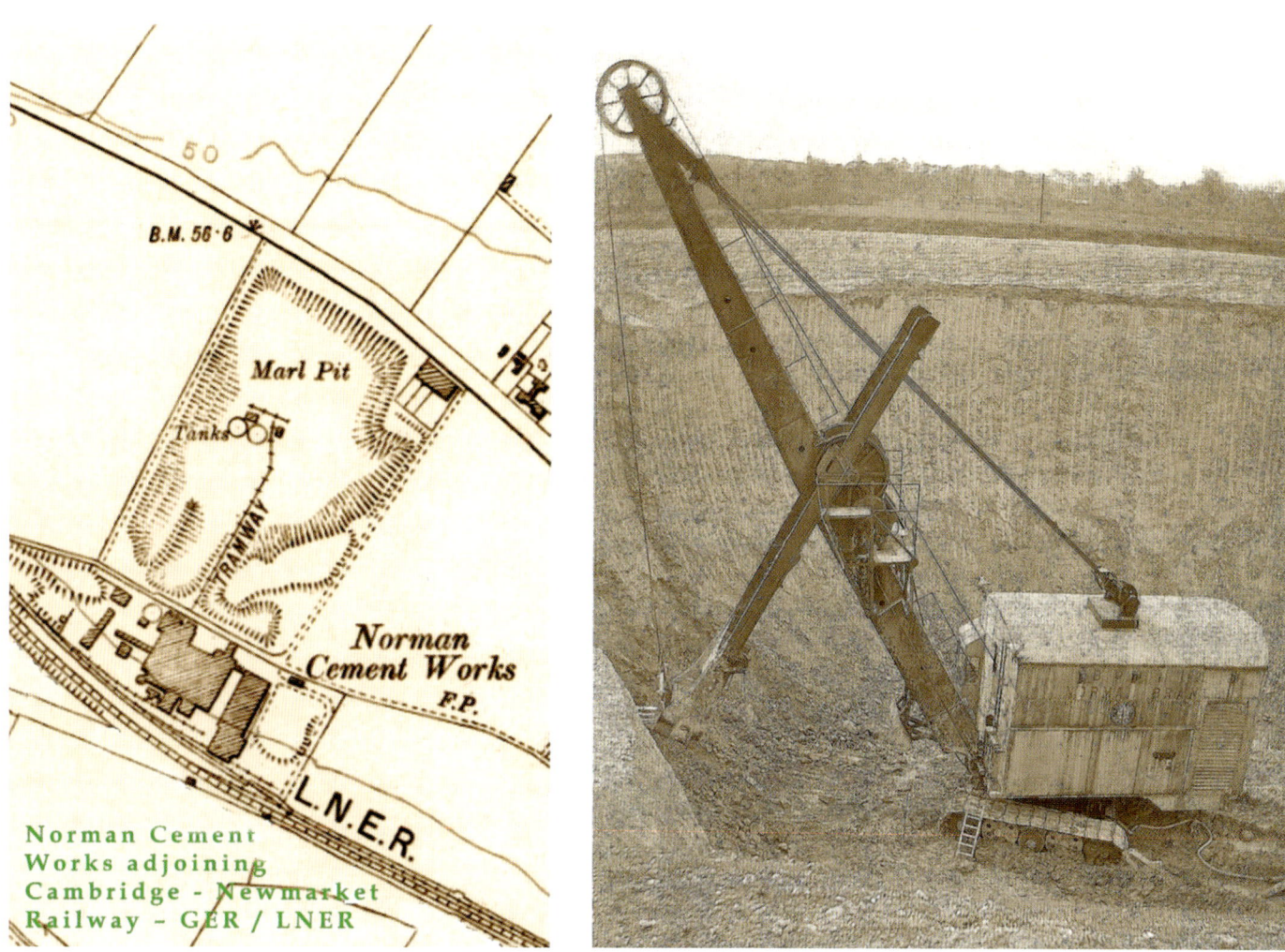

Fig 84: (left) OS 6 inch map – 1927; (right) Ruston-Bucyrus electrically-powered crowd shovel – 1956.

I grew up in Cambridge and near the village of Cherry Hinton; my principal means for exploring the nearby countryside and its railways was on a bicycle. Overlooking the Norman Cement Works was a short ride away from home and offered much to see: deep chalk pits; narrow-gauge railways on the floor of the pits; a very large excavator enlarging the chalk pit; and the Newmarket Railway adjoining the Cement Works.

I learned from exploring that in most of Cambridgeshire's cement works the chalk – or 'marl' – was dug out by large excavators, moved by tramway to the works, ground-up, mixed with gypsum and heated in large rotary kilns to create cement. This output was usually moved away from the works in bags or in bulk on a standard gauge railway link to the national railway system via the Cambridge-Newmarket railway.

I soon discovered that in the Barrington village area, about eight miles south-west of Cambridge on the line to Royston, Hitchin and King's Cross, there had been substantial cement-making in the nineteenth century. The largest chalk quarries and cement works was Barrington (East) on **Fig 85** map and in the 1950s, when I was exploring, the standard gauge Barrington Light Railway was still working. A little history explains the business:

'On 14 October 1927, the *Cambridge Chronicle* reported the opening of a cement works by the Eastwood Cement Company near the village of Barrington. Preliminary surveys indicated that there was sufficient high quality marl to sustain a cement works for an estimated 200 years. The enterprise was backed by a group of London businessmen, though the controlling interest was held by Eastwoods Ltd. A standard gauge Light Railway was authorised and built from Foxton station to the enlarged Cement Works.

'The cement works was built close to the hillside and a small two foot gauge railway was provided to bring the excavated chalk from the quarry.'

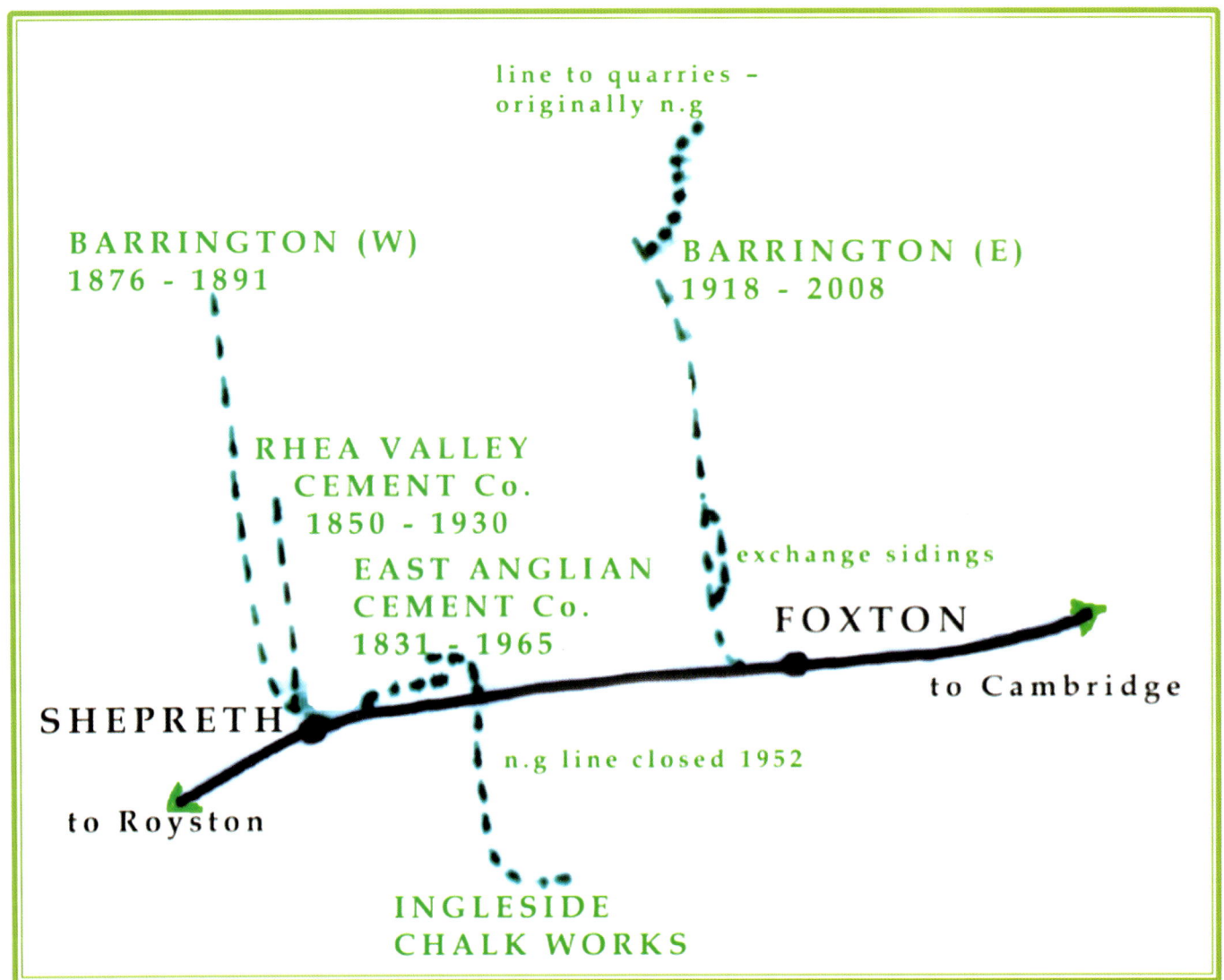

Fig 85: Sketch map (not to scale) researched and drawn by Dr Anthony Kirby (University of Cambridge).

CEMENT WORKS IN CAMBRIDGESHIRE • 85

Fig 86: The quarries in the 1960s; the Cement Works in the background is supplied by the standard gauge railway.

In the early 1960s, the cement works, owned and operated by Rugby Portland Cement Co from 1963, was modernised and the demand for chalk virtually doubled. A new quarry was opened about half a mile to the north and standard gauge lines, directly connected to the existing Light Railway from Foxton, replaced the narrow-gauge layout.

To manufacture one ton of cement requires about eight hundredweight of coal so it follows that the principal inwards traffic at Barrington is coal. Until the mid-1980s, the inward coal traffic averaged 2,000 tons per week and arrived in sixteen ton mineral wagons. About 300-350 tons of gypsum also came in by rail each week so at peak times as many as seventy loaded sixteen ton coal wagons arrived at the exchange sidings in a day requiring the 'Light Railway' locomotive to make as many as six or seven journeys to the works each day. Another aspect of the inward rail traffic up to the 1980s was spare parts for plant and machinery.

Outward rail traffic was principally cement. Bagged cement was conveyed in sacks but by the mid-1970s that business was by road transport. For the railway, from the early 1980s, most of the cement went out in bulk and was taken over by road bulk tankers by 2000.

Originally, all the Light Railway locomotives were steam powered but were progressively replaced by diesels towards the end of the twentieth century. Railway enthusiasts were generally welcomed to visit the Light Railway and on 23 and 26 June 1996 there was a two day return to steam working at Barrington. The Rugby Cement company, the Industrial Railway Society, and the Rutland Railway Museum agreed on the event and two of the Museum's preserved locomotives were used at the quarries for the two days.

Rugby Cement became part of Ready Mixed Concrete Limited then was acquired by CEMEX of Mexico in 2005. By 2005, the internal railway system had been decommissioned as no longer economically viable. CEMEX continued to operate the plant and quarry until 2008 then mothballed it, citing adverse economic conditions. Subsequently, the site was closed and partly decommissioned in 2012 and has now been re-developed for housing and landscaped.

Fig 87: Steam engines return to Barrington for two working days. The quantity of coal at the front of the picture is a reminder of the Cement Works' need for thousands of tons of coal.

Railway Companies in competition . . .

two or more stations to serve one location

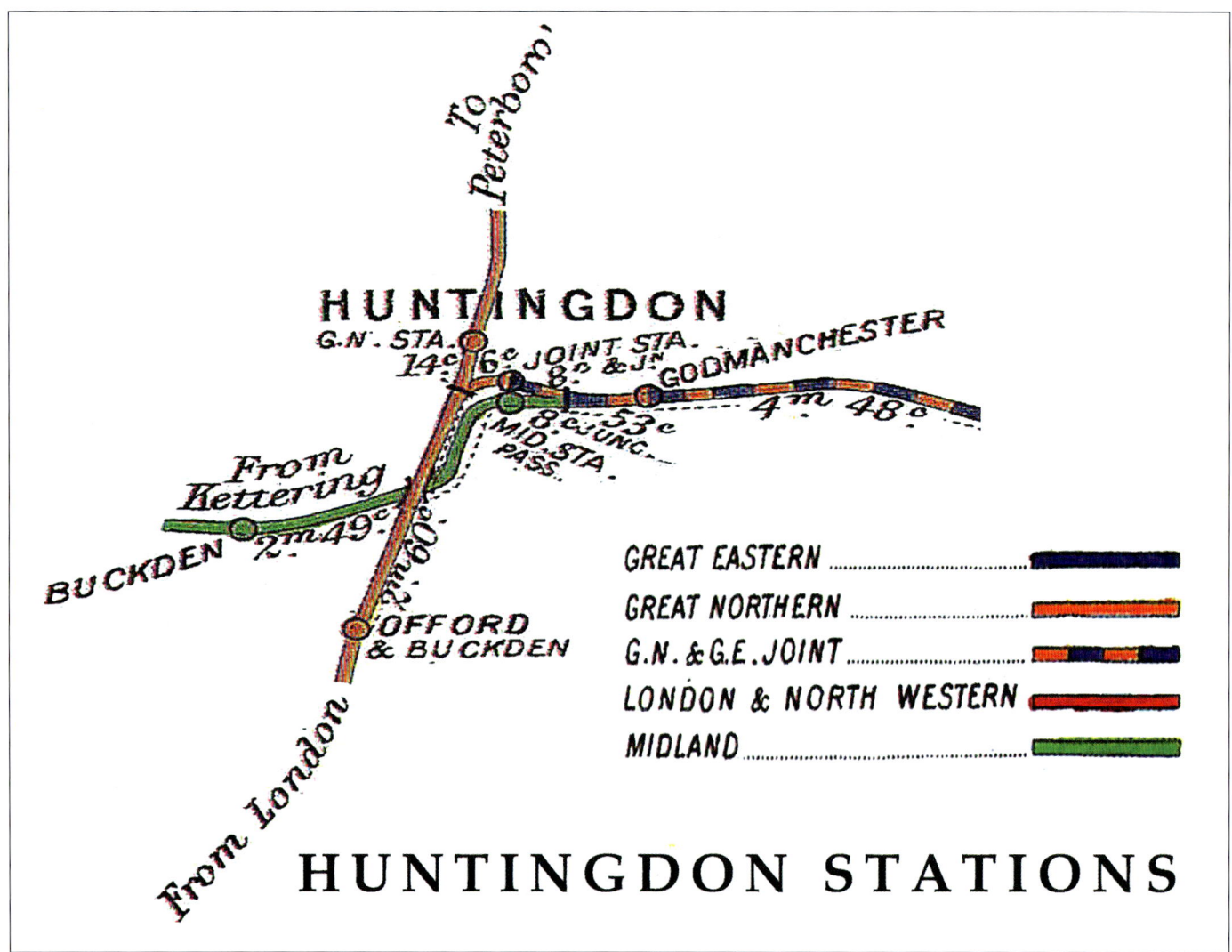

Fig 88: Huntingdon, Cambridgeshire – three Railway Companies, three Stations (edited from RCH Junction Diagrams 1900s).

Huntingdon GN Station	**Huntingdon** from 1850 to 1923 then **Huntingdon North** from 1923 to 1965 and now **Huntingdon** again.
Huntingdon GN & GE Joint Station	**Godmanchester** from 1850 to 1923 then **Huntingdon East** from 1923 until 1959 (closed to passengers) then 1962 when closed.
Huntingdon Midland Station [Pass.]	**Huntingdon East** shared with GN & GE Joint Station. For passengers not familiar with the layout at Huntingdon this confusion of stations was a conundrum!

CHAPTER 15

RAMSEY NORTH & RAMSEY EAST (HIGH STREET) STATIONS

Fig 89: Ramsey Millennium town sign.

Both GNR and GER foresaw the possibility of a through line from Somersham via Ramsey to Holme. Some of the local entrepreneurs welcomed that possibility but it never happened, principally because of lack of sufficient capital. Ramsey North, initially a GNR line, opened on 22 July 1863; Ramsey East, also called Ramsey High Street, was a GER development but completion was much slower; the Station opened on 16 September 1889. The two stations were a little distance apart as shown on **Fig 91** OS 6 inch map.

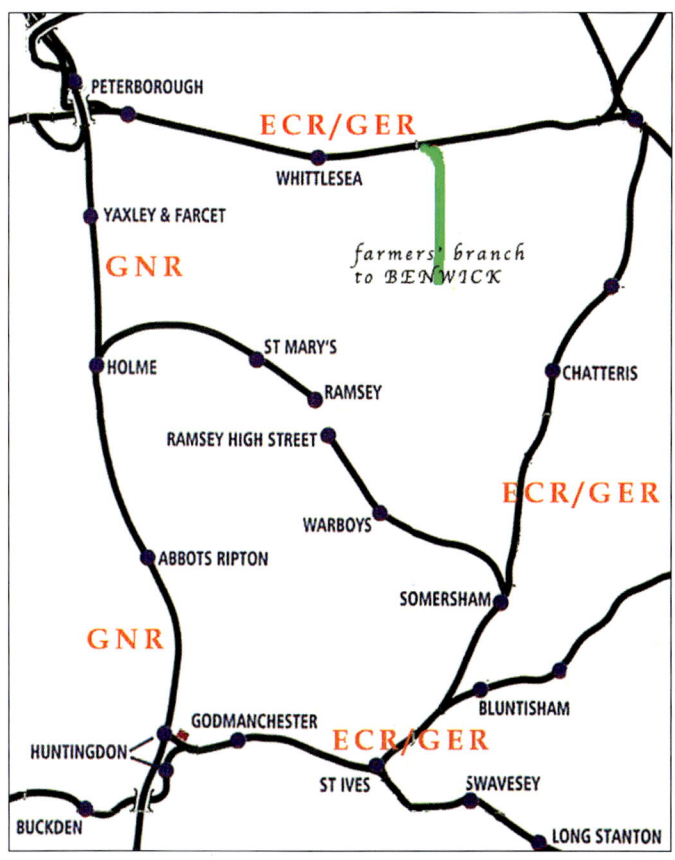

Fig 90: Peterborough-March; March-St Ives; St Ives-Huntingdon were ECR/GER railway routes north, east, and south of Ramsey. To the west was the GNR line from London to Huntingdon, Peterborough and the North.

Ramsey in Huntingdonshire was, and is, one of several small fenland market towns which developed on slightly higher land, like the Isle of Ely. Ramsey town developed around the Benedictine Ramsey Abbey – 969 to 1537 – and the market dealt in fenland vegetables, hay, wheat and cattle. By the mid-nineteenth century the town was encircled by railway routes as shown on the **Fig 90** sketch-map.

After successful draining of the fens, assisted by steam-powered pumping engines, Ramsey was a small but prosperous market town but hampered by limited transport links by fenland droves or drains. The town was a potential 'catch' for GNR and GER Railway Companies which were seeking to expand and welcomed the development of 'farmers' lines'. The whole story is too long and complex for this chapter but I commend: *Branch Lines to Ramsey*. John Rhodes. The Oakwood Press. 1986; he tells an entertaining tale.

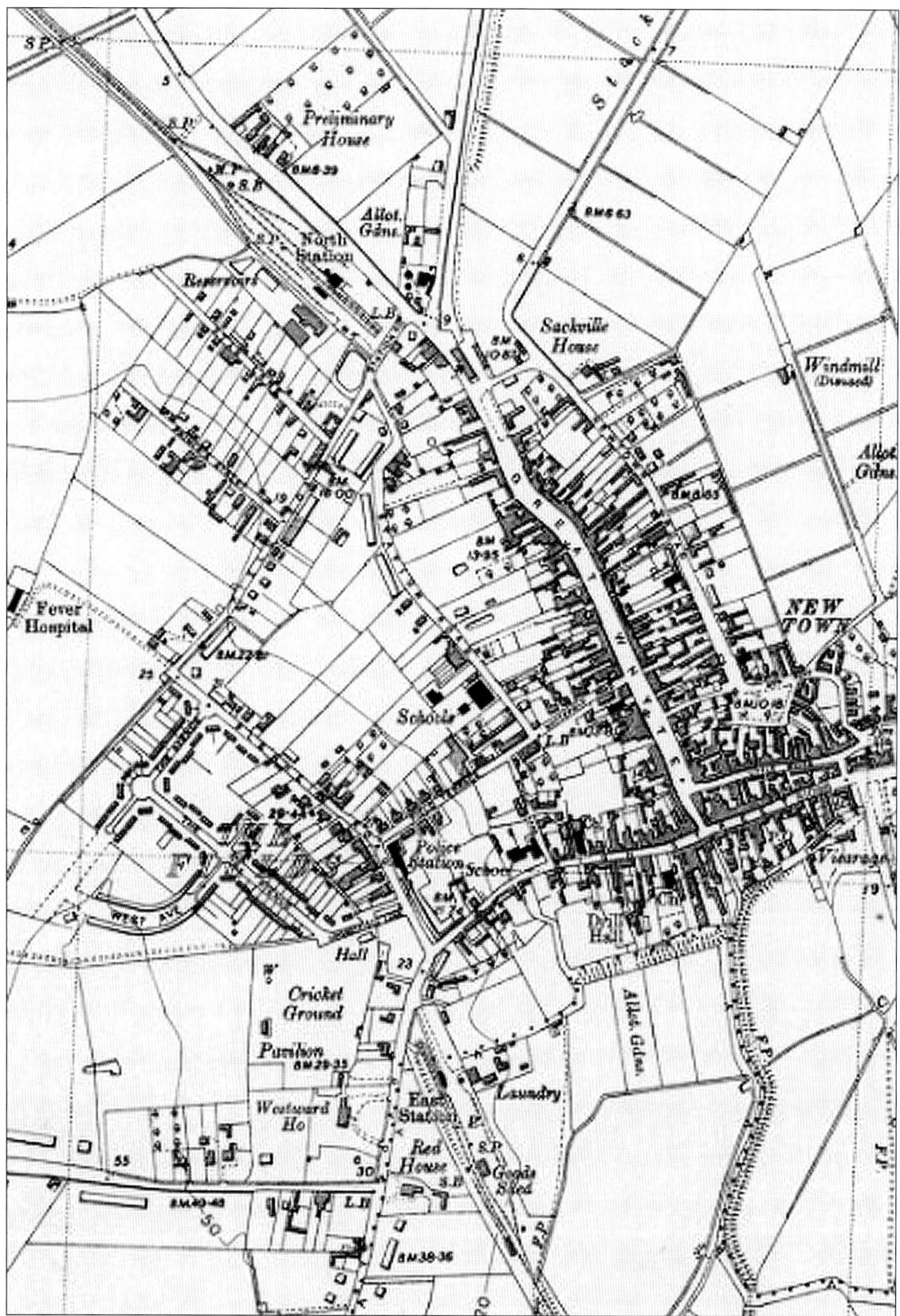

Fig 91: OS 6-inch map 1949. Ramsey East closed to passengers in 1930 but continued to be used for occasional summer excursions until the 1950s. Ramsey North closed to passengers in 1947.

Passenger and freight traffic diminished at both Ramsey stations as motor vehicles became more available and more convenient. Final closure of East Station was September 1956 and of North Station in October 1970. There is now little left to see at either site.

North Station offered better industrial potential. Coal was required by Ramsey Gas Works which adjoined the site (see **Fig 91** where the Gas Works is not named but the circular gas holders can be seen just south of 'Allot. Gdns.'). Wheat inwards and flour outwards was traffic from Tom Flowers' steam-powered roller flour mill, now converted to apartments – **Fig 92** – but still showing Flowers' initials and the date of completion.

Fig 92 (right): a late nineteenth century roller flour mill adjoining Ramsey North Station now surviving as apartments (2017).

Fig 93 (below): Ramsey East Station platform and facilities on 14 May 1937. Seven years after closure to passenger services, this picture is a fitting close to this chapter.

CHAPTER 16

FAKENHAM STATIONS

i) Fakenham Town Station and ii) Fakenham Station and subsequently
i) Fakenham West Station and ii) Fakenham East Station

Fakenham, like Ramsey in Huntingdonshire, is a long-established North Norfolk market town of a similar size to Ramsey and with two stations. **Fig 94** shows their position in the town and their OS names in the 1930s.

Fakenham's two stations served two different railway companies. Fakenham Town Station was opened on 16 August 1880 on the meandering, West to East, Midland & Great Northern Joint Railway from King's Lynn to Yarmouth. I have previously referred to the M&GNR as a 'minor railway' but it was an ambitious line determined to offer competition to the GER which was the monopolistic owner/operator of most railways in East Anglia. Because Fakenham Station had been in operation since 1849, the Fakenham Town name chosen for the M&GNR station was good marketing but geographically confusing so it was often referred to as '... the Fakenham Station in Hempton'. A chronology is:

16 August 1880	Opened as Fakenham Town
By 1898/1899	Bradshaw re-named Station as Fakenham
27 September 1948	Re-named as Fakenham West
2 March 1959	Closed

Fakenham Station is marked on the **Fig 94** map as Wells & Fakenham Railway (W&FR) because, until 1857, it was the terminus of a railway development from Dereham by the Norfolk Railway. A number of local land owners and some Directors of the Norfolk Railway financed an extension to Wells-Next-the-Sea which opened in 1857. The Station survived for passenger traffic until 1964 and the line was retained from Dereham as far as Fakenham until the 1970s for some traffic. A chronology is:

20 March 1849	Opened as Fakenham Station
27 September 1948	Re-named as Fakenham East

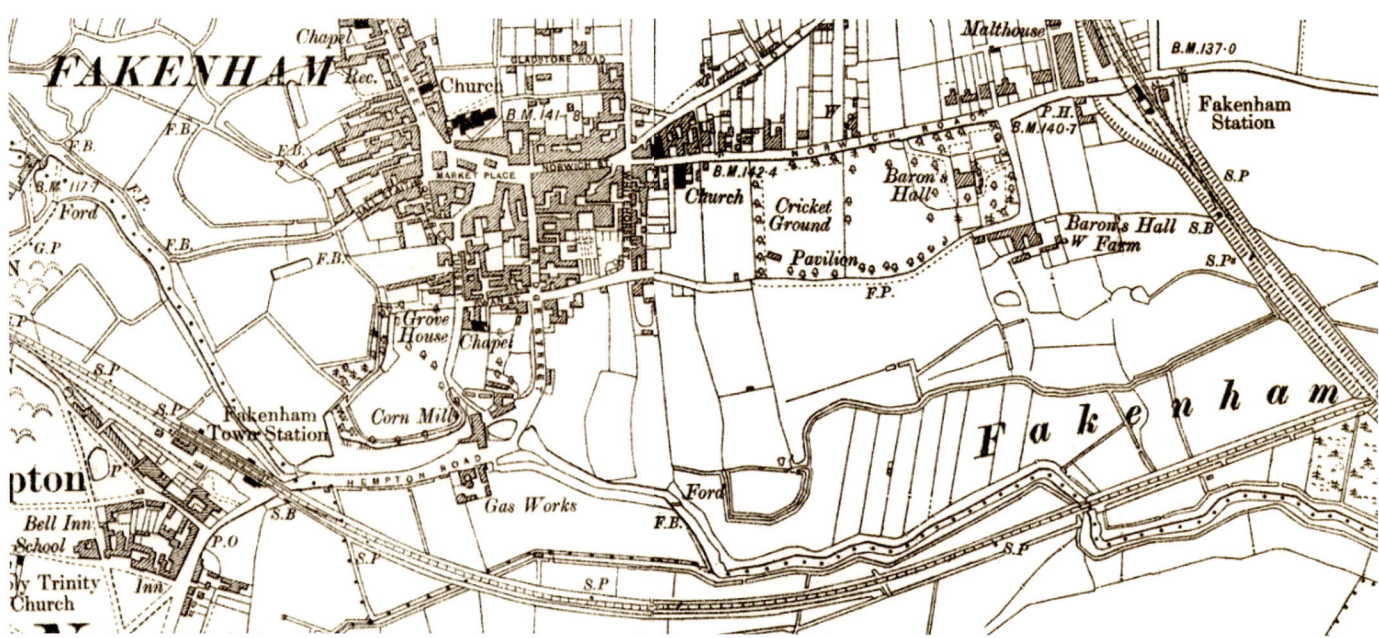

Fig 94: OS 6-inch maps: **i)** Fakenham Town Station – Norfolk XXV.NW 1936 and **ii)** Fakenham Station – Norfolk XXV.NE 1931. The two Railway Companies on the map are Midland & Great Northern Joint Railway (M&GNR) and the Wells & Fakenham Railway (W&FR).

5 October 1964	Closed for passenger traffic – track north of Fakenham to Wells was lifted but track-bed remained
mid 1950s	Closed for freight traffic

The availability of inexpensive and reliable road motor transport increased in the 1950s so closures seemed increasingly likely. It was a curious irony that Fakenham Town Gas Works – still preserved as an Industrial History Museum – was about half-a-mile from Fakenham Town Station but the coal it needed had to be transhipped at the Station, initially into horse-drawn wagons, and a siding to the Works was never built (see **Fig 94** map where the Gas Works is named).

That Station – the first to close – is now the site of an extensive Jewson's yard but a fragment of the down platform has been preserved.

Fig 95 (above): The remains of the Great Yarmouth end of Fakenham Town down platform and re-constructed name board for Fakenham West.

Fig 96 (right): Fakenham East Station with a Wells-bound DMU – mid 1950s. Fakenham East Station has entirely gone and the site built over.

CHAPTER 17

CROMER STATIONS

Cromer was and is an attractive coastal village with a small port, used for fishing and coasting traffic, and an attractive beach below cliffs on which the village grew. By the 1800s, Cromer had been 'discovered' by upper class holiday-makers who arrived by coach from Norwich. A railway was opened from Norwich in 1877 and Cromer grew rapidly – hotels, some very large, were built; a sea wall and promenade were constructed and a typically ornate Victorian pier including a concert pavilion. By 1897, Cromer was so popular that the *Cromer Express* was introduced between Liverpool Street and Cromer but Cromer's first station was – as **Figs 97** and **99** show – not well placed for the pier, the promenade and the beaches. To distinguish it from a rival station, Cromer Beach opened in 1887, the original Cromer became Cromer High in 1948 which may have sounded impressive but actually stressed the difference of locale.

Cromer Beach was a Midland & Great Northern Joint Railway (M&GNR) station and opened on 16 June 1887. Fortunately, the two principal railway companies – GER at Cromer and M&GNR at Cromer Beach – began to work together and a complicated system of junctions around Cromer was created in the early twentieth century. The **Fig 97** map shows, and dates, what happened; GER trains from Norwich and the south could use either the GER or the M&GNR stations and were able to run onto the M&GNR coastal line via Sheringham.

On 9 July 1923, a third Cromer station was opened at Cromer Links Halt; it was bleak and functional but encouraged golfers to travel by train to play at the Royal Cromer Golf Club. It was not much used and was closed on 7 April 1953 as part of BR's rationalisation.

Cromer High was closed to passengers on 20 September 1954 and to all traffic on 7 March 1960; subsequently the site has been cleared and re-developed for housing. Cromer Beach – re-named Cromer after Cromer High was closed – remains open as part of the Bittern Line from Norwich to Sheringham; as **Fig 97** map shows, all the Sheringham trains must reverse at Cromer.

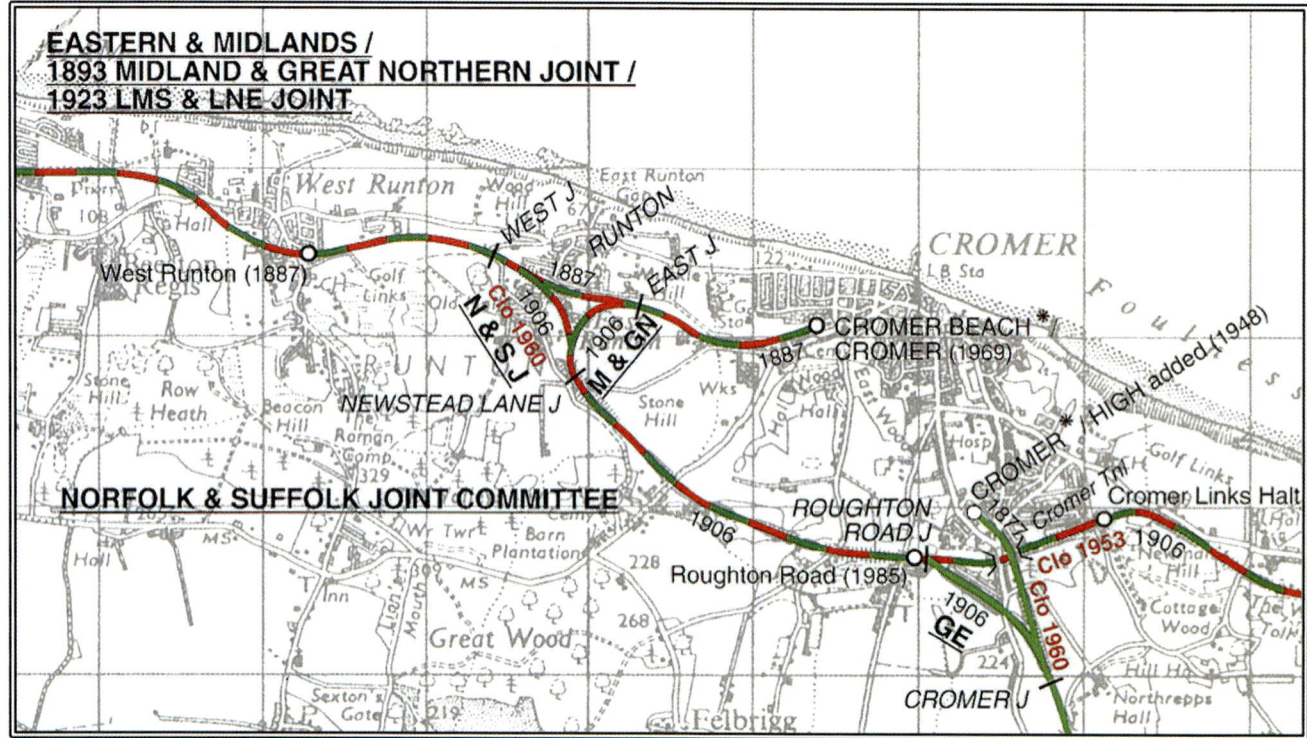

Fig 97: edited extract from *The Railways of Great Britain – A Historical Atlas*, Col. M.H. Cobb, Ian Allan, 2003.

CROMER STATIONS • 93

The detailed history of Cromer's railway connections is well told in: *The Cromer Branch*, Stanley C. Jenkins. The Oakwood Press. 1989. It is apparent from this abbreviated account that railways played an important part in the growth of Cromer and the illustrations which follow as **Figs 98**, **99** and **100** testify to this.

Fig 98 (right): Cromer High Station in 1954, shortly before closure was announced.

Fig 99 (below): Cromer High Station after complete closure in 1955. Note that Cromer 'High' was an appropriate name for this Station.

Fig 100: Cromer Beach Station – 19 May 1963.

CHAPTER 18

HAVERHILL STATIONS

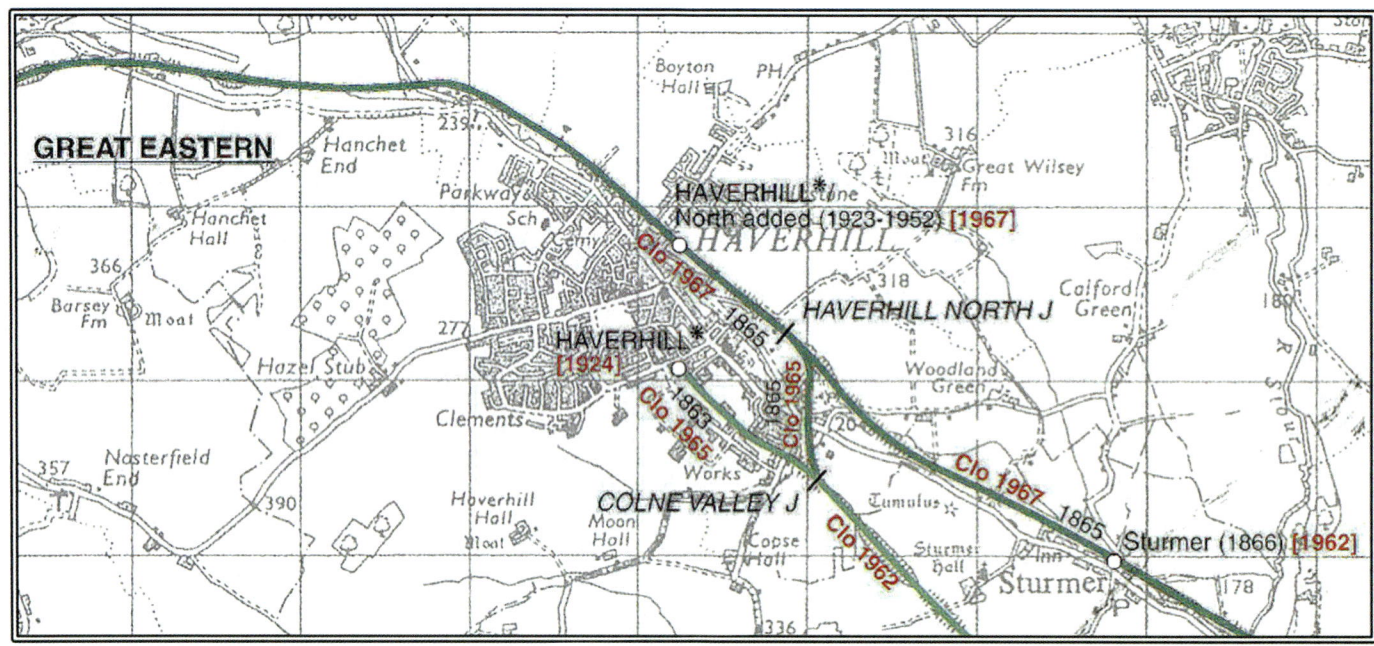

Fig 101: edited extract from *The Railways of Great Britain – A Historical Atlas*, Col. M.H. Cobb, Ian Allan, 2003.

Like Cromer, Haverhill in Cambridgeshire had two stations. Haverhill North was on the GER Stour Valley line via Sudbury to Marks Tey and Haverhill South was a terminal station for the Colne Valley & Halstead Railway (CV&HR) to Chappel & Wakes Colne. The two companies worked together if it was necessary, or useful, but the CV&HR remained fully independent until it became part of the LNER at the 1923 grouping.

Haverhill South (CV&HR) Station opened on 11 May 1863, the GER Station – latterly Haverhill North – on 1 June 1865. Neither was particularly well-placed in Haverhill so when GER installed a link between the two railways in 1865 nearly all the CV&HR passenger trains worked to and from the GER Station. Once the link was in place CV&HR ran excursions to Cambridge and to Clacton '. . . generally near the time of full moon so as to give the country folk plenty of light to get home by'.

Although the track plan in **Fig 102** appears quite generous, there were problems like the narrow single-road Loco Shed. Especially when a loco was in the

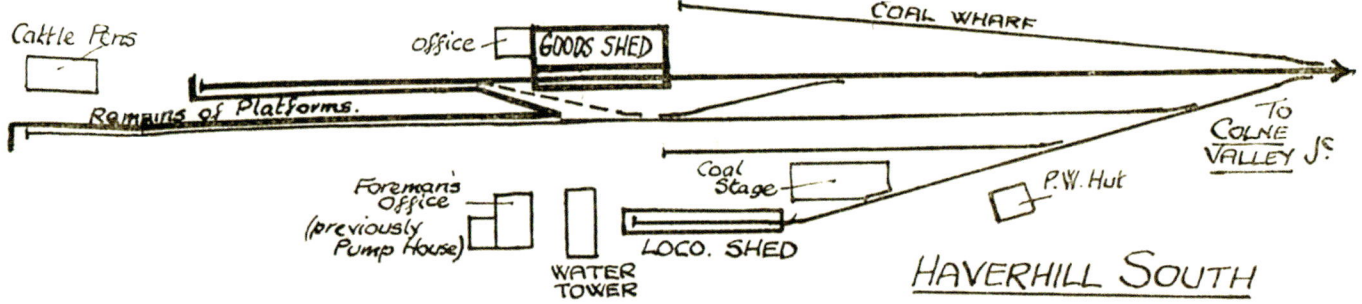

Fig 102: Sketch plan of track layout at Haverhill South (CV&HR).

shed there was very little space for any maintenance or repairs work.

CV&HR survived as an independent operator until absorption by LNER in 1923 and closure to passenger traffic in 1924. 'Probably its only true claim to fame is that it survived at all . . . [after being in a state of utter financial chaos] . . . it never killed a single passenger in a train accident or paid a dividend!' (from *The Story of the Colne Valley*, R.A. Whitehead and F.D. Simpson, Francis Ridgway Ltd, 1951).

Haverhill North, the GER Station, and the railway it served survived a little longer than Haverhill South. It was closed by BR on 6 March 1967 when the line from Shelford, via Haverhill, to Sudbury was also closed. The station site is now a Tesco supermarket and extensive car park. Today, Haverhill has a population of over 30,000 and is an industrial town but without a railway. There have been several attempts to restore a link to Shelford and Cambridge and possibly to Sudbury and thence to Colchester and London.

Fig 103: Haverhill North Station in the late 1950s.

Fig 104: Haverhill North Station and derelict track, Shelford to Sudbury, 1969.

PART 3

DEMISE – AND POSSIBLE RECOVERY

No more a 'common carrier?' Economics of railway operation? Social changes affecting railway use? Should the national railway network provide a public service?

Most of the Minor Railways explored in **Part 2 – Development** have not survived into the beginning of the twenty-first century and some of the reasons for their demise have been mentioned. It seemed logical, however, for a generic consideration of 'Demise – and possible recovery' to use some minor railways not yet discussed as potential exemplars and some of the wider issues that have affected railway operation.

The 'common carrier' problem (edited from *Index for Railways – online*):

'The 1854 Rail & Canal Traffic Act was passed to maintain some competitiveness between rail and canal systems. Railways were obliged to carry any and all goods offered to them, other than those what might damage rolling stock or where the goods were too large for the structure gauge.

'The 1854 Act and subsequent legislation caused the term "common carrier" to mean an obligation to carry goods offered no matter how small the consignment. The Act also introduced a Government-regulated system of charges for freight moved by rail, based on the weight and value of goods carried.

'These two factors, the obligation as common carriers and a Government-regulated charges structure, became the biggest obstacles to the railway's ability to compete with road transport. A single low-value consignment had to be booked in; loaded into a wagon; transported to a trans-shipment depot; transferred to another wagon possibly as its sole cargo; moved to yet another yard; attached to the local "pick-up" goods train to be dropped off at the nearest station to its destination. The revenue on this cargo probably only paid for the time of the booking clerk.

'In 1893 new Government-ordered railway rates came into force and the railways increased their charges to the maximum allowed in order to recover the losses on enforced discounts. There followed more legislation further restricting the freedom of the railways to alter their charges and leaving them no room for competition other than in any additional services and facilities they could provide and charge for.

'British main line railway companies began a period of intense competition for passenger and goods traffic. Even if goods traffic made a loss there would still be some notional contribution from each consignment toward the fixed costs of operating the railway.

'The Government control over railway rates – based on the value of the cargo carried and the obligation to carry any goods offered – became a serious problem for the railways with the growth of road lorry traffic in the late 1920s. Road haulage was not governed by "common carriers" legislation so a road haulier could offer to carry a high-value cargo at a lower cost than the railway. Or refuse to accept a cargo, especially if to accept it would mean a loss to the road haulier.

'The Transport Acts of 1953 and 1962 substantially altered the legislation relating to "common carriers" and allowed British Railways to refuse less profitable cargoes.'

By a fortunate happenchance, the edited extract below addresses the questions at the head of this page:

Railway economics must embrace the infrastructure – the rails and civil engineering on which the trains run and their support structures; the trains which use the infrastructure and the traffic which the infrastructure supports and carries. The higher the utilization, the better the infrastructure economics. Railways are at their most highly competitive when they can operate large trains, well loaded with traffic, over a heavily used network. It has generally been the case that freight business pays better than passenger business but . . . . .

Social changes affect railway use and passenger business has been materially affected by the availability of motor cars and, in larger conurbations, by the development of local public transport. Railway freight business has also been affected by the door-to-door facility offered by motor lorries. Railway cartage services once offered that facility but at considerable cost to the railway, or to the customer.

Should the national railway network provide a public service? In the nineteenth century and, pre-Beeching, in the twentieth century it was a popular perception that 'the railways' should offer a public service and most of the minor railways in East Anglia tried to fulfil that expectation. However, a fully-staffed branch line serving a number of stations and offering common carrier facilities was unlikely to generate sufficient income to cover its running costs. Beeching made that point very succinctly in his Report – BR was losing money and the Government was not prepared to fund a public service.

As Yorkshiremen still maintain: 'Yer don't get owt for nowt' so the chapters which follow explore the battles fought, and ultimately lost, by several minor railways in East Anglia. As a paying passenger I rode on several of them but clearly did not contribute enough!

CARRYING THE FREIGHT – FROM EGGS TO ELEPHANTS

Railways were Common Carriers until the Transport Acts of 1953 and 1962

They were bound by law to accept any freight traffic that was offered . . .

.... cats, dogs, beer and butter, eggs, elephants,

hay to the City of London stables,

manure and maggots,

coins to-and-from the Royal Mint,

gunpowder, cut flowers, bananas, fish,

coal, iron ore, sand-and-gravel, cement,

sugar-beet, milk, small/soft fruit, orchard fruit,

market-garden produce,

homing pigeons, calves, piglets and pigs, lambs,

cattle and sheep, mink,

trunks and other personal luggage-in-advance,

the Royal fish . . . . . .

the list is almost endless . .

ROAD HAULIERS COULD ACCEPT OR REFUSE ANY OF THIS FREIGHT TRAFFIC

Fig 105: Panel created for the NRM in 1990 explaining rail/road competitiveness. The 'Royal fish' traffic was boxes of salmon labelled HM The Queen and bound for Sandringham.

CHAPTER 19

FIRST TO GO – PART OF GREAT CHESTERFORD TO NEWMARKET RAILWAY

It is important to remember that the closure of some minor railways – or parts of such railways – took place long before the Beeching Report. A good example, and an entertaining East Anglian railway story, is the closure of part of the Newmarket Railway in 1851.

Newmarket, only thirteen miles east of Cambridge, had no railway connection although the town was home to all the major British racing and training stables. There was constant inward/outward traffic of horses all over the country but until the railway came these transfers were slow and difficult.

Race meetings attracted huge crowds so the dynamics of the 'Railway Mania' encouraged promoters to suppose that Newmarket was a worthwhile goal. Robert Stephenson was appointed to direct the construction of the Railway.

Mr (later Sir) John Villiers Shelley MP, and member of the Jockey Club, explained to Parliament why the racing fraternity were keen to have a railway link with London:

'The Jockey Club felt that a railway to Newmarket would not only be a great convenience to parties anxious to participate in the truly British sport of racing but would enable Members of Parliament to superintend a race and run back to London in time for the same night's debate.'

Inspired by such ideals, favoured by the local landowners, the Bill was unopposed and received the Royal assent on 16 July 1846. Construction was started immediately on the 'main line' from Great Chesterford to Newmarket and this line opened to goods traffic on 3 January and to passenger traffic on 4 April 1848.

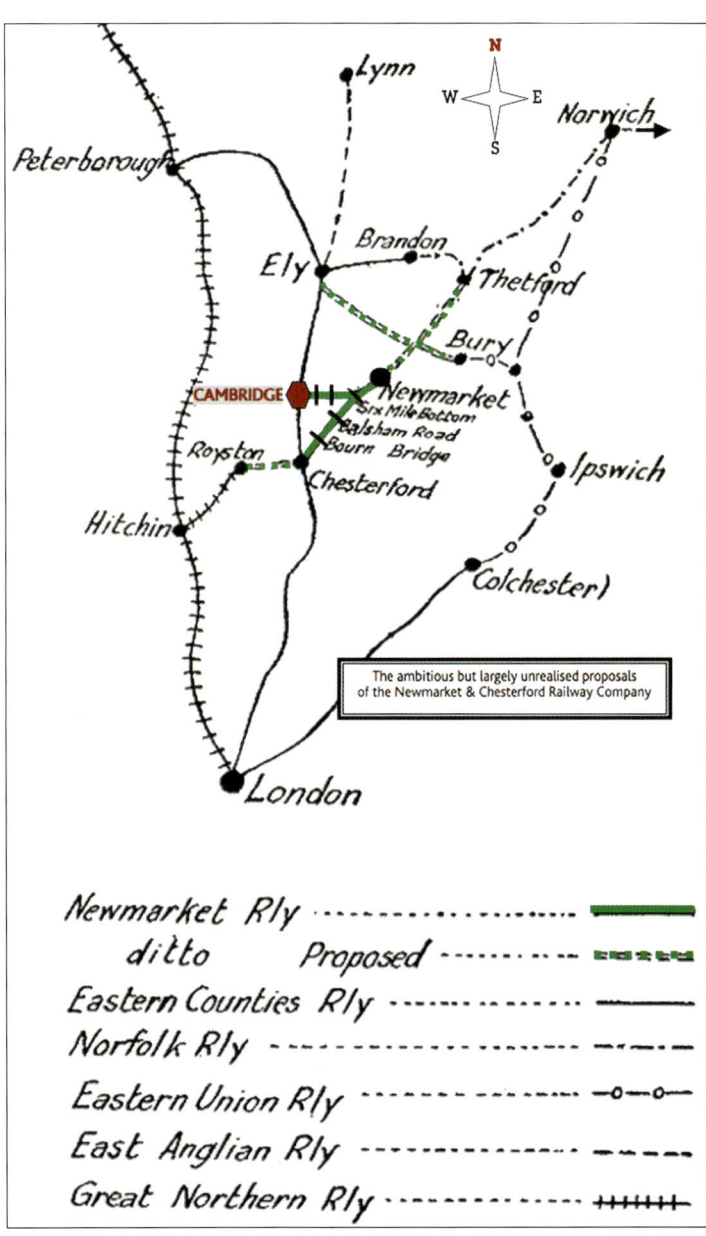

Fig 106: Sketch map of the Newmarket Railway – from Great Chesterford to Newmarket.

Meanwhile, the Newmarket Railway Directors were exploring expansions, not least because their 'main line' alone was unlikely to generate sufficient traffic and income to sustain the Railway and pay any dividends to shareholders. They were negotiating with the ECR – later to become GER and a very powerful Railway Company in East Anglia. ECR had an interest in taking over the Newmarket Railway to divert London-Newmarket and eastwards traffic via Cambridge.

The Newmarket Railway's 'main line' was generating so little income that the Railway's Committee of Management agreed to ECR taking over control of their traffic from 2 October 1848 but this agreement had to be formalised at the next ECR Shareholders' General Meeting in February 1849. The ECR Chairman, George Hudson (the so-called Railway King), did not attend the meeting. The meeting therefore ejected him from the Chairmanship *in absentia* and refused to consider an agreement with the Newmarket Railway because it seemed that the line was very nearly bankrupt.

We know today that the ECR, in working the Newmarket Railway, had been starving and bleeding it. The ECR sought to charge 1s 5d a mile for locomotive power and £600 a year for the management or rather – as the Chairman of the Newmarket Railway did not scruple to call it – the mismanagement of the line. Three months working, to 4 January, 1849, showed a gross profit to the Newmarket Company of only £704, out of which they had to pay bond interest of £2,000. The Newmarket Railway's financial problems were rendered all the more difficult because ECR held on to even this small balance of £704 on the grounds of alleged 'other claims'. In addition, the Newmarket Company had to defray out of capital the cost of maintaining their permanent way and stations and owed their contractor, and many debenture holders, considerable sums.

On 30 June 1850, the Newmarket Committee of Management closed their railway to all traffic; the Cambridge branch was not complete and Newmarket was again without a railway connection. All the engines and rolling stock went to the ECR under what the Newmarket Directors called 'an equitable arrangement' but which looks uncommonly like a case of the ECR astutely taking the locomotives and rolling stock in part-settlement of a bad debt.

At this hopeless moment, a vigorous personality, Mr Fane, who held the office of a Commissioner in Bankruptcy, took control of the Newmarket Railway as Chairman. Robert George Cecil Fane (1796-1864) was educated at Charterhouse and University of Oxford. He was called to the Bar at Lincoln's Inn in 1821 and in 1831 was appointed one of six Commissioners of Bankruptcy. Mr Commissioner Fane had already been Chairman of a Committee appointed on 22 March 1849, to investigate the work of the Newmarket Railway Company. His Committee had urged the immediate pressing on with the Cambridge branch as the Newmarket Railway Company's one hope of salvation.

When, however, at an Extraordinary Meeting of 27 July 1850, the Directors told the story of their defeatist policy of closing the line in the previous month, without even having called the shareholders together on the matter, Mr Commissioner Fane rose in his wrath and tore the Committee of Management to shreds. He showed that if running the line would probably entail a loss, keeping it shut would mean a larger loss; he criticised the mistake of making, as the pivot of the line, Great Chesterford, a small village, and not Cambridge, a large town, and robustly denounced the bungling of the various negotiations with the ECR and the Directors' tactless handling of Mr Jackson, their contractor and debenture holder. So the shareholders by a large majority cast out the Committee of Management, and Mr Commissioner Fane with his chosen Directors formed a Board to reign in their stead.

The result was magical. The line was re-opened from Chesterford to Newmarket on 9 September 1850, with rolling stock borrowed from the ECR. Better still, Fane made an arrangement with the ECR to accommodate, when opened, the Cambridge branch at Cambridge Station and so avoid the expense of a separate station and staff there. In addition, Mr Fane got Mr Jackson, the contractor, to agree to complete the line to Cambridge for a sum not exceeding £9,000, on being furnished with a certain quantity of rails and sleepers which, Fane stated, the Company would have at its disposal.

This last phrase covers an ingenious move of Mr Fane's. The original main line from Great Chesterford to Newmarket was laid as double track. A single line was ample for the traffic so Mr Fane had one set of rails and sleepers lifted from Chesterford to the junction with the Cambridge branch. This provided some 11 miles of rails and sleepers for the branch to Cambridge – and some £7,000 worth of rails in-hand for maintenance and replacements.

The urgent desire of the energetic Mr Fane to get the Cambridge branch open as soon as possible was met with annoying technical difficulties for the junction with ECR at Cambridge. In the Parliamentary plans, the curve at the junction was shown with a radius of 20 chains but it was found necessary to create a deviation that altered the radius of the curve to 8 chains. For this, the consent of the Commissioners of Railways was required and was applied for in July 1851. However, the Newmarket Company's compulsory powers of acquiring land had expired so the Commissioners refused to approve the deviation without the consents of the owners and occupiers of the land affected. Mr Fane believed it would save time to get the deviation approved first and then obtain the consents of the landowners. On 30 July 1851, Fane wrote to Captain Simmons RE of the Railway Commissioners' Office, the following pathetic note:

'Wednesday 30th 4 before 10
'DEAR SIR,
'As it will be impossible that the Company should make the curve without the consent of the owners of the land, no possible evil can arise from the Commissioners considering the curve first. If therefore, they could be induced to approve or disapprove the curve first, it would be the greatest possible convenience to me personally.

'Every day's delay is a question of £50 at least and the difficulty I have to deal with is enormous. The land I have to negotiate for is vested in 2 Trustees – one in Derbyshire and one in Yorkshire – in trust for a wife, nearly out of her mind – her 2 children, and afterwards for her husband, who will not see or speak to her.

'I am off for Lincoln this moment to see one of the Trustees; and to labour to get 5 or 6 consents to the sale. And then to get written consents to the curve again, would be more than one's life is worth.
Pray help me, if you possibly can.
'Yours truly, C. FANE.'

But the Commissioners were not to be touched by any such human appeal; it was very much more important to them that the correct Protocols of Procedure should be preserved so they rendered the following reply:

'OFFICE OF COMMISSIONERS OF RAILWAYS, WHITEHALL
'August 1st 1851
'SIR,
'I have been directed by the Commissioners of Railways to acknowledge the receipt of your letter of 30th ultimo and to inform you that they cannot enter into a consideration of the propriety of sanctioning the proposed deviations in the curve therein alluded to until they are satisfied that the consents required, before their authority can be given, have been obtained.
'I have, etc., DOUGLAS CALTON Assistant Secretary to: C. Fane, Esq.'

Mr Commissioner Fane, however, was not to be outdone by this red tape of the finest quality. He even succeeded in infusing some of his abounding energy into a Civil Service Department. On 7 October 1851, he got:

- the Commissioners of Railways approval of the new 8 chains radius curve
- approval of the line by the Inspecting Engineer – the fencing and the Cambridge Station junction having been completed
- on 8 October 1851 the formal consent to the line being opened for the purposes of public traffic.

The line was opened from Cambridge Station to Six Mile Bottom, and thence to Newmarket on 9 October 1851. Immediately the Cambridge line was opened the Great Chesterford to Six Mile Bottom line closed to passenger traffic.

Fig 107: surviving bridge on Newmarket Railway 1956; last train under it 1851.

CHAPTER 20

MILDENHALL BRANCH

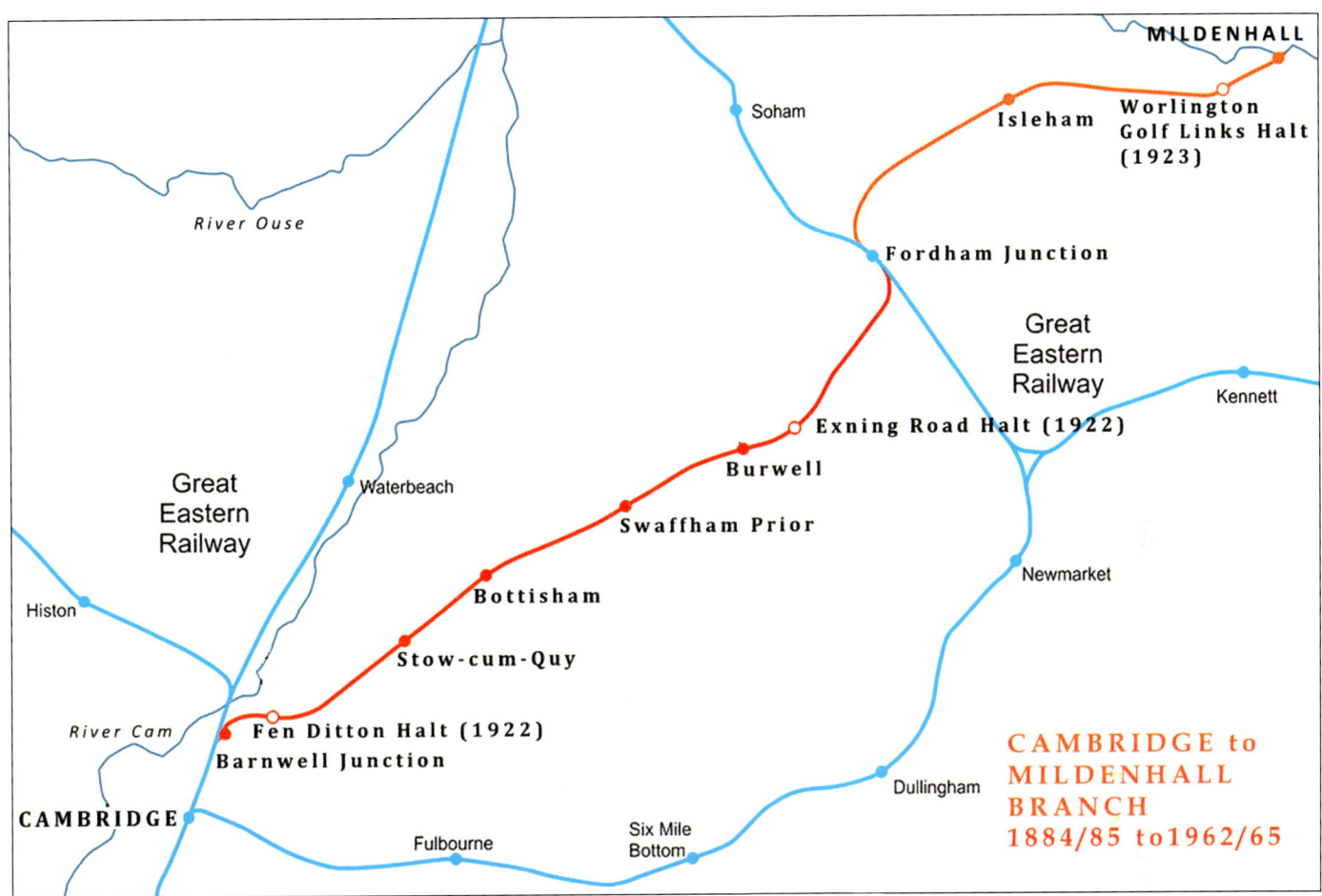

Fig 108: edited sketch plan showing the course of the Mildenhall Branch and the station names. Several of the stations were a considerable distance from the villages they were named to serve.

The **Fig 108** sketch plan nicely illustrates the 'minor' nature of the Mildenhall Branch, wandering across the edge of the fens to the south and east of the railway to the relatively small market town of Mildenhall.

The 1903 plan does show the Station well to the south of the town. I have included this map, published in *Simpson's History of Mildenhall*, Mildenhall Museum, 2012, because, when I bought the book, I assumed it would provide some background context to the building and use of the Branch Line. Alas, not so, despite the fact that Simpson's owned a printing works in Mildenhall and Alfred Simpson published his first *History of Mildenhall* in 1892 when the railway should have been very current news.

The absence of any reference to the Mildenhall Branch in Simpson's book confirmed for me that the Branch – on which I travelled on several occasions – was an idiosyncratic railway well worth including in this book, albeit in the 'Demise' section and without any 'recovery'. The Branch passenger services were ended a year before Beeching's proposed closures and although some freight services continued until 1965, they were not well used.

As with several other minor railway schemes there was one man, Charles Allix, the Squire of Swaffham Prior, who believed in the need for a railway to serve the fen shore villages to the north-east of Cambridge. Allix frequently approached senior GER officers for 'his' railway but he was rebuffed until serious flooding near Lakenheath on the Ely to Norwich main line caused considerable GER traffic losses. Allix's proposals were reviewed and a direct route from Cambridge via Mildenhall to Thetford was

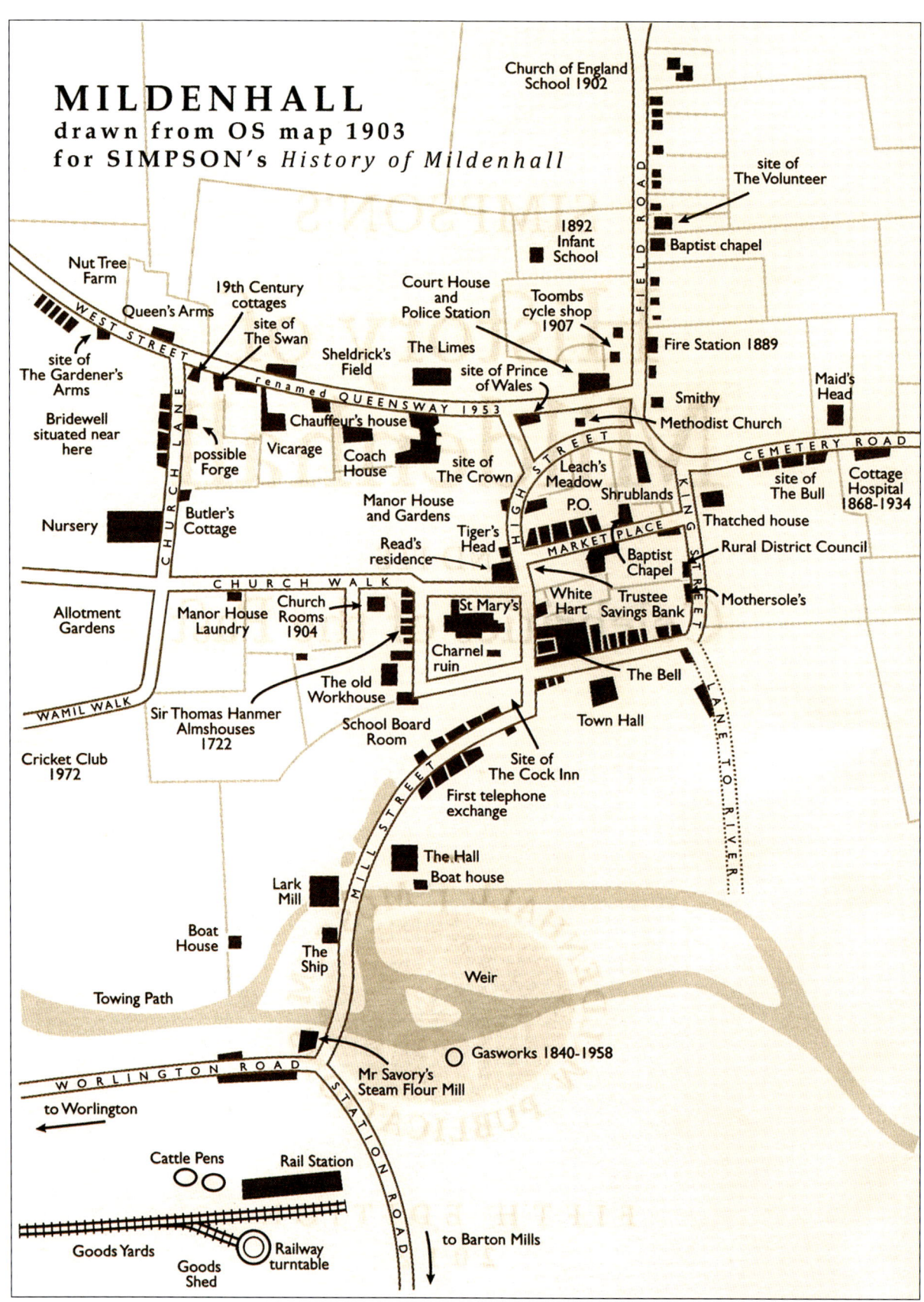

Fig 109: is a plan of the town, based on 1903 OS evidence.

Fig 110: A Mildenhall train at Platform 4, Cambridge Station on 8 December 1954. A Holden-designed LNER Class E4 2-4-0 mixed-traffic locomotive and two elderly carriages with step-down facilities for the three Halts on the Branch.

planned. However, GER was not prepared to finance the whole railway and only authorised construction to Mildenhall so the branch became another East Anglian farmers' line serving an area of sparse population.

Nonetheless, to an interested minor railway explorer like me the line was a working museum.

I little thought as I photographed the train in **Fig 110**, and subsequently travelled on to Mildenhall, that the loco hauling the train would be saved for the NRM's national collection and would become one of my responsibilities as Deputy Head of the NRM from 1987 to 1994. But that was one of the surprises which this idiosyncratic Branch line could deliver.

The next surprise was Barnwell Junction (**Fig 111**).

In **Fig 111,** the Cambridge to Ely main line runs north up the centre of the picture with Barnwell Junction goods yard to the left and the station to the right. It is a substantial station house, an awning on the branch up platform, more modest buildings on the down platform and the Junction signal box.

I say this is a 'surprise' because here is a well-equipped station and goods yard but serving a relatively under-populated area on the outskirts of Cambridge as shown in **Fig 112** but there are no platforms on the main line despite 'Junction' in the station name.

The Junction Station served an industrial area – Corporation sewage works, Exchange Iron Works, three Brick & Tile Works, Saw Mills – and a small number

Fig 111: A view from Newmarket Road bridge, Barnwell, of Barnwell Junction on 16 August 1911.

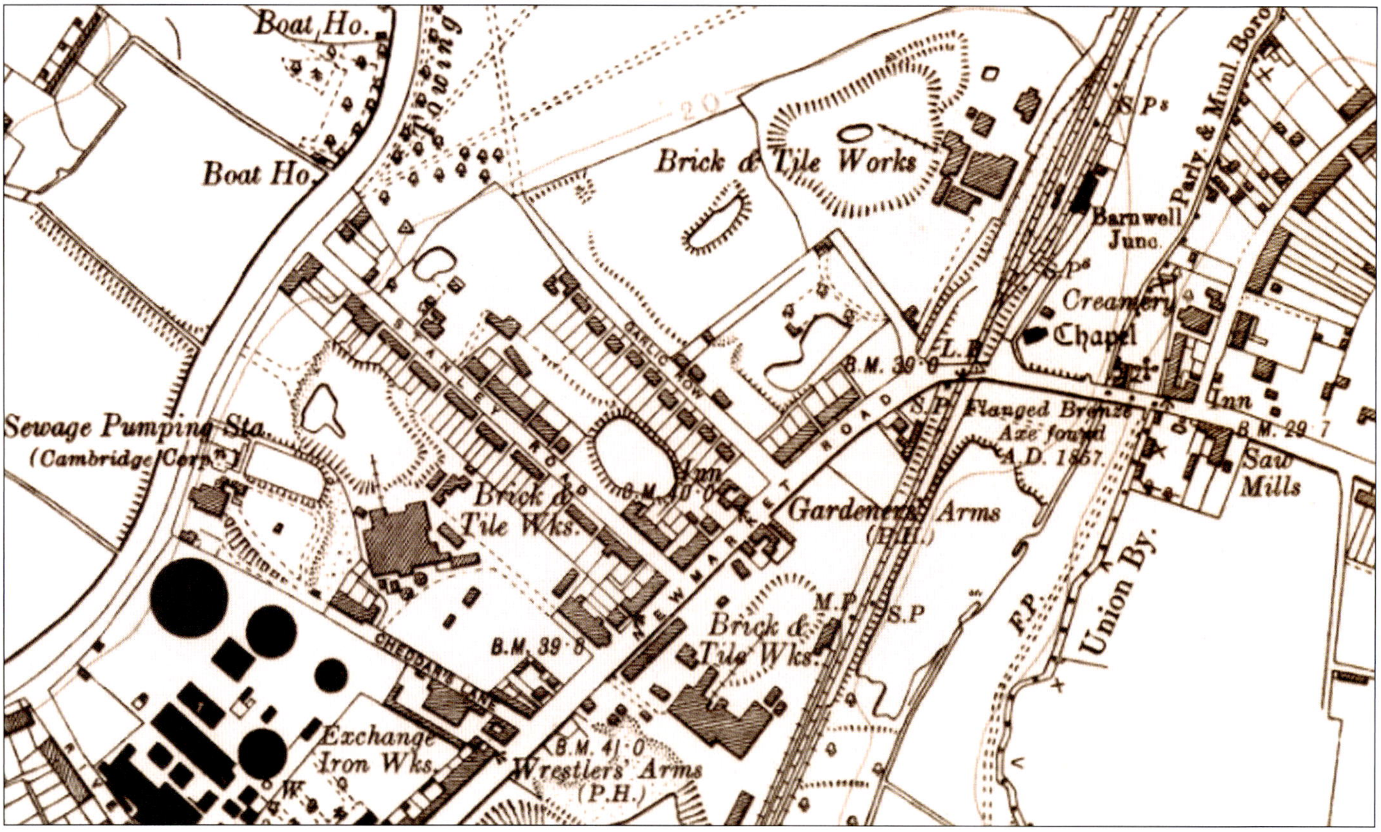

Fig 112: extract from 1927 OS 6 inch map – Cambridgeshire XL.SE.

of houses. The Chapel, named on the map and near the Newmarket Road bridge where **Fig 111** was photographed, is the Cambridge Leper Chapel. It is a twelfth century building which was originally the chapel of an isolation hospital caring for people with leprosy. Another surprise, perhaps, but nothing in the foregoing list suggests much railway business or justifies such a splendid station.

Another – and for an interested traveller a welcome – surprise is the DMU in **Fig 113** on which I travelled from and to Cambridge to explore the Branch. It was possible to sit immediately behind the driver and to see the Branch as the driver did which was a real education. Occasionally a driver drew down the blinds behind him completely excluding the front view, but in my experience that was rare. On this August journey there were few passengers so the driver opened the central door and explained the gear-changing technique he was still learning.

Fig 113: Steam out, diesel power in; a DMU at Mildenhall forming a Cambridge-bound train in August 1956.

CHAPTER 21

ALDEBURGH BRANCH

Fig 114: Garrett's stand at the Great Exhibition, Crystal Palace (1 May to 15 Oct 1851).

The Aldeburgh Branch, from Saxmundham Junction via Leiston and Thorpeness Halt to Aldeburgh was not, unusually for GER, a farmers' line but intended to serve two different markets. It opened to Aldeburgh on 12 April 1860.

The principal source of freight business and income was the Garrett Works at Leiston.

The Great Exhibition was only nine years before the completion of the Aldeburgh Branch and a stand there was a potent advocate for the international significance of Garrett's business and the need for rail links.

The other market arose from the nineteenth century demand for attractive seaside resorts and the craze for the supposed benefits of sea air and sea bathing which Aldeburgh could satisfy. Between Leiston and Aldeburgh was Thorpeness Halt, which served wealthy land-owner Stuart Ogilvie's dream of a private fantasy village. Thorpeness included a country club with tennis courts, a swimming pool, a golf course and clubhouse, the Dolphin Hotel, a large 'Meare' and many holiday homes which were built in Jacobean and Tudor Revival styles. Ogilvie invited GER to provide a station for an expanding resort.

Fig 115: part of Thorpeness viewed from the Meare in the foreground. The Meare – Ogilvie's choice of name – is 60 acres in extent, no more than 3ft deep, and includes islands; it offers exciting and safe boating for children.

Fig 116: extract from parts of two OS 6-inch maps – Suffolk LX.NE & LXA.NW - 1928. Thorpeness Halt is a little distance from the village and GER did not match the village style and implicit wealth in their Halt – see **Fig 117**.

Fig 117: Thorpeness Halt; a DMU for Saxmundham and Ipswich has just departed on 26 June 1965. The elderly GER carriage on the right is the Waiting Room which Ogilvie requested should be added to the Halt.

Aldeburgh, the Branch terminus, was once an important Tudor port and its shipbuilders were responsible for Francis Drake's *Golden Hind*. But the River Alde silted up and, as vessels grew larger, the port was no longer accessible. By the nineteenth century, there was some coastal fishing and the growing attractions of an historic town – the 400-year-old Moot Hall, the Norman Church, a Martello tower – and an extensive beach.

Fig 118: 12.30 ex Saxmundham arrives at Aldeburgh on 26 June 1953.

The Aldeburgh Branch still generates happy memories for those who travelled to the seaside but as road transport developed for passengers and freight the Branch did not prosper. There was never much passenger business at Thorpeness Halt and the fact that Ogilvie arranged motor transport from Leiston Station for the large functions he arranged and hosted at Thorpeness cannot have helped.

It is a measure of Ogilvie's eccentricity that, shortly before the GER-funded Thorpeness Halt opened, he formed a company called Thorpeness Vitesse Ltd to buy cars (and spare parts) to transport his visitors to and from Leiston Station. One very unusual idea was to buy a redundant London double-decker horse bus and to tow it with Ogilvie's large Daimler. The Daimler's body was modified to seat more visitors, charabanc style (**Fig 119**). The GER, and subsequently LNER, response to this alternative transport is not recorded although it may be implicit in the facilities GER provided at Thorpeness Halt. We do know, however, that when Ogilvie offered the Dolphin Hotel to LNER at a price to be agreed there was no agreement. BR closed Thorpeness Halt to all traffic on 12 September 1966; in the 1970s considerable death duties required the sale of much of the Thorpeness property.

On the same date, Leiston Station closed but the buildings and platform are still extant. The track through the station is still in occasional use carrying spent nuclear fuel from the power station at Sizewell.

Garrett's Works finally closed in 1981 but the Old Works have survived as the Long Shop Museum so this Branch has experienced losses but not total demise. Perhaps the inventive mind of Stuart Ogilvie is required?

Fig 119: Stuart Ogilvie's solution to the problem of conveying his visitors from Leiston Station to Thorpeness – a re-bodied Daimler towing a second-hand London double-deck horse bus.

CHAPTER 22

MID-SUFFOLK LIGHT RAILWAY

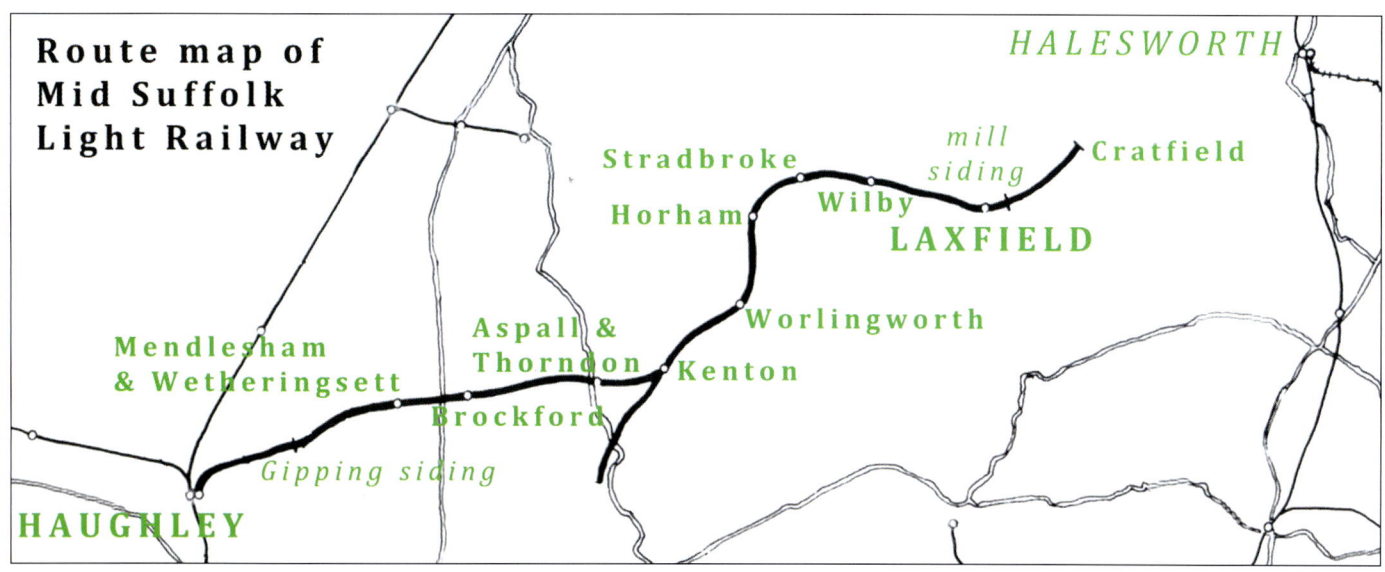

Fig 120: Sketch map (not to scale) of the 19-mile route of the Mid-Suffolk Light Railway as it was completed and operated from 1908 to 1952. The spur south-westwards from Kenton was originally planned as a railway to Debenham and thence to Westerfield and Ipswich. Development capital was so limited that the railway did not even reach Debenham and, at the eastern end, did not reach Halesworth.

The Mid-Suffolk Light Railway, popularly known as the 'Middy,' was developed and financed by local land-owners and farmers as a GER link from Haughley to Halesworth. It was promoted, after the Light Railways Act of 1896 came into effect, to alleviate the effects of agricultural depression in central Suffolk.

The first passenger train to Haughley left Laxfield a little after its timetabled departure of 07.35 on Tuesday 29 September 1908, encouraged by exploding detonators and cheers. The reports on the opening emphasised the 'Middy's' role as a means of bringing visitors and freight into central Suffolk and allowing the inhabitants to be more mobile. The principles were good, the practices less so because 'visitors' to central Suffolk were few, the locals often lacked the desire or the cash to travel away from their villages and farmers were soon complaining that the freight facilities at most stations were inadequate. However, the railway had a rural charm that pictures like **Fig 121** can recall.

For the first few years of operating there were two weekday trains in each direction – 07.35 and 12.00 ex Laxfield; 10.00 and 15.30 ex Haughley – but this service was enhanced when most trains became mixed services. However, the fastest passenger train took 62 minutes

Fig 121: Mendlesham Station, 2 May 1952.

for the 19-mile journey and the mixed trains, involving some shunting at intermediate stations, might take over 100 minutes. At first, and where previously there had only been horse transport between stations, these lengthy journeys were acceptable. But, after the First World War, as motor lorries, and public-service buses were available – as were motor cars for the better-to-do – travel on the Middy's ageing carriages became increasingly unpopular.

Nevertheless, Middy passenger and freight services were sustained, although the railway's finances were never good and did not improve when the independent company passed to the LNER in 1924. The 1930s were a difficult time for many businesses and, although the Second World War brought some more business, it generated very little income. Railway-interested photographers, like Dr Ian Allen, periodically visited the Middy and one of his pictures of Kenton Station in the late 1940s shows a busy scene (**Fig 122**).

The railway closed to all traffic on 28 July 1952.

Fig 122: A Laxfield-bound passenger train is passed at Kenton Station by a lengthy freight train bound for Haughley in the late 1940s.

Fig 123: Demise. More grass than well-ballasted railway; J15 0-6-0 65388 collecting the last wagons from the mill sidings near Laxfield in 1952.

Fig 123 epitomises the end of a working railway. In August, track-lifting began and quite soon land owners incorporated sections of the trackbed into their fields on either side. By 1970, the Countryside Commission cited the Middy as presenting fewer obstacles to reversion to agriculture than almost any other former railway in the country. I remember, when I was living and working in Suffolk from 1981 to 1987, that I explored the course of the Middy and found little to see or photograph; sometimes the only give-away was a slight hump in a country road which marked a former level-crossing.

On 28 November 1990, the Mid-Suffolk Light Railway Society was inaugurated and Paul Davey was elected Chairman. Paul had long been trying to preserve some of the Middy and in August 1990 he met farmer/landowner Tony Alston who had the remains of Brockford station site on his land. He agreed to lease the station site at a peppercorn rent and to make available two-thirds of a mile of trackbed in the Aspall direction.

So, nearly forty years after the Middy closed it was reborn and is flourishing today as Suffolk's only standard gauge heritage railway. **Fig 124** is taken from M-SLR's website:

Fig 124: The recreated Middy as a working Heritage Railway.

CHAPTER 23

HALESWORTH TO SOUTHWOLD RAILWAY

The Halesworth to Southwold Railway opened in 1879 and closed in 1929 so its demise came ninety years before this book is published. It was an unusual minor railway because it was the only narrow-gauge railway in Suffolk (3ft gauge) and its operational Head Office was in London so it was managed from afar and lacked local contacts and support.

So, dead and gone, but it actually lingered on in an almost complete state, including the remains of one locomotive and most of the passenger and freight rolling stock. In 1941 these remains succumbed to the Second World War scrap drive. Memories of what was sometimes remembered as 'The Toy Railway' lingered longer and I recall 1950s holidays in Southwold when the trackbed was a country walk and some station buildings survived.

A number of local railway-interested volunteers explored the possibility of recreating the Southwold Railway. This chapter is headed 'Halesworth to Southwold Railway' because there are now two volunteer bodies – the Halesworth to Southwold Narrow-Gauge Railway Society (HSNGRS) and the Southwold Railway Trust (SRT) – initiating developments at either end of the line to underpin a working Community Railway.

Fig 125 (below): edited extract from the Millennium Green Trust's © Website map marking Southwold Railway remains.

HSNGRS is working with Halesworth Millennium Green Trust on the remains of the SR Halesworth Engine Shed and a length of trackbed (**Fig 125**).

Fig 126: A volunteer team at work uncovering the footings of the SR Halesworth Engine Shed. The inspection pit inside the Shed is to the right back of the picture and the loco ashpit is in the foreground.

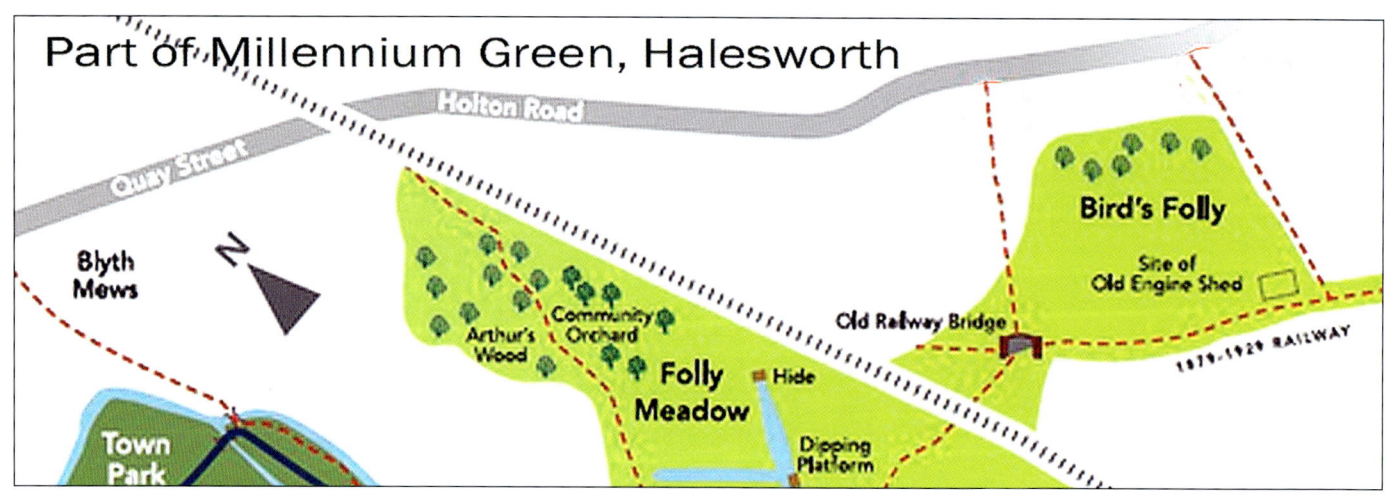

At the other end of the railway, the Southwold Station site, including the Goods Yard, has been re-developed for housing but SRT was able to purchase the site of the former Southwold Gas Works and to develop Southwold Railway Steamworks as an operational visitor centre (**Fig 127**).

So, despite its demise in 1929, aspects of a re-created Southwold Railway live on and this chapter is an appropriate introduction to 'Destiny', the final part of this book.

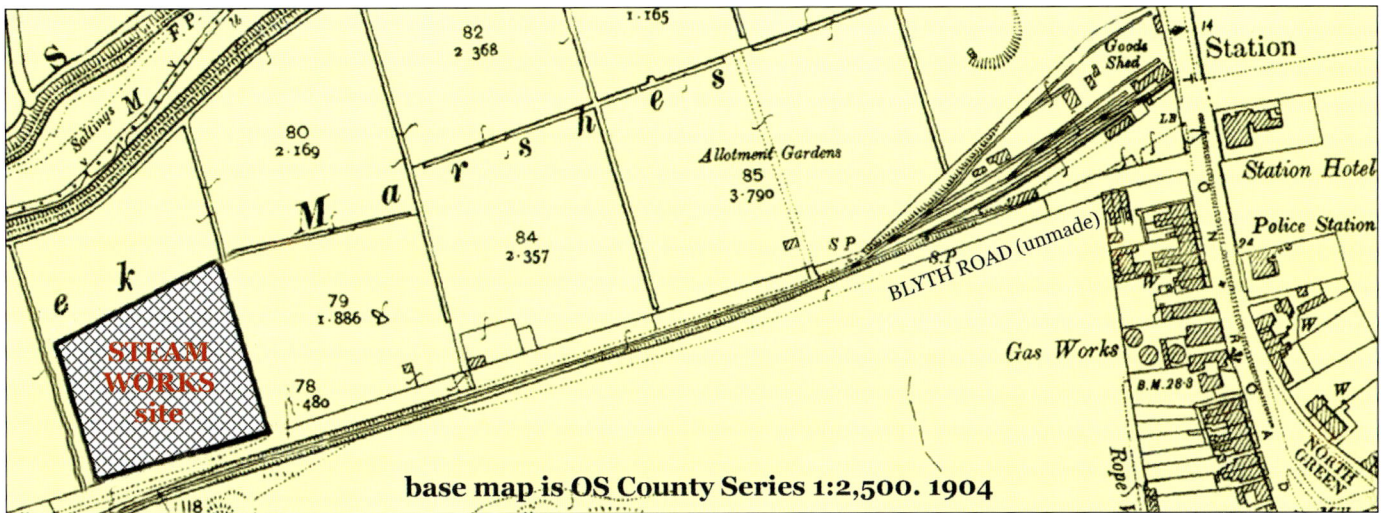

Fig 127: Site of the SRT Steamworks development on Blyth Road, Southwold, superimposed on an OS 1904 map which shows the course of the Southwold Railway and Southwold Station.

Fig 128: Architect's impression of the developed SR Steamworks site, from: John Bennett, Architect, Southwold.

PART 4

DESTINY

Some minor railways have found a new purpose

Fig 129 (above): Clare Station, Stour Valley line, closed in 1967 and now part of Clare Castle Country Park. The buildings are now Grade 2 listed and the only surviving examples of the original 1865-type station design for the railway. Platform One is a café for the Country Park, open daily and developed in the Station's 1865 Booking Hall.

Fig 130 (right): LNER Clare Station Platform Ticket – 1950s.

CHAPTER 24

ALDEBURGH BRANCH

Servicing the building of Sizewell C Nuclear Power Station?

I am very aware that I am quoting current news in this chapter and that by the time the book is published it may be 'fake news' but, at present, it is part of the story of minor railways in East Anglia. I have already recorded, in Chapter 21, that Aldeburgh Branch is still retained as a long siding to Leiston and thence, by a spur from the original route, to Sizewell B Nuclear Power Station.

Google reports that the proposed Sizewell C Nuclear Power Station is to be built by EDF on the Suffolk coast adjoining the operating nuclear power station (Sizewell B) and one being decommissioned (Sizewell A). EDF [Électricité de France] Group claims on its current website to be a global leader in low-carbon energy and to cover every sector of expertise, from generation to trading and transmission grids. EDF claims to be the leading industry operator and delivers competitive solutions that successfully reconcile economic growth with climate protection.

The *New Civil Engineer* journal, from which **Fig 131** comes, reports significant local opposition to EDF's £14bn project:

'The Sizewell C Joint Local Authorities Group (JLAG – Suffolk County Council and Suffolk Coastal District Council) are concerned about the lack of detail in the plans in response to EDF's third round of public consultation. They cannot support the project in its current state.'

At the same time, 27 actors, writers and business leaders have published an open letter in *The Daily Telegraph*, voicing concerns about the environmental impact of the Sizewell C project. The letter states:

'. . . the project must make better use of marine and rail transport to avoid the need to build new roads for construction traffic. . . if [Sizewell C] cannot be delivered by sea and by rail, without encroaching on Suffolk's SSSIs, the RSPB's Minsmere Reserve, the heritage coast, and carving-up farms and communities, it should not be delivered at all.'

The Sizewell C project is estimated to create 5,600 construction jobs at its peak, plus another 500 in supporting roles. Once in operation, the power station is expected to create a further 900 permanent jobs in Suffolk. It will include two reactors (known as the UK EPR) and be capable of generating 3,260mw of low carbon electricity which is enough to power around 6m homes.

Fig 131: a screen visualization by EDF (the Company proposing to build Sizewell C) from *New Civil Engineer* journal 22 March 2019.

Railway options are included in some of the EDF proposals but are very unspecific – 'Red Option, Green Option, Blue Option' – and do not scan readily. I am therefore including an OS-based map (**Fig 132**) from Suffolk County Council's *Sizewell C Accommodation Campus Study* commissioned from consultants Boyer with Cannon Engineering in July 2017.

Perhaps EDF, like President Reagan in 1964, can claim:

'To some generations much is given; [from] of other generations much is expected. This generation [of Suffolk folk] have a rendezvous with destiny . . .'

Or perhaps, by the time you read this book, you will know, as President Trump could doubtless have advised me, that much of what I have researched and written for this chapter is fake news!

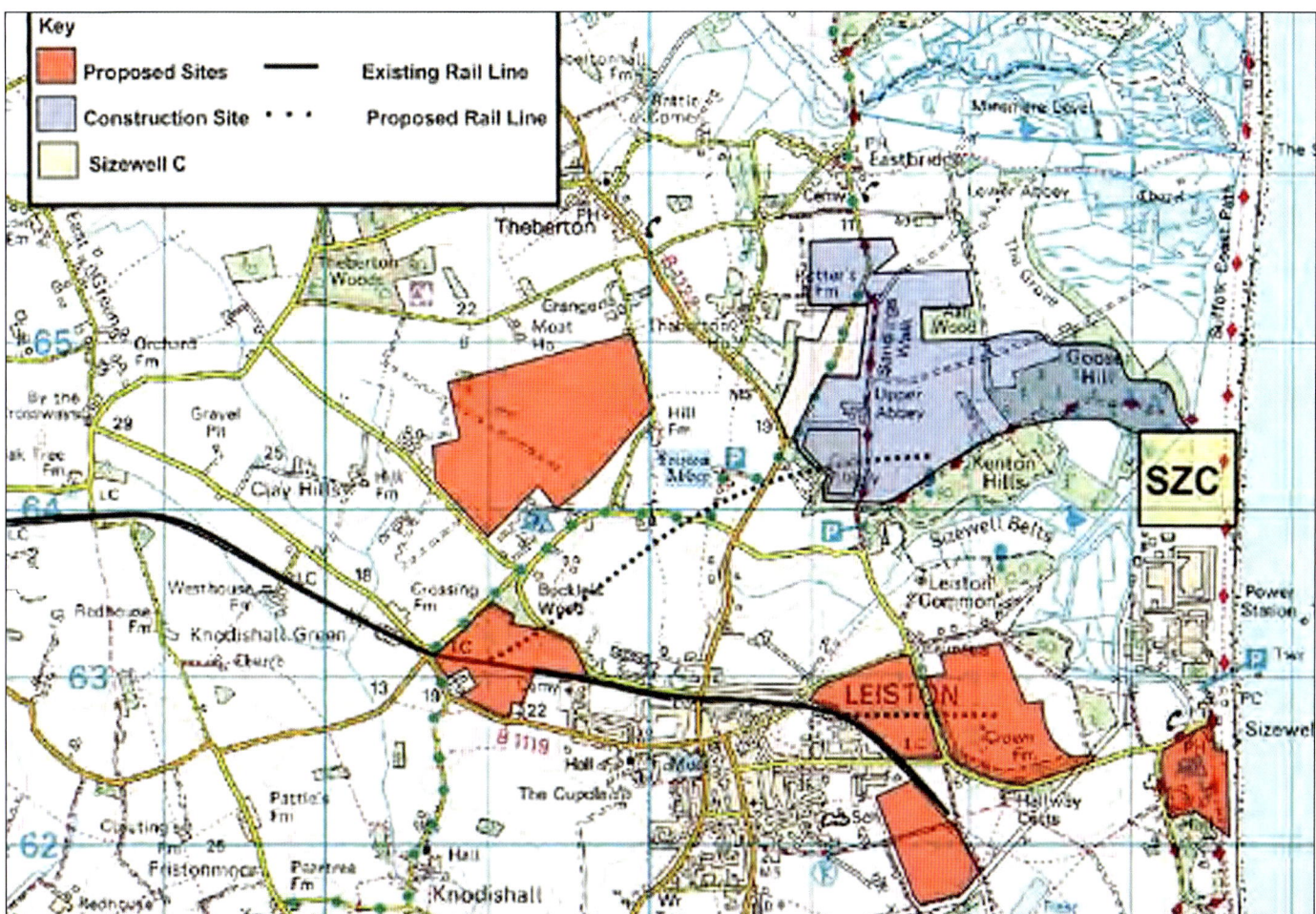

Fig 132: summary of proposals for construction sites and accommodation provisions – 'campuses' – circulated by Suffolk County Council in July 2017. A new railway connection to the southern end of the construction sites is shown as a spur off the existing Aldeburgh Branch to the west of Leiston Station.

CHAPTER 25

PRESERVED HERITAGE RAILWAYS

A heritage railway is a preserved or tourist railway which is run as a tourist attraction, is usually but not always run by volunteers, and often seeks to re-create railway scenes of the past.

I had intended this chapter to be a list, including some of the minor railways I have explored in the book, and am gratified that the list is longer than I had originally anticipated. The length is partly explained by the inclusion of narrow-gauge and miniature railways. For definitions it is generally accepted that:

- Standard gauge   4ft 8½ins
- Narrow-gauge   3ft 6ins to 1ft 11⅝ins
- Miniature gauge   15ins to 5ins

For the bulk of this book, and with the exception of the 3ft gauge Southwold Railway, I have ignored any railways less than standard gauge. But it is fitting to have the extensive list which follows in the 'Destiny' part of the book because the routes of several standard gauge minor railways have been revived at a smaller gauge.

Standard gauge railways
- Colne Valley Railway, Castle Hedingham, Essex
- Epping Ongar Railway, Ongar, Essex
- Mid-Norfolk Railway, Dereham, Norfolk
- Mid-Suffolk Light Railway, Brockford, Suffolk
- Nene Valley Railway, Wansford, Cambridgeshire
- North Norfolk Railway, Sheringham, Norfolk

Railway centres and museums
- Bressingham Steam and Gardens, Diss, Norfolk – a Nursery Garden and Steam collection including operating Standard, Narrow and Miniature gauge railways set up in 1946 by the late Alan Bloom MBE.
- East Anglian Railway Museum, Chappel & Wakes Colne Station, Essex – A standard gauge operating railway based at Chappel & Wakes Colne Station on the Sudbury - Marks Tey section of the Stour Valley line.
- Mangapps Railway Museum, Burnham-on-Crouch, Essex – a privately-owned heritage railway centre developed by the Jolly family on Mangapps Farm. It includes 0.75 miles of operational standard gauge railway.
- Railworld Wildlife Haven, Peterborough, Cambridgeshire – Founded by Rev Richard Paten (1932-2012) in 1985 as 'Museum of World Railways,' changing its name to 'Railworld' in 1992 and now

Fig 133: A drone view of Mangapps Railway Museum from Mangapps' current Website.

called 'Railworld Wildlife Haven' in reference to its change of focus towards its landscaped nature. There is a small collection of locomotives and railway memorabilia, all of which require extensive work.
- Whitwell & Reepham Railway, Reepham, Norfolk – a former M&GNR Station opened in 1882 on the line from Melton Constable to Norwich City station. It was closed to all railway services on 1 May 1964 and was derelict until purchased by railway enthusiast Mike Urry in 2007. The site is being progressively developed as a working steam centre and a tourist attraction.

Narrow-gauge railways
- Halesworth to Southwold Narrow-Gauge Railway Society, Bird's Folly, Halesworth, Suffolk – see Chapter 23
- Southwold Railway Trust, Southwold, Suffolk – see Chapter 23
- Southend Pier Railway, Southend-on-Sea, Essex – a 3ft gauge railway, owned and operated by Southend-on-Sea Borough Council, and extending for 1.25 miles along Southend Pier which, at 1.34 miles, is the longest pleasure pier in the world and now a Grade II* listed structure. Services are operated by two diesel-hydraulic locomotives, each with 5 trailer coaches and a driver control unit at the other end.

Miniature gauge railways
- Audley End Railway, Essex – A 10¼in -gauge circuit built by Lord Braybrooke, then owner of Audley End House, and opened on 16 May 1964. The railway runs for 1.5 miles through woodland adjacent to the House now in the ownership of English Heritage.
- Bure Valley Railway, Aylsham, Norfolk – a 15 inch gauge railway built on the standard gauge trackbed of the Aylsham to Norfolk Railway which opened on 1 January 1880 and was closed by BR on 6 January 1982.

Norfolk County Council (NCC) had a policy to attempt where possible to convert disused railway lines into long distance, traffic-free footpaths. NCC purchased the line from Norwich through to Aylsham via Lenwade, Reepham and Cawston. The Section from Aylsham to Wroxham was purchased by Broadland District Council.

Fig 134: 3ft gauge Southend Pier diesel-hydraulic train built by Severn Lamb in 1986.

A 15 inch gauge railway was built because it only needed half of the trackbed and so left space for a footpath. The railway was fenced off leaving a safe footpath.

The Bure Valley Railway opened on 10 July 1990 and has now run successfully for 30 years.

- Wells & Walsingham Light Railway, Wells-next-the-Sea, Norfolk – a 4-mile long 10¼in gauge railway between Walsingham and Wells. It was built on the trackbed of the standard gauge Wymondham to Wells Branch which was closed progressively from 1964 to 1969.

  The miniature railway was the brainchild of a local railway enthusiast, Lieutenant-Commander Roy Francis. It opened on 6 April 1982 and continues to operate today. The current website states that 'The Railway operates a Timetable Service 7 days a week from March 2 until 3 November 2019' and then lists '2019 - 2020 Departure Times'.

- Wells Harbour Railway, Wells-next-the-Sea, Norfolk – another 10¼in gauge railway established by Lieutenant-Commander Roy Francis in 1976. When it is working the railway provides a useful alternative to the 1,200-yard walk from Wells-next-the-Sea to Wells Harbour.

Fig 136: Wells & Walsingham 10 ¼in gauge railway – mid 1990s.

Fig 135: Bure Valley Railway; narrow gauge train and footpath sharing a former standard gauge trackbed.

CHAPTER 26

CYCLEWAYS, FOOTPATHS, A BUSWAY

I have been exploring and walking along the trackbeds of disused railways for many years so it is encouraging, in the 1980s and subsequently, that local authorities have supported such developments.

In 1977, a voluntary group of cyclists came together in the Bristol area and formed the charity Sustrans. By 1986, helped by Avon County Council, they had created the first ex-railway cycleway, the Bristol & Bath Railway Path. It was a 'green route' which became the precursor of the National Cycle Network.

Sustrans took advantage of government schemes to provide temporary employment, and some grant-aid, to build similar 'green routes'. British Waterways collaborated with Sustrans to improve towpaths along some canals for walkers and cyclists.

By the early 1990s, Sustrans had a growing number of supporters, and a network of national routes was emerging. In 1995, it was granted £43.5m from the Millennium Lottery Fund to extend the National Cycle Network to smaller towns and rural areas as well as launch the 'Safe Routes to Schools' project, based on earlier state projects in Denmark.

In Norfolk, the County Council developed Marriott's Way as a 24.6-mile footpath, bridleway and cycle route. It follows the routes of two disused railway lines – GER from Aylsham to Themelthorpe and MG&NR from Themelthorpe to the site of Norwich City Station (closed by BR in 1969). It is open to walkers, cyclists and horse riders. Marriott's Way is named after William Marriott, who was Chief Engineer and Manager of the Midland and Great Northern Railway (M&GNR) for 41 years. The M&GNR was a very rural network affectionately known as the 'Muddle and Go Nowhere' line.

Figs 138, **139** and **140** illustrate the accessibility of some of the minor railway remains in East Anglia but the 'remains' are still railway-like. My memories of the St Ives Branch – the Loop – and of Long Stanton Station, described in Chapter 9, suffered a blow when I learned that the long-closed but still extant railway was to be converted to a Busway into Cambridge,

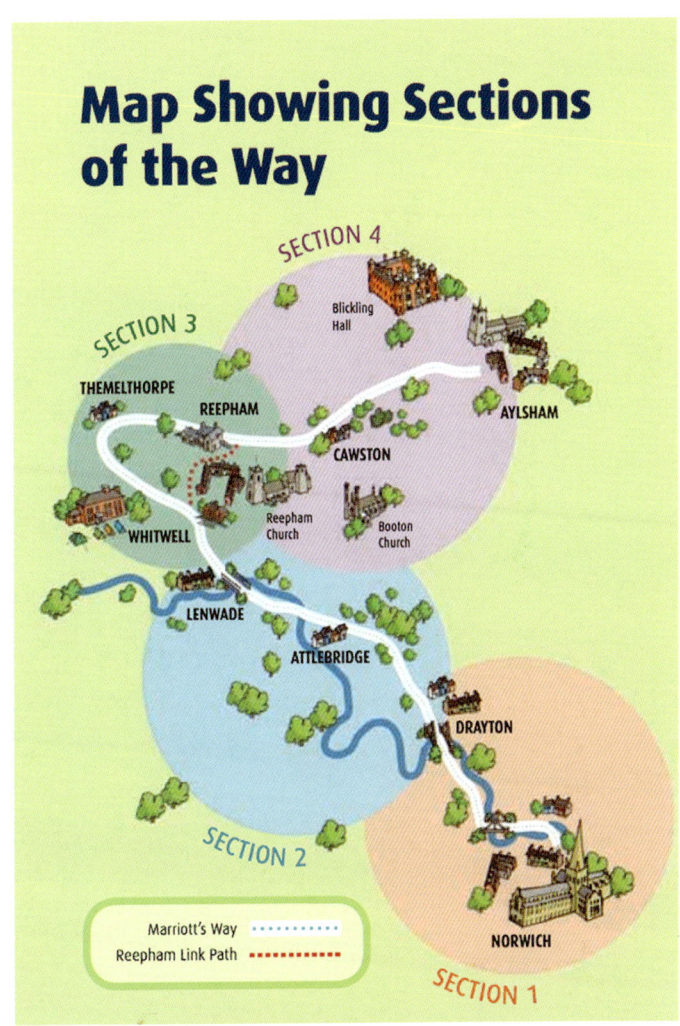

Fig 137: map from downloadable PDF for Marriott's Way.

However, my researches for this book allowed me to explore this Busway in 2018 and I learned a great deal. I had been staying with a friend in Swavesey and drove to Long Stanton to discover the Busway in Swavesey. I was looking for the past as I remembered it so **Fig 141** shows the past and the present.

Station Road was a useful reminder but there was no station and certainly no station car park any more. The 'Guided busway drop-off area' was an alternative and, I learned from my friend, an additional sign requested by villagers. It ensured that those unfamiliar with the

Fig 138: cycleways, footpaths and bridleways along former railway trackbeds often include railway features which are a stimulus to memories of the past. This is Marriott's Way in North Norfolk, formerly the Midland & Great Northern Joint Railway.

Fig 139: List's embankment on the narrow-gauge Southwold Railway, Suffolk – a big earthwork on a little railway.

Fig 140: Platform remains of Thorpeness Halt, 2017: Aldeburgh Branch, Suffolk. The trackbed is now a footpath

village were guided to the right place for unloading passengers – but no car parking!

I drove on towards Long Stanton and recalled that I should be crossing an over bridge so stopped to photograph the Busway. Better still, as **Fig 142** shows, there was a double-deck bus approaching. An impressive new use for a soundly-built railway bridge as the abutment wing in the lower right hand side of the picture shows.

Long Stanton was very different from what I remembered; I found the remains of the Station but it was no longer serving the Busway and it was now called Longstanton – **Fig 143.**

Initially I was a little lost, because the traffic-lights controlled junction, where there had previously been a level crossing controlled by the adjoining signal box, was very different from what I remembered fifty years

Fig 141: Busway signs in Swavesey in 2018.

Fig 142: Busway double-deck bus bound for Cambridge; next stop will be Longstanton.

Fig 143: the 2018 remains of Long Stanton Station – see Chapter 9 for pre-Busway pictures.

Fig 144: busway Longstanton Park & Ride 2018. The bus is heading for Cambridge. The remains of the original Long Stanton railway station (**Fig 143**) is the building at the back of the picture immediately to the left of the bus.

ago! I drove on and soon found road signs directing me to Longstanton Park & Ride, parked and photographed the changes for **Fig 144**.

There were several weather-proof frames containing guidance for would-be passengers. A pity that the paper inside the frame was sagging and a little crumpled but I did my best – **Fig 145** – to illustrate this story!

Finally I decided to explore the 'Station' or busway Waiting Room and I was pleasurably impressed. **Fig 144** shows the exterior of the building, inside it was fitted out with seats, very clean free-entry WCs, machines offering drinks and crisps/chocolates/biscuits, a panel explaining 'how the building works' and another detailing the different woods and other materials used in the build. Photography was difficult because of the amount of reflected light but I have done my best with **Fig 146**.

I was impressed with what I found at Longstanton and the general operation of the Cambridge-St Ives Busway. I still enjoy heritage railways so researching and writing this book has been a pleasure which I hope will be shared by readers.

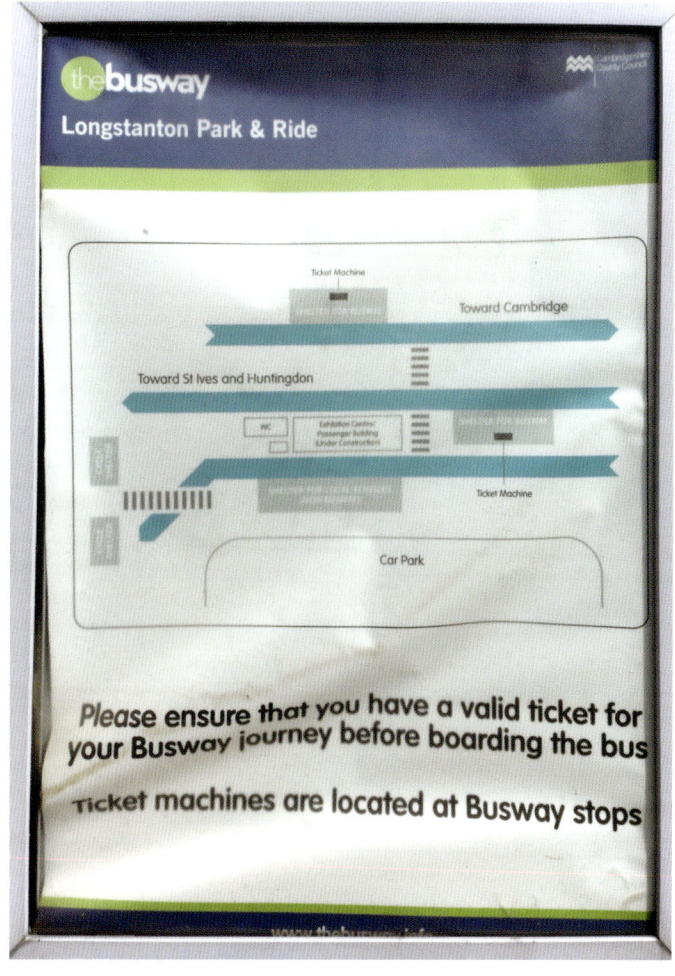

Fig 145: passenger guidance frame + poster for busway Longstanton Park & Ride 2018.

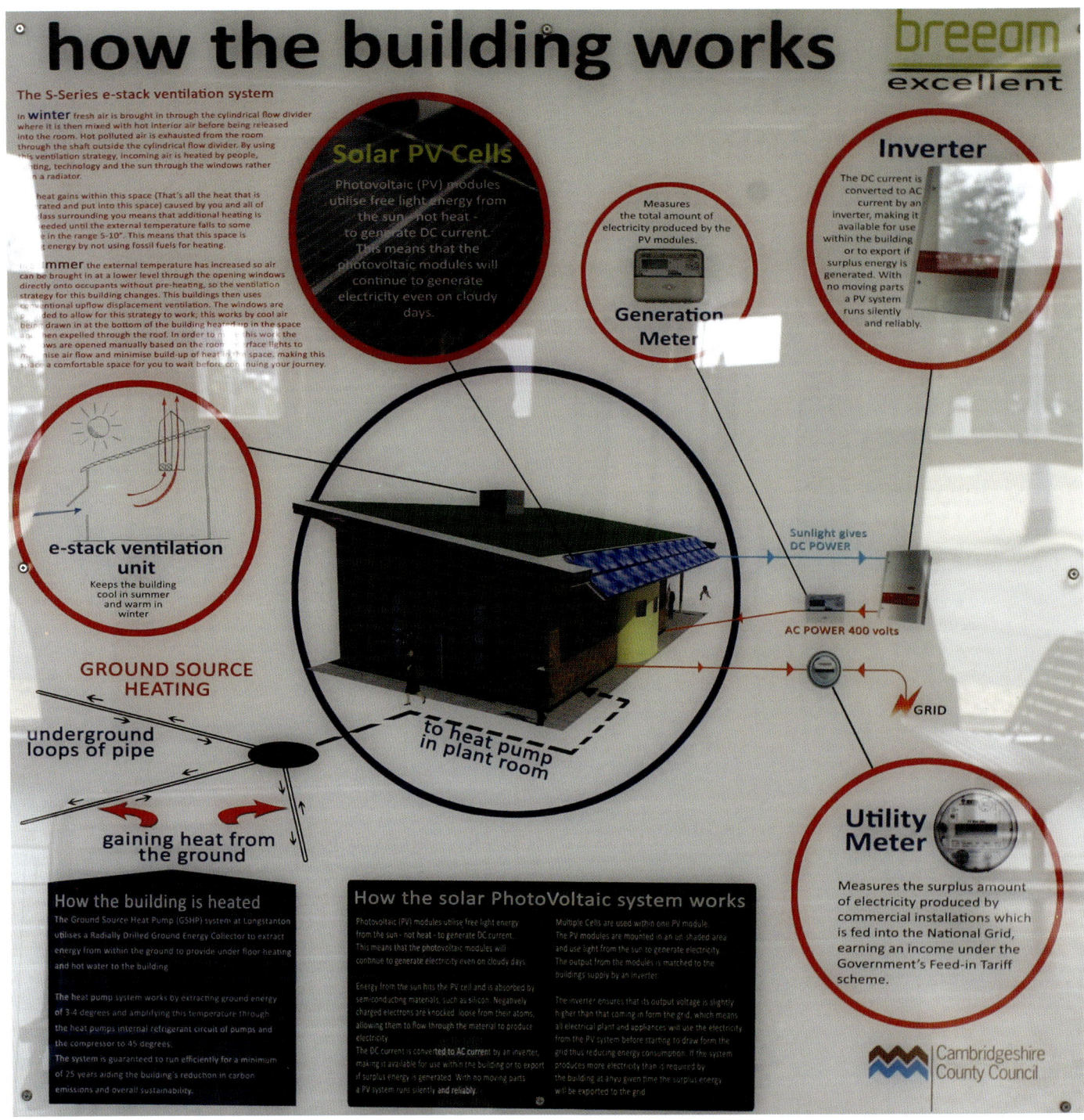

Fig 146: Longstanton busway stop building and 'how the building works'.

We must be prepared to move with the changing times so 'Destiny' for minor railways may mean 'Demise', new opportunities, different uses like the footways, bridleways and cycleways or new civil and mechanical engineering when a minor railway becomes a busway.

I have remembered the railways of fifty or more years ago but it seemed percipient to conclude the book with two contrasting pictures. Would we prefer the facilities at Longstanton (**Fig 147**) or Thorpeness Halt (**Fig 148**)?

CYCLEWAYS, FOOTPATHS, A BUSWAY • 129

Fig 147: Longstanton busway waiting area, 2018.

Fig 148: GER installed a Waiting Room at Thorpeness Halt in response to a request from Stuart Ogilvie – see Chapter 21.

PART 5

MEMORIES – MORE ILLUSTRATIONS OF 'MINOR' RAILWAYS

Memories are important for recalling heritage and past history so this book concludes with several pictures of and from minor railways which were not in the main text but are not forgotten.

Fig 149: GER 0-4-0T Steam tram engine 7132 hauling a freight train on the Wisbech & Upwell Tramway in the 1930s at Upwell. A typical GER minor railway built for agricultural traffic and passengers; the shielded wheels and motion of the tram engine permitted operation on an un-fenced roadside tramway.

Fig 150: undated Wisbech & Upwell passenger train, probably in the 1930s, passing Upwell Church. The passenger service was to and from Wisbech Station to Upwell via Boyce's Bridge, Outwell Basin and Outwell Village and in an 1899 timetable there were 6 daily trains; "*on Sunday the train does not run.*"

Fig 151: Halstead Station on the former Colne Valley and Halstead Railway, opened in 1860, had close relations with the GER but remained independent until it became part of the LNER in 1923. Some of the story of the CV&H R is in Chapter 18 (pp 94-95) but this picture is included to show the active business of a minor railway station in a small Suffolk market town in the late 19th century.

Fig 152: Framlingham Station, on 19 July 1952, was the terminus of a branch line from Wickham Market; the line closed to passengers on 1 November 1952 and to goods traffic on 19 April 1965.

A mixed train at the platform but little evidence of much busyness at this station. Framlingham, like Halstead, was a busy market town and the branch line, opened in 1859, was at first well used. But, as with most other minor railways in this book, motor lorries, buses and cars eventually took away most of the railway's traffic. However, this picture illustrates the sturdy architecture, neat trackwork and general tidiness initiated by the GER and LNER and then BR but, alas, there was little revenue!

Fig 153: Ramsey North Station, 12 August 1972, was closed to passengers on 6 October 1947 and to goods traffic in December 1973.

Chapter 15 (pp 87- 89) explains how, and why, the small village of Ramsey supposedly benefitted from two stations. Ramsey North was relatively busy with agricultural traffic but **Fig 153** is remarkably empty of *any* busyness apart, perhaps from the large grain warehouse serving a nearby steam-powered roller flour mill.

Demise is on its way; the flour mill is now apartments but a visit to the station site in 2019 while researching for this book revealed that only the warehouse remained; the rest is bare, weedy open space.

To end, however, on a humorous note. **Fig 154** is not in East Anglia but is on a minor railway in India where agricultural business still has precedence!

Fig 154: Priorities in 2006.

LIST OF ILLUSTRATIONS

Illustrations are from my collections or, with their permission to use, from the late Dr Ian Allen, John Aves, Tim Edmonds, Anthony (Tony) Kirby, David Lee, John Mann, Blake Paterson, Online Transport Archive (Peter Waller), Ken Penrose, Prof. Peter Rowlinson and Commissioning Editor John Scott-Morgan.

I am a long-time keen photographer, and have accumulated my collection from contacts with the above, my time working on BR in the 1950s and 1960s, at the National Railway Museum (1987-94); and as an active member of the Railway Study Association since 1988. I always try to contact all possible copyright holders and check any unacknowledged illustrations with forensic image search engines. If any have been missed my sincere apologies and would those concerned please contact me at <robsb@wfmyork.demon.co.uk>.

Fig No	Caption	Acknowledgements
Cover	Abbey and West Dereham Station, Stoke Ferry Branch	Author's collection
1	Saxmundham Junction Signal Box. A DMU, from which this picture was taken on 26 June 1965, is taking the Aldeburgh Branch which curves away to the right and becomes single track. The double track main line is the East Suffolk line from Ipswich to Saxmundham, Halesworth and Lowestoft	Courtesy Blake Paterson
2	Bartlow Junction: 4-wheel railbuses offered interested passengers a front seat beside the driver's enclosed cab.	Courtesy Blake Paterson (OTA)
3	Railway beginnings in East Anglia in 1844	Edited with thanks from *East Anglia's First Railways*. Hugh Moffat. Terence Dalton. 1987.
4	Norfolk & Suffolk, which are the principal counties of East Anglia, the northern part of Essex and most of Cambridgeshire westwards to the vertical black line.	Author's collection
5	Tollesbury Pier Station, Kelvedon & Tollesbury Light Railway c1930.	OTA
6	BR 4-wheel railbus leaving Wickham Bishops Station *en route* for Maldon East c1964.	OTA
7	Mixed train at Haughley Junction, Mid-Suffolk Light Railway, 28 July 1915.	Ken Nunn collection; courtesy John Scott-Morgan
8	is a sketch plan of the GER/LNER (copied with thanks from the LNER Encyclopaedia online) with a number of what I consider to be minor railways highlighted in green.	LNER Encyclopaedia online
9	Map (from Wikipedia) illustrating the competition for passenger and goods business between the Great Eastern Railway (in blue) and the Midland & Great Northern Joint Railway in red.	Wikipedia – the free encyclopaedia
10	A platform face uncovered at Norwich City Station by the Friends of Norwich City Station (FONCS). Their hope for the future is to uncover all the railway-related elements of the site and turn it into a memorial garden.	FONCS
11	[Table contiguous with the text so no caption necessary]	© Rob Shorland-Ball
12	A visual summary of the minor railways – in green – chosen for this book	© Rob Shorland-Ball

Fig No	Caption	Acknowledgements
13	Sketch map of railways to and from King's Lynn and those minor railways serving the Harbour and Docks.	Based on a drawing by the late Roger Hateley.
14	Illustration from the *Illustrated London News* (1846) showing the first terminus of the Harbour Branch, south of the River Nar at its confluence with the Great Ouse. Two vans are on the railway alongside a two-masted barque; stevedores are loading or transhipping cargo	Author's collection
15	Coal was big business for the Dock Railway and for Alexandra Dock, illustrated at the north end of the Dock in 1877. The dumb-buffered private owner wagons include some owned by Midlands, North Eastern and South Yorkshire collieries. Coal was coming by rail to King's Lynn and thence by sea to other East Anglian ports and to London.	Courtesy Mike G. Fell OBE and Irwell Press
16	In May 1993 the very last train left the Dock Railways system.	Courtesy Mike G. Fell OBE and Irwell Press
17	ABP © map of the Port of King's Lynn in 2019 – roads replace railways throughout the Port.	Courtesy ABP Website
18	LNER poster promoting King's Lynn.	Author's collection
19	An historical map of the railways serving Yarmouth and Lowestoft	Author's collection
20	Google map – course of River Waveney is highlighted.	Courtesy Google maps
21	Man-made navigational aids – like Oulton Broad and the Haddiscoe Cut from St Olaves to Reedham – join the meandering River Waveney to the River Yare. The Cut, excavated in the nineteenth century, provides a direct route between Lowestoft Docks and Norwich.	Author's collection
22	Map extract from Railway Executive – Eastern Region. Civil Engineer. March 1950.	Author's collection
23	Yarmouth near Vauxhall Station, July 1969 – see Fig 24 © 6-inch OS map.	Courtesy Blake Paterson (OTA)
24	extract from © 6-inch OS map. Norfolk LXVI.SE ca1946.	© OS. Author's collection
25	a railcar at Yarmouth.	Author's collection
26	[caption integral with text]	© Rob Shorland-Ball
27	[caption integral with text]	© Rob Shorland-Ball
28	Suffolk X.NE [Lowestoft] 1906. © OS Six-inch-to-the mile map.	© OS Author's collection
29	Lowestoft Central Station in the 1950s	Author's collection
30	North Pier and the Shingle Mill – just north of 'ET' of 'MARKET' with its network of sidings. © OS 6-inch map extract from sheet X.NE 1951.	© OS Author's collection
31	Sketch map of Lowestoft Harbour in the 1960s showing the network of minor railways serving the Harbour and industries around it as well as the passenger station – Lowestoft Central.	Author's collection, courtesy Robert Maltster
32	The landward end of South Pier and The Royal Hotel opened in 1849. An 1869 Guidebook reports that '. . . the bathing establishment is on the best principle, the baths being supplied with salt or fresh water by a steam engine, which also supplies water for other purposes'.	Author's collection; courtesy Robert Maltster
33	A rather time-worn plaque celebrating the 19th century roller skating rink.	© Rob Shorland-Ball
34	South Pier – a Family Entertainment Centre with fish and chips conveniently to hand next door	© Rob Shorland-Ball
35	Plan of the Port of Lowestoft, edited from ABP Website 2019.	Courtesy ABP Website

LIST OF ILLUSTRATIONS • 137

Fig No	Caption	Acknowledgements
36	1960 sketch map showing the River Blyth, winding its way to the North Sea through extensive tidal salt marshes. From 1879 to 1929 the Southwold Railway followed the Blyth valley from Halesworth to Southwold	© Rob Shorland-Ball
37	Southwold Harbour on map extract edited from © OS County Series 12,500 for 1927.	Author's collection
38	Southwold Railway mixed gauge weighbridge on the Harbour Fish Quay.	Courtesy John Scott-Morgan
39	Halesworth GER standard gauge station on the left and Southwold Railway goods shed and transhipment platform centre and right. Standard gauge wagons are on the track in the centre but the narrow-gauge tracks are empty, possibly because of a shortage of SR wagons that may be awaiting emptying at one of the SR stations.	Ken Nunn collection; courtesy John Scott-Morgan
40	List's Cutting, looking towards Blythburgh and Southwold, 2013.	© Rob Shorland-Ball
41	SR Steamworks development on Blyth Road, Southwold, superimposed on a 1904 © OS map which shows the course of the Railway and Southwold Station	Courtesy John Bennett, Architect, Southwold
42	Extract from © OS 1-inch New Popular Edition, 1945-1947. The map has been tilted to the right to encompass the whole of the Railway from Kelvedon Station (GER and then LNER) to Tollesbury Pier projecting into the River Blackwater. Compass North follows the grid lines.	© OS. Author's collection
43	Tolleshunt Knights Station – 1951.	OTA (courtesy Eavis)
44	Tollesbury Pier Station c1907; Station Master, Jack Gallant, from Tollesbury is at the Waiting Room door. When necessary, he rode down on the train to carry out duties here as there was no permanent employee.	OTA
45	Tollesbury Pier.	Author's collection
46	LNER/BR 68616 J67/1 0-6-0T shunting a mixed train at Kelvedon. 29 July 1950. The three passenger vehicles are bogie tram carriage E60461, brake thirds E62262 and E62261.	Ken Nunn collection; courtesy John Scott-Morgan
47	Map of Wilkin & Sons Jam Factory in Tiptree showing the railway siding. © Wilkin & Sons from the Company website.	Courtesy Wilkin & Sons Website
48	'An Edwardian curiosity' near Kelvedon on 31 March 1910.	Ken Nunn collection; courtesy John Scott-Morgan
49	Tollesbury Pier Station and potential development facilities.	Ken Nunn collection; courtesy John Scott-Morgan
50	Map of the Benwick Branch edited from a larger version (otherwise unacknowledged) in <u>The Benwick Branch</u>, Peter Paye, John Masters. 1998.	Author's collection
51	Terminus of the Benwick Branch – early 1920s. Motor lorries working with the railway here but, as motor lorries became larger and more sophisticated, the double-handling implicit here was replaced by farm-to-market journeys and the railway was cut out.	Author's collection
52	is a view to the right of the earlier picture, taken from the motor road in **Fig 51** in the summer of 2018.	© Rob Shorland-Ball
53	A cropped map illustrating some of the network of minor railways around Cambridge, St Ives, Ely and March. 'The Loop,' always so-called by local railway men, was between Cambridge, St Ives, Somersham, Chatteris (not named on this map) and March.	© Rob Shorland-Ball

Fig No	Caption	Acknowledgements
54	A view of Long Stanton Station, looking DOWN towards St Ives and taken by the author from the UP home signal which is shown as 'SP' on the **Fig 55** © OS record of the site in 1903.	© Rob Shorland-Ball
55	Taken from © OS 6 inch 1903 map – Cambridgeshire XXXIII.SE.	© OS. Author's collection
56	Another useful reference view of Long Stanton Station from the UP home signal – in 1947.	OTA
57	The Goods Yard at Long Stanton in the very early 1920s during the East Anglian fruit season.	OTA
58	Interior of the station office.	© Rob Shorland-Ball
59	Clerical and Manual Staff at Long Stanton 1962. From left: Charlie Grumbley (Porter); Graham Burling (Clerk); Albert (Alby) Cousins (Goods Porter & Shunter); Victor Burling (Chief Clerk); Charlie Ingle (Porter). Picture by Rob Shorland-Ball (Cut-Flower Clerk).	© Rob Shorland-Ball
60	Cut flower boxes. SMs Moulton then Edlington would probably have been critical of stacking in this scene. But the picture shows the style and size – say 4ft to 5ft long – of the corrugated cardboard boxes we handled.	© Rob Shorland-Ball
61	Edmundson ticket dating press.	© Rob Shorland-Ball
62	Pre-printed Edmundson ticket showing destination with ticket number on face and Edmundson press date on back.	© Rob Shorland-Ball
63	LNER Empty Wagon direction label.	Author's collection, courtesy Graham Burling
64	Taken from © OS 6 inch 1903 map – Huntingdonshire XXXIII.NE.	© OS. Author's collection
65	An aerial view of Swavesey Station during the 1947 floods.	Courtesy Carolyn Redmayne, Swavesey
66	Elsenham – 08.55 train (drawn by LNER 68530 Class J69/1 0-6-0T) departs for Thaxted on 14 July 1951, fourteen months before closure. Behind the train is the back of the wooden waiting shelter on the LNER UP platform and the brick building ahead of the train is the Booking Office.	Ken Nunn collection; courtesy John Scott-Morgan
67	Sir William Gilbey – whose UK-made gin was highly regarded in the 1900s – lived at Elsenham Hall.	© Rob Shorland-Ball
68	© OS 6-inch map 1951 – Essex nXXIV Thaxted.	© OS. Author's collection
69	Thaxted Station shortly after opening in 1913.	OTA
70	An apparently well-equipped terminus station, including a brick-built Engine Shed which housed the one engine in steam that worked the Light Railway. Thaxted was a sub-shed of Cambridge Shed and the usual practice was to change the engine each weekend. The out going engine went north to Cambridge on Saturday evening and the replacement arrived on Monday morning. There were no Sunday services.	Author's collection
71	Mill Road Halt in the early 1950s. A truly 'economical' Halt. The low platform – accessed from the trains by steps attached to the coaches – is barely longer than the passenger waiting room.	OTA
72	An edited map from the IRS book; the branch to Stoke Ferry was just over seven miles in length.	Industrial Railway Society
73	Abbey Station – © OS 6-inch map –Norfolk LXIX.SE. Note 'Keeble's Sidings' which was the start of the independent Wissington Railway.	© OS. Author's collection
74	From the IRS book – the extent of the Wissington Railway in the 1930s and 1940s.	Industrial Railway Society

LIST OF ILLUSTRATIONS • 139

Fig No	Caption	Acknowledgements
75	Stoke Ferry Station c1910; the terminus of the line was closed to passenger services in September 1930.	Industrial Railway Society
76	0-6-0ST No 1700 *Wissington* (Hudswell Clarke Foundry. Leeds 1938) picking up a truck of potatoes from a road-side siding. May 1957. Note the very overgrown track and the points to the siding hidden in the verdure.	Industrial Railway Society
77	During the 1956/1957 sugar beet campaign, a loaded train *en route* to the Wissington Factory passes a pick-up siding.	Author's collection – courtesy Dr I. Allen
78	Sedge Fen unsurfaced fenland drove and fragments of the Wissington Railway, early 1960s The sturdy and newly-built loading platform marks the succession from rail-borne to drove-borne traffic.	Industrial Railway Society
79	The extent of Garrett Works in the early 1900s.	Author's collection
80	Crossing point for the Leiston Works Railway into Leiston Station goods yard sidings in 2010.	© Rob Shorland-Ball
81	The surviving track-bed of the Leiston Works Railway in 2010.	© Rob Shorland-Ball
82	Garrett's own loco, SIRAPITE, on the Works Railway.	Courtesy Long Shop Museum, Leiston
83	© OS 6 inch map – Suffolk LX.SW 1950. Snape Maltings and the industrial railway branch from Saxmundham Junction to Snape Goods Station.	© OS. Author's collection
84	(left) © OS 6 inch map – 1927. (right) Ruston-Bucyrus electrically-powered crowd shovel – 1956.	Author's collection
85	Sketch map (not to scale) researched and drawn by Dr Anthony Kirby (University of Cambridge).	Courtesy Dr Anthony Kirby
86	The quarries in the 1960s; the Cement Works in the background is supplied by the standard gauge railway.	Courtesy Dr Anthony Kirby
87	Steam engines return to Barrington for two working days. The quantity of coal at the front of the picture is a reminder of the Cement Works' need for thousands of tons of coal.	Courtesy Dr Anthony Kirby
88	Huntingdon, Cambridgeshire – three Railway Companies, three Stations (edited from RCH Junction Diagrams 1900s).	Author's collection
89	Ramsey Millennium town sign.	© Rob Shorland-Ball
90	Peterborough-March; March-St Ives; St Ives-Huntingdon were ECR/GER railway routes north, east, and south of Ramsey. To the west was the GNR line from London to Huntingdon, Peterborough and the North.	Author's collection
91	© OS 6-inch map 1949. Ramsey East closed to passengers in 1930 but continued to be used for occasional summer excursions until the 1950s. Ramsey North closed to passengers in 1947.	Author's collection
92	A late nineteenth century roller flour mill adjoining Ramsey North Station now surviving as apartments (2017).	© Rob Shorland-Ball
93	Ramsey East Station platform and facilities on 14 May 1937. Seven years after closure to passenger services, this picture is a fitting close to this chapter.	Author's collection
94	© OS 6-inch maps: **i)** Fakenham Town Station – Norfolk XXV.NW 1936 and **ii)** Fakenham Station – Norfolk XXV.NE 1931. The two Railway Companies on the map are Midland & Great Northern Joint Railway (M&GNR) and the Wells & Fakenham Railway (W&FR).	Author's collection

Fig No	Caption	Acknowledgements
95	The remains of the Great Yarmouth end of Fakenham Town down platform and re-constructed name board for Fakenham West.	© Rob Shorland-Ball
96	Fakenham East Station with a Wells-bound DMU – mid 1950s. Fakenham East Station has entirely gone and the site built over.	OTA
97	Edited extract from _The Railways of Great Britain – A Historical Atlas_, Col. M.H. Cobb, Ian Allan, 2003.	Author's collection
98	Cromer High Station in 1954, shortly before closure was announced.	OTA
99	Cromer High Station after complete closure in 1955. Note that Cromer 'High' was an appropriate name for this Station.	OTA
100	Cromer Beach Station – 19 May 1963.	OTA
101	Edited extract from _The Railways of Great Britain – A Historical Atlas_, Col. M.H. Cobb, Ian Allan, 2003.	Author's collection
102	Sketch plan of track layout at Haverhill South (CV&HR).	Author's collection
103	Haverhill North Station in the late 1950s.	© Rob Shorland-Ball
104	Haverhill North Station and derelict track, Shelford to Sudbury, 1969.	Courtesy Nick Catford 1969 (Disused Stations)
105	Panel created for the NRM in 1990 explaining rail/road competitiveness. The 'Royal fish' traffic was boxes of salmon labelled HM The Queen and bound for Sandringham.	© Rob Shorland-Ball
106	Sketch map of the Newmarket Railway – from Great Chesterford to Newmarket.	Author's collection
107	Surviving bridge on Newmarket Railway 1956; last train under it 1851.	© Rob Shorland-Ball
108	Edited sketch plan showing the course of the Mildenhall Branch and the station names. Several of the stations were a considerable distance from the villages they were named to serve.	Author's collection
109	Is a plan of the town, based on 1903 © OS evidence.	Author's collection
110	A Mildenhall train at Platform 4, Cambridge Station on 8 December 1954. A Holden-designed LNER Class E4 2-4-0 mixed-traffic locomotive and two elderly carriages with step-down facilities for the three Halts on the Branch.	Author's collection
111	A view from Newmarket Road bridge, Barnwell, of Barnwell Junction on 16 August 1911.	Courtesy collection M. Brooks
112	Extract from 1927 © OS 6 inch map – Cambridgeshire XL.SE.	© OS. Author's collection
113	Steam out, diesel power in; a DMU at Mildenhall forming a Cambridge-bound train in August 1956.	© Rob Shorland-Ball
114	Garrett's stand at the Great Exhibition, Crystal Palace (1 May to 15 Oct 1851).	Author's collection
115	Part of Thorpeness viewed from the Meare in the foreground. The Meare – Ogilvie's choice of name – is 60 acres in extent, no more than 3ft deep, and includes islands; it offers exciting and safe boating for children.	© Rob Shorland-Ball
116	Joined extract from parts of two © OS 6-inch maps – Suffolk LX.NE & LXA.NW - 1928. Thorpeness Halt is a little distance from the village and GER did not match the village style and implicit wealth in their Halt – see **Fig 117**.	© OS. Author's collection
117	Thorpeness Halt; a DMU for Saxmundham and Ipswich has just departed on 26 June 1965. The elderly GER carriage on the right is the Waiting Room which Ogilvie requested should be added to the Halt.	OTA

LIST OF ILLUSTRATIONS • 141

Fig No	Caption	Acknowledgements
118	12.30 ex Saxmundham arrives at Aldeburgh on 26 June 1953.	OTA
119	Stuart Ogilvie's solution to the problem of conveying his visitors from Leiston Station to Thorpeness – a re-bodied Daimler towing a second-hand London double-deck horse bus.	Author's collection
120	Sketch map (not to scale) of the 19-mile route of the Mid-Suffolk Light Railway as it was completed and operated from 1908 to 1952. The spur south-westwards from Kenton was originally planned as a railway to Debenham and thence to Westerfield and Ipswich. Development capital was so limited that the railway did not even reach Debenham and, at the eastern end, did not reach Halesworth.	Author's collection
121	Mendlesham Station, 2 May 1952.	OTA
122	A Laxfield-bound passenger train is passed at Kenton Station by a lengthy freight train bound for Haughley in the late 1940s.	Courtesy Dr I. Allen
123	Demise. More grass than well-ballasted railway; J15 0-6-0 65388 collecting the last wagons from the mill sidings near Laxfield in 1952	Courtesy Dr I. Allen
124	The recreated Middy as a working Heritage Railway.	Courtesy MSLR Website
125	Edited extract from the Millennium Green Trust's © Website map marking Southwold Railway remains.	Author's collection
126	A volunteer team at work uncovering the footings of the SR Halesworth Engine Shed. The inspection pit inside the Shed is to the right back of the picture and the loco ashpit is in the foreground.	Courtesy HSNGRS
127	Site of the SRT Steamworks development on Blyth Road, Southwold, superimposed on an OS 1904 map which shows the course of the Southwold Railway and Southwold Station.	© OS Author's collection
128	Architect's impression of the developed SR Steamworks site, from: John Bennett, Architect, Southwold.	Courtesy John Bennett, Architect, Southwold
129	Clare Station, Stour Valley line, closed in 1967 and now part of Clare Castle Country Park. The buildings are now Grade 2 listed and the only surviving examples of the original 1865-type station design for the railway. Platform One is a café for the Country Park, open daily and developed in the Station's 1865 Booking Hall.	Author's collection; courtesy Clare Castle Country Park
130	LNER Clare Station Platform Ticket – 1950s	Author's collection
131	A screen visualization by EDF (the Company proposing to build Sizewell C) from *New Civil Engineer* journal 22 March 2019.	Courtesy *New Civil Engineer* journal
132	Summary of proposals for construction sites and accommodation provisions – 'campuses' – circulated by Suffolk County Council in July 2017. A new railway connection to the southern end of the construction sites is shown as a spur off the existing Aldeburgh Branch to the west of Leiston Station.	Courtesy Suffolk County Council
133	A drone view of Mangapps Railway Museum from Mangapps' current Website	Courtesy Mangapps Railway Museum, Burnham-on-Crouch, Essex CM0 8QG
134	3ft gauge Southend Pier diesel-hydraulic train built by Severn Lamb in 1986.	Jim Linwood: Creative Commons Attribution-2.0 Generic License

Fig No	Caption	Acknowledgements
135	Bure Valley Railway; narrow-gauge train and footpath sharing a former standard gauge trackbed.	Author's collection
136	Wells & Walsingham 10 and a ¼ inch gauge railway – mid 1990s	Author's collection
137	Map from downloadable PDF for Marriott's Way	Courtesy Norfolk County Council
138	Cycleways, footpaths and bridleways along former railway trackbeds often include railway features which are a stimulus to memories of the past. This is Marriott's Way in North Norfolk, formerly the Midland & Great Northern Joint Railway.	© Rob Shorland-Ball
139	List's embankment on the narrow-gauge Southwold Railway, Suffolk – a big earthwork on a little railway.	© Rob Shorland-Ball
140	Platform remains of Thorpeness Halt, 2017; Aldeburgh Branch, Suffolk. The trackbed is now a footpath	© Rob Shorland-Ball
141	Busway signs in Swavesey in 2018.	© Rob Shorland-Ball
142	Busway double-deck bus bound for Cambridge; next stop will be Longstanton.	© Rob Shorland-Ball
143	The 2018 remains of Long Stanton Station – see Chapter 9 for pre-Busway pictures.	© Rob Shorland-Ball
144	Busway Longstanton Park & Ride 2018. The bus is heading for Cambridge. The remains of the original Long Stanton railway station (**Fig 143**) is the building at the back of the picture immediately to the left of the bus.	© Rob Shorland-Ball
145	Passenger guidance frame + poster for busway Longstanton Park & Ride 2018.	© Rob Shorland-Ball
146	Longstanton busway stop building and 'how the building works'	© Rob Shorland-Ball
147	Longstanton busway waiting area, 2018	© Rob Shorland-Ball
148	GER installed a Waiting Room at Thorpeness Halt in response to a request from Stuart Ogilvie – see Chapter 21.	© Rob Shorland-Ball
149	GER 0-4-0T Steam tram engine 7132 hauling a freight train on the Wisbech & Upwell Tramway in the 1930s at Upwell.	Author's collection
150	Undated Wisbech & Upwell passenger train, probably in the 1930s, passing Upwell Church.	Ken Nunn collection; courtesy John Scott-Morgan
151	Halstead Station on the former Colne Valley & Halstead Railway, opened in 1860, had close relations with the GER but remained independent until it became part of the LNER in 1923.	Author's collection
152	Framlingham Station on 19 July 1952 was the terminus of a branch line from Wickham Market; the line closed to passengers on 1 November 1952 and to goods traffic on 19 April 1965.	Author's collection
153	Ramsey North Station, 12 August 1972, was closed to passengers on 6 October 1947 and to goods traffic in December 1973.	Author's collection
154	Priorities in 2006.	Author's collection

SELECT BIBLIOGRAPHY

The following books, often confined to the history of a specific railway, have underpinned this book and are acknowledged here.

Title	Author	Publisher	Date
Aldeburgh Branch. The	Peter Paye	The Oakwood Press	2012
An Illustrated History of the Port of King's Lynn and its Railways	Mike G Fell OBE	Irwell Press	2012
Benwick Branch. The	Peter Paye	John Masters	1998
Branch Line Age. The – The minor railways of the British Isles in memoriam and retrospect	C J Gammell	Moorland Publishing	1976
Branch Line Metamorphosis	J D Mann	J D Mann	1974
Branch Lines to Ramsey	John Rhodes	The Oakwood Press	1984
Branches & Byways – East Anglia	John Brodribb	Ian Allan Publishing	2000
Colne Valley & Halstead Railway	R A Whitehead and F D Simpson	The Oakwood Press	1988
East Anglian Branch Line Album	Dr Ian Cameron Allen	Oxford Publishing Co.	1977
Forgotten Railways Volume 7: East Anglia	R S Joby	David & Charles	1985
Impermanent Ways: The Closed Lines of Britain, Volume 9 – Eastern Counties	Jeffery Grayer	Noodle Books	2015
Light Railways in England & Wales	Peter Bosley	Manchester University Press	1990
Lowestoft – East Coast Port	Robert Malster	Terence Dalton Ltd	1982
Mid-Suffolk Light Railway. The	Peter Paye	Wild Swan Publications Ltd	1986
Minor Standard Gauge Railways	R W Kidner	The Oakwood Press	1971
Re-shaping of British Railways. The	Richard Beeching	HMSO	1963
Snape Branch. The	Peter Paye	The Oakwood Press	2005
Southwold Railway 1879-1929. The	Rob Shorland-Ball	Pen & Sword Transport	2019
Stoke Ferry Branch. The	Peter Paye	Oxford Publishing Co.	1982
Story of the Colne Valley [Railway]. The	R A Whitehead and F D Simpson	Francis Ridgway Ltd	1951
Thaxted Branch. The	Peter Paye	Oxford Publishing Co.	1984
Tollesbury Branch. The	Peter Paye	Oxford Publishing Co.	1985
Wissington Railway. The – A Fenland Enterprise	Roger Darsley	Industrial Railway Society	1984

INDEX

The list of CONTENTS on page 5 is a useful guide to the whole book.

As well as an important reference resource an Index should be enjoyed, too, as a guide to unusual topics not previously noted. Glance through the entries and follow up one or two which seem to be unusual or whimsical:

Three Horseshoes and Benwick Branch; Busway – Longstanton Park & Ride; From Eggs to Elephants; Gilbey's Gin; Leiston Works Railway; Six Mile Bottom; Thorpeness – a fantasy village

Explore, and enjoy!

Aldeburgh Branch 2, 6, 19, 22, 79
    Chapter 21 107, 109, 110
    Chapter 24 118, 125
Arthur James Keeble 71
Associated British Ports (ABP) 8, 26, 39
Barrington Light Railway 19
    Chapter 14 83, 84
Beeching Report 14, 15, 17, 59, 99, 143
Benwick Branch 52 Chapter 8 53
British Railways (BR) 8, 14, 17, 59, 74, 75, 97, 143
British Transport Commission (BTC) 8, 15, 26, 37
Busway Longstanton Park & Ride 127
Cambridge / Cambridgeshire 7, 12, 54-65, 68, 83-84, 86, 94-95, 99-101, 103, 105-106, 120, 123, 126-127
Clare Station 117
Colne Valley Railway 19, 120
Cromer 18 22 Chapter 17 94, 120
Diesel Multiple Units DMUs 7, 60
Diesel Railbus(es) 7
Downham & Stoke Ferry Railway
    Chapter 11
Essex 12, 19, 22, 47-50, 67, 120-121
Eastern Counties Railway [ECR] 8, 11, 35, 36, 87, 100, 101, 113
Elsenham to Thaxted Light Railway
    Chapter 10
Fakenham 18 Chapter 16
From Eggs to Elephants 98
Gilbey's Gin 66

Great Chesterford Chapter 19
Great Eastern Railway (GER) 11, 17
Great Northern Railway (GNR) 23, 87
Great Yarmouth 11, 17-18, 22, 28
    Chapter 6 42, 91
Halesworth 2, 8, 19, 41-45, 111
    Chapter 23 121
Haughley Junction 16, 19
Haverhill 19 Chapter 18
Hunstanton 22
Huntingdon 65, 86, 87
Kelvedon Tiptree & Tollesbury Light
    Railway 8 13 Chapter 7
King's Lynn 19 Chapter 5 54, 71-73, 90
Leiston Works Railway Chapter 12
London 11, 12, 19, 21, 23, 25, 28-30, 33-36, 42, 47, 50, 53-54, 58, 63-68, 71, 75, 84, 87, 95, 99-100, 110, 114
Long Stanton / Longstanton 7
    Chapter 9 123-129
Lowestoft 2, 8, 22, 28 Chapter 6 143
Lowestoft Central Station 30, 35
Melton Constable 18, 37, 121
Mid Suffolk Light Railway 8, 15, 16, 18, 19 Chapter 22 120
Midland & Great Northern Joint
    Railway (M&GNR) 18, 90, 92
Mildenhall Branch Chapter 20
Newcastle 22, 23, 25, 58
Newmarket 11, 17, 83, 84 Chapter 19
Norfolk 8, 11, 12, 17, 18, 24, 30, 32, 35, 71, 72, 90, 120-124

Norwich 11, 18, 23, 29-31, 34, 35, 39, 92, 103, 121, 123
Preserved Heritage Railways
    Chapter 25
Ramsey 19 Chapter 15 90
Richard Garrett & Son Chapter 12
River Blyth 39, 42
River Waveney 30, 31, 34, 35
Saxmundham Junction 2, 79, 81, 107 129-146, 101
Sizewell C Nuclear Power Station
    Chapter 24
Snape Maltings Chapter 13
Southwold Railway 9, 18, 19, 39, 41-46
    Chapter 21 120, 124, 143
St Ives Loop Chapter 9
Stoke Ferry 19, 49, 50 Chapter 11
Stuart Ogilvie 107, 110, 129
Suffolk 12, 19, 22, 34, 37, 39, 81, 82, 108, 114, 118, 119, 121, 124, 125
Swavesey 7, 63-65, 123, 125
Thaxted 19 Chapter 10 143
The Royal Fish 98
Thorpeness – a fantasy village 107, 108, 110, 125, 128, 129
Upwell 19, 49, 50
Wells 22, 90, 91, 122
Wilkin & Sons, Tiptree Chapter 7
William Abel Tower 71 Chapter 11
Wissington Light Railway
    Chapter 11